AN ACTOR AND HIS TIME
JOHN GIELGUD

To Ralph & Mu Richardson
with gratitude and affection

AN ACTOR AND HIS TIME
JOHN GIELGUD

In collaboration with
John Miller and John Powell

APPLAUSE
NEW YORK • LONDON

An Actor and His Time by John Gielgud
© 1979, 1996, 1997 John Gielgud
ISBN 1-55783-299-4

Library of Congress Cataloging-in-Publication Data

Gielgud, John. 1904-
   An actor and his time / John Gielgud.
     p.   cm.
   Originally published: London : Sidgwick & Jackson, 1979.
   Includes index.
   ISBN 1-55783-299-4
   1. Gielgud, John, Sir. 1904-   2. Actors--Great Britain-
-Biography.   I. Title.
PN2598.G45A3   1997
792'.028'092
[B]--DC21   97-31701
                                           CIP

APPLAUSE BOOKS

211 West 71st Street
New York, NY 10023
Phone (212) 496-7511
Fax: (212) 721-2856

10   9   8   7   6   5   4   3   2   1

Contents

LIST OF ILLUSTRATIONS

Where sources are not credited, photographs are from the personal collection of John Gielgud; the names of the photographers are no longer available.

LIST OF ILLUSTRATIONS

Preface to the 1997 Applause Edition

Since the last reprint of *An Actor and His Time* in 1989, John Gielgud has continued to delight audiences in various media. On stage and television he portrayed Sir Sydney Cockerell in *The Best of Friends;* he starred in television adaptions of John Mortimer's *Summer's Lease* and Chekhov's *Swansong;* BBC Radio invited him to celebrate his 90th birthday by recreating his King Lear with a star-studded supporting cast; and, perhaps most rewardingly of all, he finally achieved the long-held ambition he mentions in these pages of filming *The Tempest.*

In Peter Greenaway's dazzling version, significantly entitled *Prospero's Books*, Sir John carried off the extraordinary feat of speaking all the other characters' lines as well as his own, right up until the reconciliation scene at the end. The arduous making of this stunning film is described at length in his later book *Acting Shakespeare.*

He has also contributed a moving performance in *Shine* as young David Helfgott's inspirational piano teacher at the Royal College of Music in London; and added a final coda to his long association with *Hamlet* by appearing in Kenneth Branagh's 1996 film as Priam with Judi Dench as Hecuba. In the 90th Birthday BBC Radio Tribute I presented for *Kaleidoscope* in 1994, Sir Alec Guinness looked forward to us all celebrating his mentor's 100th birthday in 2004. In the meantime we have these memories of an extraordinary life in the theatre, which has enriched the lives of audiences and the work of his fellow-actors for so much of the twentieth century.

John Miller

Foreword

When I first embarked on writing an autobiography in 1938, I was greatly dismayed to find how difficult it was to express myself truthfully, accurately, tactfully, straightforwardly, and, I hoped, readably. Since that far off time I have written two more books about the theatre as well as this one, in which I collaborated with John Miller and John Powell, working with them to develop a series of television and radio talks we had concocted together some months before. Proud of my luck in being a member of the Terry family, I was always anxious to jot down my recollections of them, and to share my admiration of so many of their brilliant contemporaries with readers who might enjoy similar enthusiasms to mine.

Despite my all too evident deficiencies in grammar, phrasing and style, I have still managed to find a good deal of pleasure in exploring the chequered mazes of authorship and reminiscence. I can only hope to have contributed in my own small way to the fascinating memories of the seventy years of my theatrical and film career.

John Gielgud
March 1989

Chapter One

1904-1921

Edwardian childhood — Theatrical ancestry — The emotional Terrys — Ellen Terry, 'the Great Star' — 'Golden Fred' Terry — The famous actor-managers, Tree and du Maurier — The legendary actresses

The house where I was born, in April 1904, was steep and chilly. It stood in the Old Brompton Road, in South Kensington, and the horse-drawn traffic, vans, cabs and carriages roared and clattered along outside, noisier even, I seem to remember, than the lorries and cars so soon to take their place. In winter the bedrooms and bathrooms were particularly cold. I hated the tepid baths and the icy, linoleum-covered floors which surrounded them; the occasional hipbath, allowed only when I was ill, and taken in front of the nursery fire, with a big towel being warmed on the high fender, was a luxury to which I greatly looked forward.

Winter too brought the fogs, impenetrably thick. I would find my way home holding one hand in front of me for fear of colliding with someone coming in the opposite direction, while with the other I tapped along the railings with a stick.

In the main, though, my memories of a London childhood are happy ones. I remember the uniforms worn by so many different kinds of people. Maids wore caps and aprons; messenger-boys, who delivered parcels and telegrams and whose arrival, with news of accidents or deaths, was always dreaded, had pillbox caps worn on one side with a strap under the chin. Then there was the muffin-man with his big dinner-bell and the tray on his head covered with a green baize cloth, and the knife-grinder with his wheel and treadle. The coalmen had grimy faces under black shiny caps, with broad flaps at the back to protect their necks and shoulders, and black corduroys buckled under the knees, like Alfred Doolittle in the second act of Shaw's *Pygmalion*. The huge coalcart would grind to a halt at our front door and the men, jumping down to unload the sacks, would carry them on their shoulders through the gate and shovel their contents into the cellar through a round hole covered by a metal plate.

Dressing and undressing were lengthy procedures in those days and I tended to dispose of them as rapidly as possible. There were so many accessories to cope with — vests and long underpants, sock-suspenders, buttons, braces, cufflinks, collar studs, detachable collars, waistcoats and ties. Tying a bow was always a great problem, for made-up bowties were considered caddish and deplorable. Women had to wrestle with an equally formidable series of garments: drawers and petticoats, hooks and eyes, corsets, camisoles; hats, veils, muffs, handbags, card-cases and umbrellas in the daytime; teagowns or long dresses with flowing skirts, elbow-length gloves, aigrettes and fans in the evening. The fine details of costume absorbed me even before I came to observe them in the theatre with a professional eye.

Sunday was the day on which we children were expected to spend some of the time with my father. During the week he left for the City early every morning and did not return until six o'clock, when he would sometimes call on us in the nursery for half an hour and occasionally play the piano for us. He had a charming gift of playing by ear and could improvise quite ambitiously on classical themes. After Sunday lunch, when he presided over a large joint which my grandmother, Kate Terry, and an aunt or two were often invited to share, my father would set out on a long walk, usually accompanied by me and one of my brothers. For these excursions, of course, more dressing-up was required: hats, gloves, mufflers and overcoats in cold weather; boots and galoshes in wet weather; walking-sticks and straw hats in the summer months.

We walked a great deal in my boyhood. No one I knew had cars until the twenties, though I do have a vivid memory of an excursion with my grandmother in a hired electric brougham, a strange contraption without a bonnet, whose driver sat high in front and steered by means of a long curved handle. A tremendous storm broke as we were proceeding along Chiswick High Street. Enormous hailstones hit the roof of the brougham and bounced off the pavements as we sat huddled together, expecting to be electrocuted by the lightning at any moment. The machine was completely immobilized for ten minutes and the unfortunate chauffeur was soaked to the skin.

Sunday walks with my father often included visits to museums and picture galleries. Sometimes we went to concerts, either at the Queen's Hall or the Albert Hall, which was nearer home. At the Albert Hall we always had to sit on the very hard benches by the organ, because my father was convinced that they were the only seats not affected by the dreadful echo. I was apt to fidget a good deal during a long performance and would complain afterwards to my brother that I found the theatre a far more exciting place, but now I am infinitely grateful for that introduction, forced on me by my father, to the fascination of music and pictures. At the Albert Hall I heard the great Chaliapin, then at the end of his long career, a magnificent giant of a man with wavy white hair who surveyed a tiny notebook through his gold lorgnette as he checked the words of his programme. I was greatly impressed too by the pianists — Rosenthal and Rachmaninov — and by the beauty of Kreisler's violin playing, from the moment when he first lifted the instrument to his shoulder, to the awed silence of the audience as he lowered it at the end of the piece, before the applause crashed out and he smiled and bowed with infinite grace and charm. Vladimir de Pachmann was exquisite as an interpreter of Chopin, though his antics on the platform were somewhat grotesque. He would grimace and mutter to himself and sometimes to the audience. 'Chopin crying,' he would exclaim during a sad nocturne, for the benefit of the people sitting in the three front rows. On one occasion he refused to begin until two men (his 'keepers,' my father told me) were brought on to the platform to readjust his piano stool. They were even required to slip two pieces of writing paper under one leg of the piano which Pachmann maintained was not correctly balanced.

One Sunday morning my parents took me to Hyde Park before lunch. We passed the smart riders in Rotten Row to reach the carriage and drive by Hyde Park Corner. Here, between Hanover Gate and the Achilles Statue, so-called Society was to be seen between the hours of eleven and twelve disporting themselves in the fashionable promenade known as Church Parade.

Several distinguished ladies were pointed out to me, including Mrs Asquith, the wife of the Prime Minister. I had seen her once before at a Royal Academy Private View, hopping like a raven in a black feathered hat from one gallery to another and criticizing the exhibits in a raucous voice. I was fascinated by the sight of another lady, heavily made up, with black patches on her cheek and chin like an eighteenth-century marquise, and very fantastically overdressed and hatted. 'Ah!' my mother whispered, 'that is Lady Alexander. She is dressed by the famous courturiers Reville and Rossiter and they say she is given her clothes by them for nothing because she is such a good advertisement.' Lady Alexander's husband, Sir George, who died in 1918, was, of course, the famous actor-manager of the St James's Theatre, and had brought to it a long series of distinguished productions. The theatre in King Street had an elegant auditorium, decorated in green and gold, but rather steep and clumsily designed: pillars unfortunately obscured the stage from a number of seats.

Lady Alexander managed to survive the disappearance of Church Parade and, long after the Great War was over, continued to exploit her dress-sense. I saw her again one night at a ball at Claridges, still wearing the black patches (but now crowned with an elaborate white wig), tightly corseted under a sheath of white satin, and foxtrotting with a succession of very personable young men. My last memory of her is curiously grotesque and somewhat tragic too. In 1945 I was directing a revival of *Lady Windermere's Fan* at the Haymarket Theatre, and was sitting in the stage box on the opening night in my usual state of trepidation when I suddenly noticed a figure in the front row of the stalls that could only be Lady Alexander, though all I could see was the back of her white coiffure, her upturned nose and the collar of a purple velvet cloak hunched about her shoulders. During the intervals she did not move, but a number of people went up to her and she seemed to talk with animation. When the play was over and the auditorium began to empty, two men suddenly appeared from nowhere. They lifted Lady Alexander from her seat, wrapping her cloak round her as if she were a doll about to be packed into a box for Christmas, and carried her bodily past the rows of empty seats. Then, pushing open the door which led from the stalls to the box where I was still sitting, they rushed past me with their burden up the steps leading to the ante-room. From here there is a long passage leading to the Royal Entrance in Suffolk Street, where her car was obviously waiting. The incident was over in a flash but it was a strange farewell appearance for such a sensational personality, and it haunted me for days after.

My mother was the daughter of Kate Terry-Lewis, the eldest of her four daughters, only one of whom, my aunt Mabel, went on the stage. In 1893, when she was twenty-seven, my mother married Frank Gielgud, who was a stockbroker. She had four children, Lewis, Val, myself and my sister Eleanor, who was three years younger than me.[1]

Grandmother Kate — she of the electric brougham — was the eldest child of Ben and Sarah Terry, both actors, and her next sister was the great actress Ellen Terry, Irving's leading lady for a quarter of a century. Mother's sister was Marion Terry, a beautiful actress, and her brother Fred, the youngest of that generation, also had a distinguished career on the stage.

Grandmother was herself a successful actress.[2] As a child she worked with the Charles Keans, then with Fechter in London and Manchester. She played about a hundred parts before she retired in 1867, at the age of twenty-three, to marry my grandfather, Arthur Lewis, who was a very fashionable haberdasher with a shop called Lewis & Allenby's in Conduit Street. He had a beautiful house, Moray Lodge, on Campden Hill, was an amateur painter and singer and a friend of Dickens and Mark Lemon. Grandmother Kate reigned on Campden Hill as Mrs Arthur Lewis and entertained in a very big way, with concerts and enormous parties. There was a conservatory, terraced garden, a billiard room and so on. And then Arthur Lewis lost all his money. After his death, my grandmother lived very simply and rather resentfully in an ugly little house in West Cromwell Road, and she had no grand clothes and did not give parties any more. She played bridge and had paying guests. This was a sad end to her career but she never grumbled or groused. She must have hated being out of the picture, even though many people *still* recognized her and paid court to her.

Recently I was returning from a trip to America, and on the way from Heathrow to Central London in the car I passed the end of the street where my grandmother had lived. Her old house was being systematically demolished by bulldozers, and as the brick wall crashed down, I could suddenly remember the look of every single room in the house, my aunt giving me biscuits from a box on a high shelf in her bedroom, and my grandmother sitting up in bed in a flannel nightgown with a white pig down her back.

My grandfather died at the turn of the century, before I was born, but I knew my grandmother well; she did not die until 1924. She saw me in quite a number of plays, and now, of course, I wish I had asked her more about her stage career, but she was then an old lady and I did not connect her with the theatre in the way that I connected Ellen and Marion and Fred, who were still acting when I was a child. But she took me to the theatre a great deal when I was a boy, usually to matinées, where she demanded — and received — a certain amount of respect from the management. They used to give her the Royal Box and we would sit there together. Tea was sent and we would sometimes go round afterwards and see the actors.

My grandparents on my father's side were both Polish but spoke perfect English, and my great-grandmother, Amela Aszpergerowa, had been a successful actress in Lithuania, famous for her Shakespearean roles. Her husband Wojciech was also a famous leading actor. Their daughter married Adam Gielgud, my grandfather, who had been born at sea during his parents' flight from the Polish revolution of 1830, when the Counts Gielgud lost their family seat — a castle, Zamek Gielguda, on the River Memel. Adam came to England with his wife in the 1850s or 1860s and lived there until finally retiring to Switzerland where they both died. He was a war correspondent. He had a little beard, I remember, and was very charming. My grandmother, who spoilt me rather when she was in England, was a devout Catholic. She wore a black velvet bag with a silver clasp which hung on a chain from her waist. I once went to stay with them in Vevey, where they lived in a *pension*, and my grandmother took me to see Francesca Bertira in a silent film. Often we would go to a wonderful cake shop in Montreux where they had delicious ices and coffee with cream on top. I was very greedy then, as I still am.

I was very fond of my Gielgud grandparents and they were very sweet to me, but I do not think they ever talked to me about the theatre; I did not feel that they had much to do with it — any more than my father's brother who shot big game in Africa, or his sister who was married to a very well-known academic painter in Krakow and who had nine children. Her eldest son was killed in the First War fighting against the British, while my brother was in the British Army fighting on the other side.

I had never thought that my father's side of the family was a very important influence on my acting, though Marguerite Steen, in her book about the Terry family, suggests that my Slav side was of great value to me, helping to make me more original as a performer. It is certainly true that my father had more sense of humour than my mother. He had something of the Slav temperament and was inclined to be moody. He could be very enchanting but also rather forbidding, and had a far less easy temperament than my mother. He may have given me a certain edge. If I had been a pure Terry, with the emotional facility of that family, my acting talent might have developed in a more conventional way. I have always had a tremendous feeling for Russian literature, ballet and music. I was highly amused by a comment Bernard Shaw made once in a letter to Edith Evans, when we were playing together in *The Seagull* and Shaw refused to admit that I was any good at all. Indeed, he thought my performance was so dreadful that the play was ruined every time I came on the stage. I suppose he had no idea that I had a Lithuanian background on my father's side which might have given me an insight into Russian plays and literature. 'Of course,' he wrote, 'John Gielgud, although he can be very good when he is rightly cast, couldn't possibly play anything by Chekhov, being a Terry.'

Among the Terrys Ellen was, of course, the 'Great Star'.[3] She led a somewhat irregular private life. She did occasionally come to our house, but my mother thought her restless and fidgety, and preferred the acting of her sister Marion. I fell madly in love with Ellen the first time I ever saw her on the stage. I decided that the restlessness.was part of her glory, because what I remember most about her is her movement, although she was then in her seventies, deaf, rather blind and very vague. But when she came on you really believed that she was walking on the flagstones of Venice or in the fields of Windsor. She moved with an extraordinary spontaneity and grace, holding her skirts gathered in two hands or bunched up over one arm, and crossed the stage with an unforgettable impression of swiftness. In her great days it was always said that the lines in *Much Ado*- 'For look where Beatrice like a lapwing runs/Close by the ground to hear our conference' — were exactly applicable to her. Shaw said that she had a genius for standing still, when she was not making the most beautiful movements. Irving insisted on this, because he was very slow and she was very swift. She was a Pre-Raphaelite actress. She had sat for painters like Rossetti, and she had known and talked with all the great men of her time — Tennyson, Browning, Ruskin, Wilde — and had learned a great deal from them. Yet she had a real humility. When you met her, you felt that she was ready to learn from children, or from anybody else with whom she came into contact. She also had a wonderful sense of humour which the rest of my aunts and uncles certainly did not.

My grandmother had a kind of heavy humour, but I always felt that she was slightly jealous of Ellen's enormous fame. She had been so very successful herself when she was young, but had given it all up to marry and have children and become a respectable victorian matron. Ellen had three marriages, several love affairs and two illegitimate children and, although she and Irving were honoured guests in my grandparents' house, there was never that intense devotion between the sisters that biographers would like to suggest, though I was told that when my grandmother died Ellen went down and sat in her room for two or three hours, quite alone with her.

Ellen's humour, frankness and generosity were all slightly suspect to Marion, Fred and Kate who, though they were all fine actors, took the theatre dreadfully seriously. This made them extremely good in rubbish. They performed in very fustian plays. They all inherited Irving's love of romantic melodramas in which they acted with great skill and conviction. Marion was a great comedienne, marvellous in farce because she herself had no humour at all. Even though the whole family was so talented, they must have considered Ellen rather a scrapegrace. Indeed, it was a wonder that she managed to be received in all the great houses of England and America when her two children, Edith and Gordon Craig, had no official father.[4]

I was fortunate in seeing Ellen four or five times on the stage. I was only dimly aware of how difficult it was for her to go on acting: at that time she found it almost impossible to remember her lines and she could hardly see. It was said that she had strained her eyes when she was living with Edward Godwin, the father of her two children. Godwin was an architect, a thoroughly unreliable man who often failed to come home at nights, and Ellen would sit up working on his plans and drawings by candlelight.

All the Terrys had very bad memories. Marion, at the end of her life, used to go to play the big scene from *Lady Windermere's Fan*, with my aunt Mabel Terry-Lewis, her niece, at charity matinées, and I remember my mother trying to hear her go through her words at our house. She kept making endless mistakes, although she had known the part for many years.[5] However, they all had a lot of skillful ways of covering their lapses of memory, as many old actors do. Irene Vanbrugh, in her last performances, had the same trouble, but she would shout or stamp her foot or look at the other actor, making it seem as if he was the one who had dried up. This was a much more common occurrence in my days as a youthful playgoer. The prompter was often a good deal in evidence, particularly on first nights, and the audience did not mind, they thought it was all part of the fun. When I saw Ellen Terry as the Nurse in Doris Keane's *Romeo and Juliet* in 1919 she could hardly remember a word, and Basil Sydney and Leon Quartermaine, who were playing Romeo and Mercutio respectively, whispered every line in her ear, and then she said the line herself and it sounded as if she had just thought of it. One would have thought it would have made her nervous, but she *still* had confidence in her charisma and in the audience, and managed to enchant them just the same.

I have heard very little about her performance as Hermione in *The Winter's Tale*, one of the last big parts she played in 1906, just before her Jubilee. Tree did not play in it, though it was produced in his theatre. A man called Charles Warner played Leontes. There are some beautiful photographs of Ellen as the statue, but there is no record that I have been able to find which really discusses her performance, and I would imagine that by that time she was probably too old to create a completely new success. Perhaps when she chose the play for her Jubilee year she remembered that she had made her very first appearance on the stage *all* those years before as the boy Mamillius in the same play, with Mrs Charles Kean as Hermione wearing a Greek wreath round her head and a crinoline with many layers of petticoats. But Ellen Terry went on playing Portia and Queen Katharine in *Henry VIII* almost until the end of her life in charity matinées and at Stratford. She probably had to go on appearing a little too long, but once she stopped acting for good she was sad and began to fail. I once visited her at her lovely farm in the country, but I felt that she was restless there, and could only really be happy when she was working in the theatre.

I saw her once on the Palace Pier at Brighton, playing the Trial scene from The *Merchant of Venice*. She had to be wheeled down that long pier in a bath chair to reach the theatre; but when she came striding on in the Trial scene you would never have thought she was a semi-invalid and an old lady, except that she had white hair under her scarlet cap. She achieved the most perfect phrasing when speaking Shakespeare, a kind of frankness which made it seem as if she had just been taught the passage in the next room by Shakespeare himself. I heard her do the 'Mercy' speech many times at charity matinées, and she never failed to thrill her audience, although she often hesitated from forgetfullness.

One of her great gifts was that she could, as Shakespeare does, suddenly drop from a very high style of speech, manner and behaviour, into something so homely and human that the whole audience was immediately touched by it. Shakespeare often demands this method: 'Dost thou not see my baby at my breast, That sucks the nurse asleep?,' 'All the perfumes of Arabia *will* not sweeten this little hand,' and 'Pray you, undo this button'. Those very simple words, when they are suddenly contrasted with the linguistic grandeur around them, can have the most superb effect on the stage. Ellen Terry knew exactly how to change gear in order to achieve the right result.

When I was a boy, I heard her read Beatrice in *Much Ado* at a private house in Grosvenor Square. Ellen came on in evening dress and a cloak, sat with a lot of amateurs on little gold chairs, and started reading very solemnly. After a scene or two she dropped the book in her lap and started to act, and it was wonderful to see this old lady suddenly turn into a young woman of twenty-five. The other actors were thrilled too, but they were also rather put out when, in the church scene, she rushed over to embrace poor Hero, a timid young girl, and a gold chair fell over, and the evening became something of a shambles.

The Terrys all had mellifluous voices which could break very easily, and a great gift for tears — a gift I seem to have inherited. Edward Gordon Craig, Ellen's son, always maintained that Ellen could not resist making an audience cry; and there was some truth in it. At the same time, she was perfectly aware of the humbug. In a scene of pathos, when she was weeping real tears for the benefit of the audience, she would turn around and whisper jokes with the actors behind her hand. She was terribly mischievous; even towards the end of her career, in 1902 when she was playing *in The Merry Wives*, she put a pin in the padding Herbert Tree was wearing as Falstaff. He got through just one scene before his whole stomach collapsed. Ellen was simply delighted! She was always full of childish fun — running down the stairs late for her cue, with her dresser doing up her dress at the back. She once said to me, 'Oh, I fell down in St Martin's Lane this morning and I was laughing so much the policeman couldn't pick me up.'

A landlady with whom I once stayed in digs in Edinburgh told me that she had had Ellen Terry to stay for a week. Ellen was always answering the door, talking to the coalman and being enchantingly interested in everybody. When the bill was presented on Saturday night it was only 8 pounds, but Ellen gave the landlady a cheque for 80 pounds. The landlady insisted on giving it back to her and was very angry that Ellen's lady companion, who was travelling with her and was supposed to look after her, had not taken the trouble to be there when the bill came to make sure there was no mistake.

It was perhaps Ellen's unconventional approach to life that made her such a great actress, and yet all her successes, except in Shakespeare, were in sentimental melodrama. When she tried to tackle contemporary plays — *Brassbound* and *Alice Sit-by-the-Fire* were both written for her by Shaw and Barrie — she could not remember the lines. Besides that, it seems that her personality was much too big for modern plays. Max Beerbohm said that she blew them out of the window with her bonny English warmth. As Lady Cicely in *Brassbound*, the part needed very precise phrasing and a certain discipline which cramped her style. Of course, for old-fashioned plays she had been able to rewrite her part and she often did. Her prompt-books show how she used to hack about plays like *The Dead Heart* and *Ravenswood, as* Irving and Fred Terry used to do. Many of the old actors used a script merely as a basis for improvisation and would embroider parts and situations to suit their own style.

The Terry family were very loyal at supporting each other's performances. We all used to be there on their first nights. *Romeo and Juliet* was really Ellen's last professional engagement in London, in 1919, with Doris Keane playing Juliet. As we went into the theatre my grandmother arrived. Marion Terry came in from another door, and they kissed each other, of course. Then, I could not think why, they both turned and went by opposite doors into the theatre, down different staircases. Grandmother came into the auditorium first, and the gallery, which in those days always applauded celebrities at first nights, began to clap and she smiled and waved her hand. Then Marion came in from the other side, and also got a very good round of applause. In the interval I said in a loud voice to Marion, 'Grandmother had a wonderful reception,' and Marion replied, 'Yes, dear, I expect they thought it was me.' It was a very typical Terry sweetness. I do not think they were maliciously jealous, but there must have been, of course, a certain competition. Marion sometimes had to succeed Ellen in a play. She was supposed to be very good in Shakespeare, although I think she never played it in London. My father saw her once in Stratford as Rosalind and admired her acting very much, more than he admired Ellen's in fact. I do not know whether my parents were slightly disapproving of the Bohemian life that Ellen led, or whether it was just the restlessness and fidgets my mother complained of, but they were less enthusiastic about her than they were about Marion and Madge Kendal.

Fred Terry, who was known as 'Golden Fred,' was a great jolly man, and always very kind and helpful to me.[6] But he could be alarming too — he had a most violent temper. He was an enormous eater, gourmand, gambler, as well as a splendid actor and a great personality. He married the beautiful Julia Neilson, who was a very affected, mannered actress, but who had moments of charm. He used to make her life hell at rehearsals and his company was terrified of him. To me his productions were the last link with the Irving tradition. Fred worshipped Henry Irving.[7] I saw his productions of *The Scarlet Pimpernel* and *Sweet Nell of Old Drury* and, later on, *Much Ado,* and they seemed to have an extraordinary sweep about them, and an immense care for detail. He used to kill his company with hard work, making them rehearse all day. A new play might take as much as a year to prepare because Fred could not learn his lines and insisted on directing himself, getting into fearful rages and losing his hat by sitting on it in the stalls. All the noises behind the scenes — royal processions approaching or the Massacre of St Bartholomew — were rehearsed and executed to perfection. Make-up, clothes, scenery and lighting — everything was meticulously harmonized.

Fred and Julia toured the provinces in competition with Martin Harvey and his wife, who were also very popular. Both Fred and Martin Harvey had been members of Irving's Company, and they followed his traditions and became great provincial stars. Fred gambled his profits away while Julia spent all hers on dresses and bric-a-brac. They lived in a big house on Primrose Hill, crammed with beautiful furniture, glass and china, ate enormous meals and became vastly fat. The last time I saw them, in *The Pimpernel,* they could no longer dance the minuet. Instead, they sat on chairs on each side of the stage while the company very nervously performed the dance under the eye of the boss, who was obviously going to give them hell the moment the curtain came down. It was rather sad and funny. But Fred, in his own way, was a great actor.

He was not very happy in modern clothes, and he had a very naïve approach to the theatre. He used to come and see plays that I was in, usually standing in the back of the pit so as not to be recognized. He was fearfully shocked by *The Constant Nymph* because one of the characters was an unmarried Bohemian creature who lived with a composer in the Tyrol with a lot of illegitimate children. Fred would be violent about anything in a play that he did not think was manly and noble. The heroines were white, and the villains were black, and that was that. But he had an enchanting quality. He was funny, engaging and a real card in many ways.

Many of the Terrys appeared in the Shakespeare Tercentenary performance at Drury Lane in 1916. It was a marvellous occasion and I shall never forget it. There was an amazing programme, including the whole of *Julius Caesar*. Henry Ainley played Antony and Harley Granville-Barker had rehearsed the crowd. Du Maurier and Edmund Gwenn were the First and Second Citizens: in fact, everybody in the crowd was a well-known actor or actress. H. B. Irving was marvellous as Cassius. The programme began with some music, and after *Julius Caesar* there was also a pageant made up of tableaux from Shakespeare plays in which all the actors in London appeared, framed in scenery used in the pantomime that year. Great pillars, set on broad steps, rose through the floor of the stage at Drury Lane. The players came up with their backs to the audience from below the stage and halted on the first tier, turning round to reveal themselves — to enormous applause of course — and then moving on again to make place for another group. At the very top of the steps was a bust of Shakespeare on a pedestal, and on one side stood Ellen Terry as Comedy in white, with Genevieve Ward, a very famous old actress, as Tragedy in black on the other, both holding masks, and the company all went up in groups to lay wreaths before the statue.

Fred Terry walked on in the *Much Ado* excerpt, and Ellen and Marion appeared as Portia and Nerissa. There was a story that Genevieve Ward, who was a terrible old battle-axe, made a scene because she found she was asked to share a dressing-room. She saw the list up on the board when she came into the theatre, and did not notice the other names. When she opened the door of the room she found that she had been asked to share it with Ellen Terry, who peered over her spectacles and said, 'You always were a cat, Ginny!'

It was in the interval of this performance that Frank Benson, who played Caesar, was knighted.[8] After the murder scene, King George V summoned him to the Royal Box. There was no sword, so someone rushed round the corner to Simmonds, the theatrical costumiers in King Street, Covent Garden, to borrow one. The King then knighted him, whereupon great cheers rose from the huge company behind the curtain. Sir George Alexander came out to announce to the mystified audience that Benson had been knighted, and of course the audience went mad too. It made a tremendous climax to the occasion.

The Edwardian theatre of my boyhood was dominated by the great actor-managers like George Alexander, Herbert Beerbohm Tree and Gerald du Maurier.[9] At the time I accepted their style of acting completely and I suppose I longed to be like them. I thought that was the way to act. I was inclined to prefer the panache of Fred Terry (or Robert Lorame in *Cyrano)* to the naturalistic but brilliant acting of du Maurier or Hawtrey, though I also admired the latter's very different style. But I had no conception of the various methods necessary to achieve such fine results. Du Maurier often put on rubbish, just as Fred Terry did. They both catered to the public taste for plays by sentimental dramatists like J. M. Barrie. Barrie is quite out of favour now. Although his plays are beautifully constructed, there is a chocolate-box side to them which is embarrassing to the modern public, but which people adored when they were written. I saw *Dear Brutus* on its first night in 1917 and afterwards in several revivals. When I directed and acted in it myself during the Second War I kept remembering how marvellous du Maurier had been as the painter Dearth. I could not touch him in the part.

Du Maurier swept away a good deal of fustian. When he staged *Interference* in the twenties he played a long dumb-show scene in which he found a murdered man before the police arrived. It was a ten-minute episode during which he kept the house enthralled. If only he had brought such skill and expertise to Ibsen and Chekhov! But he had little appreciation of great plays. He did not read much and he did not like the theatre to be taken too seriously. He preferred to give the impression that the stage was just a way of earning a living on the side, though in actual fact he was not particularly happy outside the theatre. My Aunt Mabel, who worked with him once or twice, was a very accomplished actress, but she had the same slightly snobbish attitude towards the theatre. She told me once that she had been in love with Guy du Maurier, Gerald's brother, who wrote the famous play *An Englishman's Home*, and was killed in the First War. I said, 'But surely you must have been in love with Gerald?' and she replied, 'In love? With an *actor?*' She took the attitude that acting was a sort of recreation and she even once asked to be excused from playing a matinée in order to go to the Derby. Du Maurier allowed her to go.

Aunt Mabel was the youngest of my mother's three sisters.[10] She was also the prettiest and the most elegant, though somewhat sharp-tongued and opinionated. At my grandmother's house there was a full-length portrait of her by John Collier, in which she was sitting in an imposing chair, dressed in a long black velvet ballgown. As a boy, I was particularly fascinated by her because I knew she had formerly been an actress. In 1905 she had married and given up the stage to live in the country with her husband, Ralph Barley, a captain of Territorials and, presumably, well-to-do. When I was in my early teens they invited me down to stay with them in their manor-house in Dorsetshire. There were white doves on the lawn, a dairy where I would greedily lick cream from the open bowls, and delicious meals. But I was absurdly homesick and dismayed by the quiet of the country, where I had seldom been except on family holidays. I can remember sitting in the downstairs lavatory gazing ruefully at a decorative plaque over the washstand which announced, in raised capital letters, 'East or West, Home is Best.' But I liked helping to pick mushrooms in the wet fields and bringing them back to eat for breakfast. In the evening Mabel would descend in a becoming teagown and lie on the sofa with her feet up. Reassured by her charm, I became more than ever convinced that the theatre was the career I wanted to pursue. To my great delight, my aunt decided to stage a series of performances of a one-act play by Gertrude Jennings, *The Bathroom Door.* It was at that time considered, I suppose, a little daring, since all the characters appeared in dressing-gowns, night-gowns and pyjamas. I played the juvenile and Mabel was naturally the Prima Donna. We acted in village halls for the benefit of the local Women's Institute and it was all a great success.

After the First War Mabel's husband died and she decided to employ her boundless energies by returning to the stage. She reappeared in the early twenties in a comedy by H. M. Harwood, *A Grain of Mustard Seed,* and made an immediate success. Her style and technique were quite unimpaired by her long absence from the theatre.

Her carriage and diction were always faultless and she continued to act for the next twenty years, both in London and New York, in a succession of aristocratic roles which fitted her to perfection.

As a young boy I often caught a glimpse or two of the great theatrical figures of my parents' time, Sir Squire Bancroft and Sir Johnston Forbes-Robertson.[11] I would pass them as they strolled along Piccadilly in their curly-brimmed top hats and frock coats, one with wavy white hair and a monocle dangling from a moiré ribbon, the other cadaverous, with sculptured Burne-Jones features. Bancroft had retired with a fortune many years before I was born and when Lady Bancroft died he went to live in the Albany. From there he would walk each morning to his bank, where he would demand a slip with the amount of his current balance, which he would diligently examine before proceeding to lunch at the Garrick Club.

Somewhat morbidly fascinated with mortality, he always visited the bedside of friends who were ill, bearing a large bunch of black muscat grapes. He was also a faithful attendant at funerals and memorial services (as well as fashionable theatrical first nights) and was heard to remark, on his return from a cremation service — in those days something of a novelty — 'A most impressive occasion. And afterwards the relatives were kind enough to ask me to go behind.'

Perhaps the most legendary theatrical figures of that time were the international star actresses, those great creatures whose names alone could fill a theatre. I saw Eleonora Duse[12] in *Ghosts* at the New Oxford Theatre in Tottenham Court Road, long since demolished. I stood at the back of the packed theatre at a matinée. Every actor in London was there and the feeling in the audience was unforgettable, a mixture of respect and awe, a sense that we would never see this great woman again. When Duse came on, the atmosphere was already electric, and she could hardly fail to make the most wonderful impression. I did not know the play very well, but Duse looked infinitely sad and distinguished with her white hair, and wearing a plain black dress with a shawl draped over her shoulders. I remember that her acting seemed very, very simple. She had marvellous hands and all her movements were weary and poetic. Here was a legendary figure whose career had spanned fifty or sixty years of the nineteenth-century theatre, and she succeeded, to my mind, in living up to her legend, although she was evidently old and tired.

Many years later, in 1952, at a cocktail party in Hollywood, I was introduced to Charlie Chaplin. He took me aside and began to talk to me about his boyhood in London when he used to see Tree's productions from the gallery at His Majesty's. For some reason we talked about Duse. Chaplin described an occasion on which he saw her act. He began to imitate the actor who had appeared that night with Duse. He whipped out a chair and sat astride it and began to jabber bogus Italian. In a brilliant mime, he showed how the actor was enthralling the audience with a long speech when suddenly the curtains behind began to move and a little old lady came out very quietly and glided across the stage and put her hands towards the fire. Duse. And at this point the poor actor who had seemed so remarkable a moment before was completely blotted out.

The rare appearances of Sarah Bernhardt in London were just as sensational.[13] Someone once said that the atmosphere in the theatre before the curtain went up on a play of Bernhardt's was like a cage of tigers about to be released. She had a marvellous voice with an extraordinary range, This is confirmed by her gramophone records, crude as they seem now. She and Duse both worked in so many countries where the language was not their own, and where they could not count on being understood, that they had to rely on their voice skills to convey the meaning of a scene. As I do not know any Italian I could not judge Duse's diction or phrasing. In *Ghosts*, it did seem to me that she was far too romantic, not at all the kind of hard-boiled Northern hausfrau that Mrs. Alving should be, but she was magically interesting.

There is a charming story about Ellen Terry and Bernhardt. After a performance at the Lyceum, Ellen and a friend, Graham Robertson (who tells the story in his reminiscences, *Time Was*), were passing the theatre where Bernhardt was playing. Ellen had a big bag of eggs. Ellen said, 'Isn't Sally B. dead yet? Let's go in and watch the last act.' So they went and sat in the pit and, after the last curtain, went round to see Bernhardt. She was extremely upset to learn that they had been in the pit and also that they had not seen the whole play. They were just about to leave when Ellen cried, 'Oh, my eggs!' and they had to rush back to the front of the house to retrieve the eggs from the pit.

Probably the most august figure and one of the last *monstres sacreds* of the Victorian era was Dame Madge Kendal.[14] I once saw her driving down Shaftesbury Avenue, red-faced and imposing, in full evening dress. For some reason her car was lighted up inside, and there she sat, bolt upright, her hair parted in the middle and screwed back into a bun, her neck and shoulders in handsome décolletage with a sparkling necklace at the throat, and her bodice tightly corseted; with the cleft between her breasts exposed as in a portrait by Ingres — an awe-inspiring sight.

Many people, including my own father, had considered Mrs Kendal the finest actress in England, a mistress of comedy and domestic drama surpassing even Ellen Terry. She seldom ventured into the classics, however, and the photographs of her as Rosalind-Ganymede — with her husband as Orlando sporting a resplendent Victorian moustache — suggest a rather overcorseted, buskined Amazon.

On her eightieth birthday Dame Madge was asked to record a speech for broadcasting, and chose to read a speech from *As You Like It*. Arriving at the BBC she was received with respectful ceremony. The director showed her where to stand and pointing to the microphone explained politely, 'That, Dame Madge, is your Orlando.' To which the old lady replied, with a gracious smile, 'Ah, my husband was better looking than that.'

One of my earliest theatrical memories is seeing Oscar Asche in *Chu-Chin-Chow*.[15] I must have been about twelve when I went with my parents. We sat in the dress circle and I was overwhelmed by the production, which fulfilled my most cherished pictorial enthusiasms, first inspired by the drawings of Edmund Dulac, Arthur Rackham and Kay Nielsen which had illustrated my books of fairy tales. Scenery and costume were far more important even than the acting to my youthful eyes.

Asche, who was the star of *Chu-Chin-Chow*, and made a fortune out of it, was also a remarkable director. One effect I remember particularly was the opening procession of servants carrying big bowls of food, like a Veronese painting; and there were donkeys and camels and beautiful girls in yashmaks. Asche himself played the wicked king of the robbers and sported gold fingernails, while his wife, Lily Brayton, wore an enormous fuzzy black wig and transparent Oriental draperies.

It was wartime and the troops, home on leave from the trenches, adored *Chu-Chin-Chow*. The theatre was full of khaki and blue, and there was one scene which never failed to bring the house down. It was set in the slave-market and featured tiers of beautiful girls with very little on. This scene prompted a witticism of Tree's, 'More navel than millinery!' I used to go to *Chu-Chin-Chow* again and again, standing for hours in the pit queue and spending all my pocket money.

I had not seen much Shakespeare and though there was not a big public for the classics in those years, I did see the Benson Company in *As You Like It* at the Coronet Theatre in Notting Hill Gate. Tree had created a great fashion for Shakespeare, from the time when he built and opened his own theatre, Her Majesty's, in 1900, until he went to America in 1915. After that, no other manager dared to compete, though Granville-Barker,[16] from 1912 to 1914, did three sensational productions of Shakespeare at the Savoy, one of which, *A Midsummer Night's Dream*, I was lucky enough to see. These productions were considered very avant-garde and appealed only to a limited, high-brow audience. The general public was not interested in Barker's simple approach after Tree's lavishly spectacular productions with real rabbits and fountains and Richard II riding a real horse through the streets of London. Tree put on a great Shakespeare festival every year, at which he used to invite various touring companies to appear in his theatre, and there would be seven or eight Shakespeare plays staged there over a couple of weeks.

At the end of the First War, James Bernard Fagan took the Court Theatre and put on a series of classics, but unfortunately he starred his wife, who was not a very good actress. Although he had Maurice Moscovitch as Shylock and Godfrey Tearle and Basil Rathbone as Othello and Iago, the venture was not financially successful. It was not until the thirties that, by a lucky chance, I was able to bring Shakespeare back to the West End as a commercial success.

I was of course, always enamoured of the theatre, because my family was so closely connected with it. My mother knew Henry Irving, who died the year after I was born, for he often used to visit my grandparents. I was fascinated by the idea that Ellen Terry and Gordon Craig were my near relations and I read all Craig's books. I had a model theatre, for which I used to design scenery, and my brother and sister and I would make up the plays together and speak the lines from behind the scenes.

I was also a tremendous fan of the ballet throughout my adolescent years. When I was at school at Westminster my great friend was Arnold Haskell. He and I used to escape from school on our afternoons off and, in our silk top hats and tail coats, climb up to the gallery at the Coliseum to see matinées. This was just at the end of the First War. There would be one ballet in the middle of a variety programme and Diaghilev was only too glad to secure the engagement for his famous Russian dancers who had been stranded in Spain during the war. I was thrilled by the music and by Bakst's brilliant décors. I began to understand Stravinsky better and to learn a little about the technique of dancing.

I gained many of my ideas for scenery from the ballet. I could see that it was possible to have effective scenery without a lot of solidly built sets. Diaghilev was brilliantly ahead of his time in commissioning Post-Impressionist artists like Derain, Picasso and Bérard, though his early triumphs were designed by Benois and Bakst, who were more conventional artists.

As I grew up I began to think that I would like to design scenery, because I was so taken with all the decorative arts, and I did a lot of drawing in my spare time — imaginary costumes and illustrations. I remember copying out the whole of *The Lady of Shalott* and trying to make it look like an illuminated missal. I gave it to my mother as a present. It was a very amateurish effort but it was a labour of love and took many months. I collected a whole portfolio of my drawings and, very timidly, showed one or two of them to my Uncle Fred and talked about becoming a scene designer or decorator as a profession. On further enquiry, however, I discovered that I would have to learn architecture and technical drawing, and since I was hopeless at mathematics I thought, 'Oh, that's no good, I shall never be able to do that.'

I was beginning to act in a few school productions, as Mark Antony, Shylock, the Mock Turtle and Humpty Dumpty, and I did some amateur work with Rosina Filippi, a very celebrated old actress with a school in Chelsea. I also played Orlando in an open-air performance at Battle Abbey. I began to say to myself, 'What about becoming an actor?'

My parents were not altogether enthusiastic about the theatre as a profession, though they were both enthusiastic playgoers. I tried another tack. 'Supposing you let me see if I can get into one of the dramatic schools, and then, if I haven't made a success by the time I'm twenty-five, I'll do whatever you want and go on to architecture, or try to learn proper mathematics.' I did not want to go to Oxford, even though my eldest brother Lewis was at Magdalen both before and after the First War, and my brother Val at Trinity a little later, and I had fallen in love with the city. In my last term at Westminster I had felt that I was not getting very far. I was specializing in English literature and history, and was making little progress. I knew that my grandmother and aunts had all been in the theatre from their childhood and felt it might be better to go on the stage straight away. I was seventeen.

My parents finally agreed, rather reluctantly, and I wrote to Constance Benson, Sir Frank Benson's wife, who ran a little drama school close to my grandmother's house in Cromwell Road. I recited for her and gained a scholarship. I spent a year there, playing several important roles, including scenes from *Hamlet*, Sir Peter Teazle and Benedick. There were only four or five men in the school and about twenty girls and we used to split up the parts with the slimmer girls playing young men. I seemed to be getting on quite well there, although Lady Benson — a very bad actress but a splendid teacher — thought me mannered and rather effeminate (which I was) and conceited too. She rightly put me in my place. At the end of each term Lady Benson used to come and act for us herself. Once she played the Ophelia mad scene in a large Edwardian hat.

And then, in 1922, my cousin Phyllis Neilson-Terry, Fred's daughter, whom I hardly knew except that I had seen her in plays and had been introduced to her in her dressing-room (I was greatly in awe of her because she was a beautiful, statuesque creature with very pale blue eyes, and a great star in those days), suddenly wrote out of the blue and asked me to go on tour with her, as assistant stage manager, understudying four parts, at a salary of £4.10s a week.

Chapter Two

1922-1928

Touring in the North — RADA — The Poet Butterfly — Rep in Oxford — Coward and Chekhov — 'A thousand times goodnight' — Mrs Patrick Campbell: 'Gin was mother's milk to her' — Edith Evans

My grandmother Kate wrote to me of her delight that I had 'a real start in a profession you love,' and added some advice. 'Don't anticipate a bed of roses for on the stage as in every other profession there are slings and arrows to contend with. Be kind and affable with all your co-mates but if possible be intimate with none of them. This is a quotation of my parents' advice to me and I pass it on as I have proved it to be very sound. Theatrical intimacy breeds jealousy of a petty kind which is very disturbing.'

Phyllis Neilson-Terry was playing a piece called *The Wheel*. In those days, London successes were usually sent on tour with less expensive casts. Edith Evans had been in the play in London, and so had Randie Ayrton and Philip Menvale, but on tour the leading man was Ion Swinley, whom I also understudied, and another actress played Miss Evans' part.

We went on a twelve- or fourteen-week tour to Hull, Leeds, Sheffield and the North, and I lived in digs, where I was constantly frightened of making a fool of myself. In the theatre I was given dogsbody jobs — seeing costumes and props out on Saturday night and in on Monday morning, checking the lights, calling Miss Terry from her dressing-room and so on.

In the last act of the play I had four lines to speak, and had to learn to make up which I found difficult. After two hours' struggle my face would be bright orange and shiny, but the company was kind and helped me, and Swinley, with whom I acted several times later, proved to be a most enchanting man. He was rather sad and lonely; I believe his wife ran off with another man when he was fighting in the First War and, embittered by this, he drank too much. I used to go on pub crawls with him from half past ten in the morning until three in the afternoon, when everyone would return to their digs, have lunch and go to sleep until the play began in the evening. That was the main form of recreation on tour in those days, when there was usually only one cinema in a town. I found it all a little disillusioning, though not in the least discouraging.

I remember once making a *faux pas* with my cousin. I knew that she had first acted under the name of Phyllida Terson (a contraction of Terry and Neilson) and one night, trying to be funny, I knocked at her door and said 'It's your call, Miss Terson.' She did not look at all pleased. I was told later that when she was called Phyllida Terson and acting with Herbert Tree, my aunt Manon, who was in the stalls, overheard somebody in the next seat saying 'Of course, she's one of Tree's illegitimate children,' so she quickly changed her acting name to Neilson-Terry. I had no idea of the gaffe which I was committing (I have become famous for dropping similar bricks), but I tried to learn to behave more carefully. 'You must never speak aloud in theatres,' I was told, 'otherwise somebody will overhear what you say and may repeat it afterwards.' However, Phyllis forgave me and she used to help me sometimes at understudy rehearsals, teaching me how to hold her — she was six feet tall — during love scenes, in case I ever had to go on, and showing me how she bent her knees and folded herself into my arms — a useful lesson.

One night I went on for one of the parts I was understudying and the company thought I did rather well. Phyllis was kind enough to say, 'When we go to Oxford your parents are coming down. I'll put you on again in that part so that they can see you.' The principal was asked to stand down, which I do not think he can have liked very much, and on I went. I was absolutely dreadful. I realized that the first time I had succeeded through sheer nerves but the second time I had no technique to rely on. One of the actors in the company told me 'I don't think you've had enough training, you ought to go to another dramatic school,' so when I came back from the tour I went to the Royal Academy of Dramatic Art and asked if I could have an audition. I won a scholarship there in 1922.

At Lady Benson's there had been only a small drill hall, and space was limited, but at the RADA there were a good many rooms. They had just opened their little theatre and it seemed very grand. The teaching was excellent. There was a lady called Alice Gachet, who taught in French and later on 'discovered' Charles Laughton, and Helen Haye, who had, funnily enough, given me the diploma at Lady Benson's school, and Claude Rains.[1] We used to have fascinating people down to speak to us. Shaw came once, the first time I ever set eyes on him, and made a speech telling us we must never take less than £8 a week, because we would be keeping somebody else in the gutter! And Sybil Thorndike came and rehearsed us in scenes from the *Medea*.[2]

In those days Sybil had sandy hair arranged in coils round her ears, like radio receivers, and wore long, straight dresses in bright colours with strings of beads round her neck. She told me that Jason was a selfrighteous prig and I must play him as such. She exuded vitality, enthusiasm, generosity and we were all spell-bound as we listened to her.

I do not remember seeing her on the stage until *Saint Joan* in 1924, when I was lucky enough to be at the opening night, sitting with my parents in the dress circle of the New Theatre. It was an inspiring occasion — play, production, décor, acting, it all seemed perfect to me. At the end of the evening, when Sybil led on the weary actors, all looking utterly exhausted by the strain of the long performance, to take a dozen calls, I realized, perhaps for the first time, something of the agonies and triumphs of theatrical achievement.

Sybil Thorndike was surely the best-loved English actress since Ellen Terry, and these two great players shared many of the same fine qualities — generosity, diligence, modesty, simplicity. The theatre was the breath of life to Sybil — or rather the theatre, music and her deep religious faith. Blessed with immense talent, boundless energy, unremitting application and splendid health — until the last few years when she learned to triumph over increasing disabilities — she fought her way, helped by the devotion of a brilliant husband and loving family, to worldwide recognition. Her good works were man-ifold, her influence for good shone from her like a beacon, but she hated to be praised or to be thought sweet and saintly. 'I hate pathos,' she said once, 'It's soft and weak. But tragedy has fight.'

She was very fine, though to my mind unequal, in her playing of tragedy, but she was one of the few actresses of her generation who dared even to attempt it. She took the stage, whether as Lady Mac-beth or Queen Katharine or Hecuba, with a splendid stride, faultless phrasing and diction, and riveted her audiences with her superb au-thority and vocal power. In comedy she was sometimes tempted to hit too hard, but as the years passed her skill and control, under her husband Lewis Casson's iron hand, restrained and refined the execu-tion of her art to a remarkable degree.

Saint Joan, of course, was written for her, and it was her acting masterpiece, though she must have got sick and tired of hearing peo-ple say so. Her performance was unrivalled. Her tearing up of the re-cantation in the trial scene was a moment of really great acting that I shall never forget. She was as convincing in the slangy colloquial passages as in the great poetic speeches, blending the different sides of the character with unerring judgement, and never for a moment allowing sentimentality or sanctimoniousness to intrude on the sim-ple directness of her approach.

In her private life she managed somehow to retain a certain re-serve and dignity, despite an ebullient facade. She had beautiful man-ners. Genuinely interested in everyone she met, strangers as well as friends, she could bounce and flounce without ever losing her mod-esty and basic humility. The moment you were lucky enough to work with her in the theatre you knew she was a leader, but also a giver, not self-centred, professional to her fingertips, disciplined, punctual and kind. She confessed to having a terrible temper but I never saw a sign of it myself.

Her beauty grew, fittingly, in her old age, and her noble head, veiled in the white silk scarf she always wore, singled her out in any gathering, whether at theatres or parties or in church. During these last years, it was sad to see her the victim of continual pain. But mag-nificently she rose above it. 'My piffling arthritis,' she would say.

With unforgettable dignity she walked at the head of her family up the long nave of Westminster Abbey, at the memorial service for her husband. Eagerly she followed every moment of the service and, typically, waited afterwards to greet a great crowd of friends. One day, soon afterwards, I called on her to find her lying in bed, evidently in great pain. 'A bit tired today,' she said, 'for it was Lewis's anniversary yesterday, so I got them to drive me up to Golders Green and sat there for half an hour.' But she announced defiantly that she intended to come to see *No Man's Land* on the following Friday. I begged her not to make the effort and thought no more about it. When the evening came, however, during the interval I heard over the loud-speaker, above the chatter of the audience, her unmistakably clear voice: 'Do you know my daughter-in-law Patricia?' Ralph Richardson bounded into my dressing-room to tell me, 'She's here after all!' And, of course, we both had letters from her next day. George Devine told me that she came to see every one of the new plays he was presenting at the Court and would always write him vivid and constructive criticism as soon as she got home.

How fitting it was that her very last public appearance should have been at the Old Vic on its farewell night. At the end of the performance, she was wheeled down the aisle in her chair, to smile and wave for the last time to the people sitting in the theatre she had always loved so well. Lively, passionate, argumentative, always traveling, acting, learning a new language or a new poem, a magnificent wife and mother, she was surely one of the rarest women of our time. 'Oh, Lewis,' she cried once, 'if only we could be the first actors to play on the moon.'

At the RADA, after the excitement of the *Medea* and Sybil Thorndike, we did a very ambitious play which Claude Rains directed — *The Living Corpse*. It is a highly elaborate piece, with a huge cast, about a man who leaves his wife, goes to live with the gypsies and then disappears. The wife marries again, and the police find the husband in a low dive and arrest him for bigamy. In the last scene he appears with a straggling beard, wearing nothing under his huge overcoat, falls at his wife's feet to beg her forgiveness, and finally shoots himself — all tremendously Russian and melodramatic.

Rains suggested that I should take the leading role of Fedya. We borrowed all the props, rehearsed like mad and learned to sing the gypsy songs. The performance was quite a success in the end, though I cannot image how I had the courage to take on such an ambitious part. Nigel Playfair, who was a friend of my mother's, came to see me in one of the public shows.[3] He liked it and offered me a part in *The Insect Play*, by the Capek brothers, which he was putting on at the Regent Theatre.

In *The Insect Play* I had a most embarrassing part. The first act was entitled 'The Butterflies,' the second act 'The Beetles,' the third 'The Ants'. The second and third acts were splendid, but the first was a disaster. In the original production in Czechoslovakia this act had apparently been highly improper, concerned mainly with fornication. The Butterflies were frightfully lightminded creatures, having affairs, drinking cocktails, and so on. Playfair and Clifford Bax, who adapted the play, tried to alter this first act, removing the indecencies, and the result was very tame indeed. I played the Poet Butterfly, and looked terrible in a laurel wreath, white flannels and pumps. I had to come on with a battledore and shuttlecock which I failed to aim correctly. On the last night Playfair sat in a box with his back to the stage all through the first act, which depressed us very much.

As a producer Playfair was unobtrusive. I remember nothing he said, but once when I was sitting behind him at a dress rehearsal, I made a most impertinent suggestion. But he turned round and said, 'It's a very good idea, I will do that.' He had no side at all. His manners were charming and he was very easy-going. It was said that when there was a crisis, he invariably walked out of the theatre and went for a stroll until his manager had dealt with the situation. Easy-going he may have been, but he had great integrity. He was rather tubby, short-sighted, smoked an enormous pipe and wore very shabby clothes. He loved to stay at Oxford, at the inn at Godstow, and bathe in the river. He had an extraordinary flair for the eighteenth century. His production of *The Beggar's Opera* at the Lyric, Hammersmith, was enchantingly pretty, too pretty perhaps, as the squalid satire of the play was lost — Playfair's highwaymen and doxies were rogues in porcelain. But how wonderfully well he did it.

The Lyric Theatre at Hammersmith — recently rebuilt — was a beautiful old Victorian house which had been shut for ages. There was a butcher's shop alongside the theatre which stank in hot weather, and all the local boys used to bang on the dock doors with hoots sticks and make a fearful racket. It was uncomfortable and smelly, the dressing-rooms were wretched, but it had a unique atmosphere. It was an important theatre for me in my early career, as I appeared in three productions there, though they were all unsuccessful.

When *The Insect Play* ended its six-week run at the Regent, Playfair decided to put on a chronicle history play called *Robert E. Lee*, a sequel to *Abraham Lincoln*, by John Dnnkwater. *Lincoln* had been an enormous success but the sequel, which was rather long drawn out, was less satisfactory. However, Playfair engaged a huge company of twenty-five and asked me to play Lee's aide-de-camp. I was dreadfully bad. I walked clumsily, could not manage my boots, tripped over my sword, and was thoroughly ashamed of myself. But I was also understudying Claude Rains who played one of the other leading parts. Rains seemed to like me and encouraged me. I had always been enormously impressed by his acting. He had been in Henry Ainley's companies in 1918 and 1919 at the St. James's and afterwards went to the Everyman in Hampstead, where he acted a lot of Shaw — Napoleon in *The Man of Destiny*, and Dubedat in *The Doctor's Dilemma*. In both those parts he was splendid, so when I went to the Regent and found I was to understudy him, I was naturally thrilled. He was ill one day and I went on for two or three performances and seemed to do quite well. I was lucky to get the chance of playing but as a result I tended to become imitative. I had little idea at that time of playing a part with any originality.

At the end of 1923, after leaving RADA, I played Charles Wykeham, one of the dreadful boys in *Charley's Aunt*, at the Comedy Theatre. Even though I thought it would be rather fun to be in a farce, I did not enjoy it. Amy Brandon-Thomas, the daughter of the author, was determined that the play should be done exactly as it had been from the very beginning, a kind of tradition, like Gilbert and Sullivan.

In 1924 J. B. Fagan sent for me to his house in St John's Wood and asked me if I would like to go to Oxford and play six or seven parts in a repertory season there. He had taken a curious place in Woodstock Road, an archaeological museum full of stuffed animals, known locally as the Red Barn. The seats were bentwood chairs ranged on wooden planks so that when you moved the whole row shifted and squeaked. There was no front curtain, and we never knew where to put the prompter whom we always needed very badly because, as we did a new play every week, we all used to dry up and make mistakes. It was an ambitious programme, but great fun. I lived in Oxford in a troy flat in the High and earned £8 a week, a marvellous sum to me in those days.

The indefatigable Richard Goolden was in the company and Flora Robson as well. Tyrone Guthrie was also a member of the company and tried to act — not very successfully- but he was very amusing and an original personality. I played three seasons at Oxford and had some very good parts and in 1924 I did my first — silent — film: *Who is the Man?* playing a dope-fiend sculptor in a part originally written for Sarah Bernhardt.

At the end of the first Oxford season Fagan released me to go to understudy Noël Coward, who was playing Nicky Lancaster in his first success, *The Vortex.*[4] Someone had said 'Oh, I hear you play the piano a bit,' which is why I got the job (and why I got the job in *The Constant Nymph* afterwards). In fact, I can only play by ear, like my father, and have never been able to read music.

I went to see Noël at the Royalty Theatre in Dean Street, very apprehensive of course, but very thrilled to meet him. His dressing-room was filled of bottles of Chanel No. 5, with twenty dressing-gowns in the wardrobe. He had just finished writing a revue for Cochran called *On With the Dance*, which was shortly to be produced in Manchester, and Noël wanted to go up for the first night to see it, so he said I should take over Nicky Lancaster for that performance. It was my first smart, West End engagement. A few weeks later Noël decided to leave the cast to have a holiday before taking the play to

New York, and Lillian Braithwaite very kindly agreed to forego her holiday and continue in the play while I succeeded Noël. We were acting at the Little Theatre in John Street, Adelphi, one night, when a cat came on to the stage while we were playing the big emotional scene in the last act. I became so hysterical that I threw it into the audience. Fortunately the auditorium was almost level with the stage, and the cat was able to slip away.

I was very much aware that Noël was an infinitely better Nicky Lancaster than I was. It was a highly-strung, nervous, hysterical part which depended a lot upon emotion. I found it tiring to play because I did not know how to save myself. However, the play ran a long time and did good business, which was rather gratifying at that stage in my career.

Noël was always word-perfect at the first rehearsal and expected the whole company to be the same. This was all very well for him because he was usually the author too. He had terrible rows with Gladys Cooper and Edith Evans in later years because they would not learn his lines beforehand. He used to say that it wasted so much time. In my view, it is much easier to learn the words when you have the movement and the business. It is important to know how the other actor is going to speak his line so that both of you can react properly. If you start absolutely word-perfect, like a parrot, I think it makes everything flat and dull. Perhaps Noël's method suited his own plays — they are written in a very clipped, staccato style, and he nearly always played them with people like Gertrude Lawrence, an extraordinary, volatile, talented creature who invariably gave the plays a rhythm and quality of her own. She was a much greater actress than Noël was an actor, though he too was highly skilled and spoke his own words and lyrics quite brilliantly, with marvellous pace and diction.

Noël was always highly professional and very much down on anybody who was not. He adored Hawtrey, who, he said, had taught him everything he knew. Hawtrey fascinated me too. I saw him in a number of plays, and he never seemed to do anything at all. He was fat, with a lazy manner, not good-looking at all, but with impeccable timing- and a deadpan perfection in comic situations.

I went back to Oxford for the 1924-5 season. Fagan put on The *Cherry Orchard*, which had then not been seen in England except in a Stage Society production when many of the audience walked out through sheer boredom. We were all bewildered by the play, but I found the part of the student Trofimov fascinating. I thought I would make up with a bald wig and steel spectacles — Chekhov says that the student's hair is very thin. When I walked on to the stage at the first performance, I suddenly thought, 'This isn't what I thought acting was. I'm just part of a novel, or a family, or something very intimate, and I don't care what they feel about it in front, I know I have to do it this way.' It was a revelation to me. I also began to see, for the first time, that it was possible to project a personality completely different from one's own, rather than just showing off.

Although none of us understood the play there was an extraordinary sincerity about the performance, and a feeling of discovery for the young company. When Playfair came to see it he immediately offered to transfer it to the Lyric, Hammersmith, where we had a rapturous first night followed by a very mixed press. Playfair decided it was a failure and engaged a cast for a revival of *The Beggar's Opera* to replace it. But Fagan decided to move us to the Royalty Theatre in Dean Street and we ran there all through the summer. It was a great success and, for me, a thrilling engagement because it led to so many things afterwards.

In 1924, I played my first Romeo in London with Gwen Ffrangcon-Davies.[5] She had seen me in The *Insect Play* and thought I was simply awful, and when she heard I was to play Romeo she practically had a fit. Fortunately at the first rehearsal she took a fancy to me and we have been devoted friends from that day to this. She had had a very exciting career, mostly in Birmingham, as Barry Jackson's leading lady. She made her greatest success as Elizabeth Browning in *The Barretts of Wimpole Street*, but to my mind, Jackson never really exploited her potential. He was not certain that he wanted stars in his company; he believed in a repertory company — which is perhaps why I got the part of Romeo.

Gwen played everything with extraordinary skill and wit. When she played the subordinate part of Lady Herbert in *The Lady with the Lamp*, a play about Florence Nightingale with Edith Evans in the

took pupils in a mountain chalet. Throughout the first act she was making pasta, occasionally obliging with excerpts from her opera triumphs. In the third act there was a scene in which her daughter was being stoned because she had had an affair with a peasant and went into a church for refuge. She put on the Madonna's robe and crown and the peasants thought she was the Mother of God come to life and knelt down and worshipped her. In the next act the daughter returned home and her mother had to say, 'I salute my genius in you,' and fall on her knees. I thought this would be the most marvellous scene for Mrs. Campbell, but she only said sulkily, 'I suppose you want me to play the daughter.' She was then about seventy and extremely fat. It was preposterous, but typical of the way she cut the ground from under your feet, so you could not help her or advise her.

When we played together in *Ghosts*, James Agate said that she was like the Lord Mayor's coach with nothing in it! Indeed, she did very little with the part, being far too busy insulting the unfortunate man playing Pastor Manders. He was frightened to death of her and sweated furiously. She would say with her back to the audience, 'Oh, look at that old man with the sweat pouring onto his stomach.' In the great scene where I had to tell her that I had got brain disease she taught me most carefully how to say my line ('The disease I suffer from is seated here' — pointing to my forehead). She said, 'You must speak with a channel-steamer voice. Pinero showed me how to do it!' As I was preparing to say the line at the first performance, she said, in a loud aside, 'Oh, I am so hungry!' Yet, at the dress rehearsal, when one would have expected her to be most difficult, she had sailed through, knowing every line and being most impressive. She was totally unpredictable. Later on I started to direct her in a play by Rodney Ackland, *Strange Orchestra*, in which she would have been wonderful. She rehearsed for two weeks and then threw up the part because her dog was in quarantine. She used to draw funny pictures of everybody during rehearsals.

Rehearsing *Pygmalion* with Tree she must have been impossible. They were both such eccentrics. They kept ordering each other out of the theatre with Shaw in the middle, trying to cope with them. How the play ever came out I cannot imagine. I saw the revival in which she played Eliza again — she was fifty in 1914 when she first created the part. She was far too old, of course, but she did some wonderful things. I remember her knitting in the last act, very haughtily, speaking with a terrible bogus accent. She was brilliant in the tea scene. I have an idea that Shaw wrote it as a skit on her real voice, the booming contralto that everybody used to love to imitate.

When I went to see her in *The Matriarch*, she played the last act in a wheelchair wearing a big fur cloak, and a black hat with a veil. At the end of the performance — I knew how to get backstage because I had played in that theatre — I pushed the pass-door open and said, 'Where's Mrs. Campbell's dressing-room?' 'Oh, she's gone,' they said. 'Gone, how can she have? She was taking her call a minute ago.' 'Oh, she always goes out with the audience, just drops her cloak in the wings and pushes past them.'

I saw her play Ella Rentheim in *John Gabriel Borkman* in a little repertory theatre at Kew Bridge. Her dressing-room was so small that she could hardly move in it. She gave a marvellous performance in the second and fourth acts, and a disgraceful one in the other two. Mrs. Borkman was played by an actress called Nancy Price whom Mrs. Campbell disliked. They refused to take any notice of one another, which was something of a drawback since the first act consists almost entirely of a dialogue between Mrs. Borgan and Ella Rentheim. The two ladies sat in large armchairs on either side of the stage (with two prompters as near as possible in the wings) looking straight into the audience, and speaking their lines without taking any notice of each other at all. Then the second act began. Mrs. Campbell liked Victor Lewisohn, who played Borkman, and thought him a fine actor. So she suddenly blossomed and gave the most wonderful performance. She only acted to please herself, with no sense of responsibility towards an audience or her fellow actors. Yet she came to see me act quite often and used to give me wonderful tips. When I was playing *Hamlet* in New York she sent me a card — 'Give me the beauty I long for.' I asked my director to invite her to the party after the performance and she behaved with appalling tactlessness. She went up to Judith Anderson, who was playing the Queen, and said, 'Why do you sit on the bed? Only housemaids sit on the bed!' To the director, she said, 'Why has the Ghost got mumps?' (The Ghost wore a large mask.)

I was with her in New York the day Edward VIII abdicated. We had just been to see Charles Laughton in the film *Rembrandt*. When we came out, the famous Abdication speech from Fort Belvedere was being broadcast. We went into the Plaza Hotel to hear it. Mrs. Campbell burst into tears and said, 'Let's send him a telegram.' I suggested that since we did not know the ex-King and in any case he would have left Fort Belvedere by this time, it was not a good idea. 'Oh, yes, we must, we must,' she said, so we rushed to a post office.

She said to the clerk, 'Isn't this wonderful? The greatest thing since Antony gave up a kingdom for Cleopatra.' The woman took a piece of gum out of her mouth and replied, 'Oh, I guess he just wanted to go play ball.' I finally persuaded her to send a telegram to Charles Laughton instead, saying how much we had enjoyed his film.

It was in the early 1920s that the Guitrys, father and son, first appeared in London with their enchanting leading lady, Yvonne Printemps.[7] I have a vivid recollection of Lucien Guitry's acting in a drama called *Jacqueline*, produced in London in 1922, in which he played an elderly roué who strangles his mistress in the final scene. It was the preparation for this denouement in the second act that impressed me most. The scene was in a hotel bedroom where he had taken the girl for a weekend. Guitry stood over her as she lay on the bed, and she suddenly shrank from him crying, 'Oh ! You terrify me.' For a few seconds he seemed to grow inches taller and become a towering and sadistic creature. Then, suddenly breaking the tension completely, he resumed his normally charming manner for the rest of the scene. I watched him most intently, and am convinced that in fact he did absolutely nothing, not moving his hands, his face or his body. His absolute stillness and the projection of his concentrated imagination, controlled and executed with a consummate technique, produced on the girl and on the audience an extraordinary and unforgettable effect. I knew I had seen a great actor.

I met Sacha Guitry on only one occasion. In March 1939 Peggy Ashcroft and I were invited to appear at a gala given in the courtyard at the Foreign Office to celebrate the state visit of the French President, M. Lebrun. It was a tremendous affair, the last of its kind before the war, and I could not help referring to it afterwards as the Duchess of Richmond's Ball. There was a magnificent profusion of flowers, sent from Sir Philip Sassoon's garden at Lympne, masses of azaleas edging the balconies, and a positive thicket of madonna lilies dividing the stage from the auditorium.

Sacha Guitry had been invited to appear with Seymour Hicks in a sketch written by them both. Hicks was a great admirer of Sacha and had acted in English versions of several of his plays. The humour of the little piece was supposed to lie in attempts by Sacha to speak English and Hicks to reply in French. Both actors were exceedingly nervous and obviously under-rehearsed. I watched them from the wings as they kept drying up and killing each other's laughs, which were not very plentiful in any case. Appearing with them was Sacha's latest wife, Genevieve Sereville, an extremely young and pretty girl. At the morning rehearsal Peggy and I had been asked to be intro-duced to the distinguished visitors. Mlle Sereville was dressed in a very short skirt, and her stockings were rolled below the knees like a footballer's, showing a considerable expanse of thigh. We stammered a few polite words in our somewhat halting French, to which M. Guitry, an imposing figure with fur collar and gold-topped cane, made suitably gracious acknowledgment. As we moved away to find our dressing-rooms I ventured to remark to Hicks 'I say, sir, that's a remarkably attractive girl with M. Guitry, don't you think?' and was rewarded by the trenchant comment, 'Try acting with her, old boy. It's the cabman's goodbye.'

The first time I saw my name in lights was in 1928 in a farce with Hermione Baddeley. It was an appalling concoction, backed by the lady who had written it, called *Holding Out the Apple*. It contained, among many others, one immortal line: 'You've got a way of holding out the apple that positively gives me the pip.' It ran about six weeks, largely to an audience of nurses in free seats. I was next to play in a ghastly thriller called *The Skull*, and later in another drama, *Out of the Sea* at the Strand Theatre, in which I played a pianist who strummed excerpts from *Tristan* on the piano before committing suicide with the heroine on a rock. That was a disaster too. I began to feel restive.

It was agreeable to be well paid, announced in big letters at the top of the bill, but not in such wretched plays. Then I had a chance to re-place Leslie Banks in *The Lady With the Lamp* with Edith Evans and Gwen Ffrangcon-Davies.

I had never worked with Edith Evans before, but I had seen her in a number of plays and admired her enormously. We rehearsed our scenes together — I was very much in awe of her — and she kept say-ing that I was not *dirty* enough in the scene when I was carried in, dying on a stretcher. To make myself dirtier I used to strip in the dressing-room and cover myself with fuller's earth, so that when she touched me in the hospital scene she would believe that I was en-crusted with the dust of the battlefield.

Sybil Thorndike seemed to revel in her success, but Edith Evans did not. Edith was undoubtedly the greater artist of the two; Sybil was the greater woman. Edith Evans was the finest actress of our time and I am privileged to have known and worked with her so often. She was not always easy. There was something rather aloof about her. She was not a cozy person, except when you could get her alone occasionally. In Bryan Forbes' life of her she told him that she liked me only when we were alone together, away from all the frivo-lous nonsense with which I liked to surround myself. I admired her dedication. She was not gregarious, and she found it difficult to open out to people. Like Ellen Terry and Peggy Ashcroft she longed to be an ordinary woman, to have a home, a husband, perhaps children. She never had them. At different times she tried to take up dancing, farming, attempted to drive a car or skate, to do the everyday things that an ordinary woman does. But she was always driven back to the theatre — just as Ellen Terry was.

She had been first discovered by the eccentric William Poel, who cast her as Cressida, after rehearsing her first in several male parts in the same production. He had encouraged her to leave the Belgravia hat-shop in which she had been working and become a professional actress.[8] At that time she was considered plain, and leading ladies were expected to be beautiful. Edith Evans was no beauty in the con-ventional sense. Her eyes, with their heavy lids, were set with one slightly lower than the other, giving her face an enigmatic originality. But it was a fascinating canvas on which she soon learned to paint any character she chose. I remember once saying as a young actor, 'I would love a photograph of Edith Evans. I never know what she looks like, she always looks like the part.' It was probably the greatest compliment I could have paid her.

It was as Millamant, in Congreve's The *Way of the World*, that she took the town by storm. It was a unique and exquisite performance. She purred and challenged, mocked and melted, showing her changing moods by subtly shifting the angles of her head, neck and shoulders. Poised and cool, like a porcelain figure in a vitrine, she used her fan — which she never opened — in the great love scene as an instrument for attack or defence, now coquettishly pointing it upwards beneath her chin, now resting it languidly against her cheek. Her words flowed on, phrasing and diction balanced in perfect cadences, as she smiled and pouted in delivering her delicious sallies. She displayed her superb taste by perfect timing and control, never stooping to indulge an overenthusiastic audience, and disdaining any temptation to overstress an emotional moment or allow too many laughs to interrupt the pace of a comic scene.

She grew to hate her success as Lady Bracknell, though it was perhaps the most popular and famous of all her great impersonations. She was staying at my cottage in Essex one weekend just before the War when I suggested a possible revival of the Wilde play. I took a copy from the bookshelf and we read the handbag scene together to the other guests. After the laughter had died down Edith handed me back the book and remarked gravely, 'I know those sort of women. They ring the bell and tell you to put a lump of coal on the fire.'

She disliked the imitations of her trumpet tone in the famous line 'A *handbag?*' which many people seemed to think was the alpha and omega of her performance as Lady Bracknell. For me there was so much else to admire. There were the exquisite details of observation and execution; the sly look of suspicion, for instance, as she glanced at the armchair she had chosen for the interview with Worthing in the first act. In those few seconds she managed to convey both appraisal and approval, as if reassuring herself of the suitability of that particular piece of furniture as a throne for her corseted dignity, before deigning to lower herself into the seat.

She strove to create her performances from an inner conviction, trying to find the 'bridges,' as she called them, to achieve progression and climax in the characters she was determined to bring to life. 'I never make effects,' she used to say. Of course she did — but with what subtlety, skill and artistry.

In 1932 I was asked to direct — for the first time in that capacity — a production of *Romeo and Juliet* at Oxford for the OUDS, and was enriched by the privilege of working with Peggy Ashcroft as Juliet and Edith Evans as the Nurse. Of course, I was greatly in awe of Edith at first. I timidly suggested that she might perhaps be doing needlework in her opening scene with Juliet and Lady Capulet. I pictured her, I suppose, with a tapestry in a frame and a large needle threading in and out, typical romantic costume-play 'business.' I was quite wrong, though she knew at once what I was driving at. She kept a tiny piece of material between her hands which she handled very sparingly (almost hiding it in her long sleeves) using a gentle rhythmic movement to give a slight counterpoint to her first long speech without in the least detracting from it. It was my first glimpse of her remarkable instinct for selectivity.

She preferred to move very little. I do not remember any swift entrances or exits in her performances and she taught me to give up my own impatient inclination to drive actors about the stage in order to give a scene excitement long before the dialogue demanded it. You could not hurry Edith or muddle her with too many suggestions before she was ready for them. The character and its truth, the pattern of the syllables, the give and take of the vocal exchanges, these were slowly taking shape during the early rehearsals and from these basic foundations she began to develop her performance. Not until the part really began to possess her would she completely sweep in to her performance. She could not, as some actors do, patch together old material which she had tried out successfully in other plays in order to achieve a superficial short cut to a new creation.

She was always extremely reticent about the acting of her colleagues; praise from her was as precious as it was rare. Once she paid me a sublime compliment which I shall always cherish. 'Your Benedick, Johnnie,' she said after a rather stormy argument about the playing of comedy, 'that performance, you know, was seven-eighths perfection!'

Chapter Three

1929-1930

Harcourt Williams at the Old Vic — Shakespeare at record speed —
Richard II — *Lilian Baylis* — 'Which Hamlet are you?' — The
Importance of Being Earnest — *Ralph Richardson* — Macbeth

At the end of 1928 I suddenly had an offer from Harcourt Williams,
whom I knew slightly, to go to the Old Vic.[1] I was reluctant to go because of the salary, which was only £10 a week. As a sort of leading
man I was being paid about £50 a week in the West End and getting
billed above the title. Harcourt Williams was offering me a season
with several leads, though none specified in the contract. In two
minds whether to accept or not, I went to Edith Evans between performances of *The Lady with the Lamp*. Usually she never saw anybody
while she was resting, but she asked me in and gave me a long talk,
and finally said, "If you want to learn how to play Shakespeare, I
think you'd be very wise to accept it.' And so I did.

Martita Hunt was engaged to play opposite me and Gyles Isham,
who had been a very successful Hamlet as an undergraduate at Oxford, was also in the company. Lilian Baylis thought that he would
probably play it again at the Vic.[2] When it came to discussing parts
and I said I wanted to play Hamlet, she hedged and havered, though
finally I did get the part. After a few weeks, I found that I got on well
with the company, especially with Harcourt Williams, though not
with Donald Wolfit, who always disliked me very much. In fact, when
he was afterwards in management, with a great reputation in Shakespeare, he referred to me as 'the Enemy' and used to go purple in the
face at the very mention of my name. He was a powerful actor, who
had learned his business from Matheson Lang and Fred Terry, but
had also learned some of their old-fashioned actor-manager's tricks,

and he lacked any sense of humour, particularly about himself. He was jealous too, and though often effective, could, I thought, be very tasteless in his acting.

Harcourt Williams was a delightful man. He was a vegetarian and carried around a big tin of Bemax to keep him going. His devoted wife, who was a diseuse and gave recitals every year for children, adored him and was always at his right hand to encourage him. He was a very modest man. He had been with Ellen Terry, Benson and Granville-Barker and had an enormous admiration for them all. He had been a very good actor himself, and extremely good-looking too as a young man. But he was beginning to age during the two arduous Vic seasons of 1929-31 and he fired very easily. As soon as he found he could get on so well with me and with Martita — and in the second season with Ralph Richardson and Leslie French — he would invite us to go and have buns with him at lunchtime and would ask us for suggestions. I would rough out ideas for sets and Ralph for casting, and we were all encouraged to contribute and have our say.

I had walked on at the Old Vic right back in 1921 as an unpaid student between terms at the Benson school. In those days the company had been full of the sort of old actors you read about in Dickens. I was terrified of them because they were real old 'laddies,' rushing off to the bar every five minutes and using awful language. I walked on there in four plays in which Russell Thorndike played all the leads: Hamlet, Peer Gynt, Wat Tyler and Lear; four huge parts in the space of five weeks. He knew them all perfectly and acted with great wit and drive. My first speaking part was the Herald in *Henry V* with one line — 'Here is the number of the slaughter'd French.'

In 1929 my first role was to be Romeo and, just as before, it was not a success. Adele Dixon played Juliet and Wolfit was Mercutio. Williams tried to make us play very fast in order to get through the whole play in the two hours that the Chorus says it should last. The result was that we gabbled and the audience could barely hear us. This was Williams' first attempt to carry out the instructions in Granville-Barker's prefaces.

Next we did *The Merchant of Venice*, in which I played Antonio and Brember Wills was not very successful as Shylock. Then we did a version of Moliére's *Le Malade Imaginaire,* and after that *Richard II.* I could see from the company's attitude that they all thought I was going to be good in *Richard II* and I felt elated at being allowed to play the part. It ran for only about three weeks and there were hardly any notices, but I began to feel I had made a real personal success.

This was, in fact, one of the advantages of the Vic. A young actor could try his wings without being slanged or over-praised the next day. I played Macbeth later on in that first season and James Agate came to one of the matinées, representing the great *Sunday Times.* He came round to my dressing room after the murder scene and said, 'You were very good in that scene, but I know you can't do the rest of the play so I just thought I would come round and tell you now!' But mostly the critics did not come at all, and we depended for success on the loyal Vic audience.

The audiences at the Vic were very lively. There was an old lady called Miss Pilgrim who ran a stationer's shop in Islington. She had been a fan of the Old Vic for years and used to walk all the way from Islington to Waterloo Road for the first nights and many other performances. She always sat in the gallery and at the end of the performance she would sing 'God Save the King' in a very loud cracked voice. She had a wall eye, we all knew her by sight and she used to write letters to us. A year or two after I had left, when Tyrone Guthrie took over the direction, stars like Charles Laughton, Athene Seyler, Flora Robson and James Mason were in the company. Miss Pilgrim went to the stage door one night and asked everybody in the company to sign their autographs for her as they came out of the theatre. The next day they found that the paper had been folded over, and on the other side she had written a demand to the Governors that Tyrone Guthrie should be sacked.

I doubt whether Lilian Baylis had any real understanding of Shakespeare. In fact, I do not think she ever saw a play right through. I would meet her wandering about the passages during performances or she would write letters behind a curtain in the back of her box. But she always seemed to know exactly what was happening in her theatre. She never involved herself in rows over productions, apart from the invariable comment that it was all costing too much. She liked coming on to the stage herself in her cap and gown, and making rather jolly appeals to the public, telling them that they must all come to the theatre much more and that they were all bounders. She was a parochial mother-figure, but with this extraordinary belief that she was there for a purpose which it was her duty to carry out. Her opening of Sadler's Wells at the beginning of the thirties, for instance, was madness. The theatre was horrible, done up as cheaply as possible with very poor acoustics. We all dreaded it.

Our production of *Hamlet* that 1929-30 season had been so successful that Maurice Browne, who was then a producer — he had put on *Journey's End* and made a lot of money — transferred it to the Queen's Theatre in the West End. That was where I crossed swords with Wolfit. He was playing the King, and thought I had influenced Williams to cut his part for the West End, which of course I had not. But he grumbled and groused throughout the run. The weather was appallingly hot that summer and by some extraordinary chance Henry Ainley was playing *Hamlet* at the Haymarket and Alexander Moissi was playing it in German at the Globe, so there were three Hamlets in the West End together.

The Globe was next door and I went to a matinée to see the production. Moissi had a curious tenor voice. He was playing, of course, in German which I could not understand, but although I knew the part by heart I was unable to follow the text. There were some impressive things in the production, but Moissi himself was a very poor Hamlet. He appeared to be permanently sorry for himself, crying into his handkerchief in the Nunnery scene, and finally stabbing the King in the back. I was introduced to him backstage and he looked me up and down and said, through his interpreter, 'Oh, you play it in the Spanish style, I see.' (My costume had a high white collar and black trunk hose.) That was all he said. He was wearing a costume that somehow combined Peter Pan with the Middle Ages, and it did not suit him very well. But I also saw him as Fedya in *The Living Corpse* and thought him strikingly effective in it.

I was not thought of as a character actor in those days, having so often played nervous, hysterical young men. But I had a feeling that perhaps if I played a character with truth it might make me a better actor. In juvenile parts I was inclined to be an exhibitionist and for a long time my ambition was to be frightfully smart and West End,

wear beautifully cut suits lounging on sofas in French 'window comedies.' The Vic began to cure me of such ideas. When I was asked to
play Hamlet, the great juvenile part of all times, at first I thought I
would make a terrible hash of it because I felt I could give only an in-
ferior copy of the other Hamlets I had seen — about twelve by that
time. At drama school I had loved trailing my black cloak around,
posing and being emotional, but I had a feeling there was something
wrong with that.

I threw myself into the part like a man learning to swim and I
found that the text would hold me up if I sought the truth in it. It oc-
curred to me that most actors tried to whitewash the unpleasant as-
pects of Hamlet's character. The handsome, middle-aged stars of the
Edwardian theatre romanticized the part. Even John Barrymore,
whose Hamlet I admired very much, cut the play outrageously so that
he could, for instance, play the closet scene all out for sentiment,
with the emphasis on the 'Oedipus complex,' sobbing on Gertrude's
bosom. Yet Barrymore, like Russell Thorndike, had a wonderful edge
and a demonic sense of humour. Ernest Milton had the same quality.
Of all the actors in my time I felt he must be the nearest to Irving,
with the same kind of extravagance and flowery, sinister power.

The majority of people who remember my Hamlet saw it at the
Haymarket Theatre in 1944, the last time I played it in London. But
the few people alive who saw both my last and my first Hamlet say
that the Old Vic version was the better. To see a Hamlet aged twenty-
five was a new experience for the public then. The actors in the Edwardian period never played it until they were forty. John Barrymore
was forty-five when I saw him. The youthful tantrums and despair of
the opening scenes were perhaps more poignant because I was so
young. And then, as I have said, I tried to find the violent and ugly
colours in the part.[3]

In the 1944 production, which George Rylands directed, I felt I
was too old to get the same effects in the opening scenes, though I
was perhaps better in the last ones. Harley Granville-Barker had
given me a great many valuable notes about the play when we did the
Elsinore production just before the war.

In 1945 I played Hamlet for the troops in the Middle East, which was exciting because there were no critics to worry about and success or failure was unimportant. What mattered was to make them listen by trying to do it as well as possible. The trouble with the Rylands production was that I was too tired. We were performing three other plays in repertory with two performances on Wednesdays and Saturdays. At the matinée I would sleep on my sofa for ten minutes during Ophelia's mad scene, which is the only wait Hamlet has, and after the final curtain would swallow a cup of tea and start making up for the evening performance.

The most thrilling Hamlet for me was the production in New York in 1936, because I felt I was on my mettle. It was my first big chance in America, and I was presented by an American management with an all-American cast except for Malcolm Keen, who played the King, and Harry Andrews, who played Horatio. Rehearsals were thrilling because everyone seemed so excited about my performance. It was fearfully hot weather. We rehearsed on a roof somewhere and poured with sweat. I gave my all at those rehearsals, so anxious was I to impress the company.

At the time I was asked to go to America, I heard that Leslie Howard was proposing to play Hamlet there as well.[4] I said in that case I would not go. He was a great star and an Englishman and it would have been impertinent to put myself in competition against him. I signed my contract on the strict understanding that Howard would not do his production — and then, months later, he announced he would do it after all. He had an English cast, with Pamela Stanley and Clifford Evans and Lady Forbes-Robertson, the widow of the great Sir Johnston. Howard started on tour and the production I was in was the first to open in New York. My notices were interesting and reasonably kind, but though the reception on the first night had been overwhelmingly appreciative, I was doubtful of success. I remember cabling home and saying I thought we might run for six weeks with luck. Soon afterwards Howard's production opened and was not at all liked. The next day we had standing room only. It must have been a fearful blow to him and he naturally resented it very much and made speeches defending his performance. The gossip columns were full of it — it was called the 'battle of the Hamlets' — and the taxi drivers used to say to me, 'Which Hamlet are *you?*' The publicity people tried to get me to meet Howard and we were urged to go to see each other's performances, which we both refused to do.

It was slightly uncanny how our careers seemed to run on parallel lines. I met Howard only twice, and then merely for a chat and a drink, but I understudied him in a revival of *Berkeley Square* in which it was arranged that I should play some performances for him. I remember rehearsing the part but I never saw him in the theatre and I never went on. Later I was asked to play his part in *The Petrified Forest* in London and refused because I did not care for the play. Howard, of course, had made a huge success of it in America.

At the beginning of the Second War, Howard was in England. He did not go back to his home in Hollywood, he sold his polo ponies and went off to Portugal to give pro-Allies lectures. At about the same time — Christmas 1942 — I went with a concert-party company, including Edith Evans and Beatrice Lillie, to Gibraltar. We went by plane and were told that there was no danger as we should be flying through a neutral zone. A few weeks later Leslie Howard was shot down and killed — in the very same plane. A little later, when I was playing at the Haymarket, I was sent the script of a film with a note from the producers saying that Howard was to have made the film and they could think of no better substitute than me. I was horrified, flung the script across the room and would have nothing to do with it.

My New York *Hamlet* broke the Broadway record for continuous performances previously set by Barrymore — 101 performances. In fact, my record held until Richard Burton broke it in the mid 1960s, in a production directed by me, which seemed a little ironic.

Hamlet is not, however, a role that an actor should ever be asked to portray for a hundred performances on end. There is such a range of opportunity in the part that it encourages you to try all sorts of different tricks and effects. You need a very strict director to keep you in line. When I directed Burton in *Hamlet* he told me that the one thing in which I had been able to help him was knowing where the rests were, so that he did not play too long on hysteria and nerves. I tried to make him find a real line for the part. The play is so familiar that the temptation is to play up the 'show' scenes — the closet scene, the nunnery scene, the play scene, the graveyard scene — instead of making it a play with progressions in which the audience does not know what is going to happen next. It was for this reason that I loved acting Hamlet to the troops during the war. Quite unfamiliar with the story, they followed it with breathless interest, wondering what would happen next.

I have had my fill of *Hamlet* now. So many books are written about the character but I cannot read them any more. Nor, I think, could I direct the play again. When I attempted to direct Burton I found it impossible to do anything new or interesting. I was surrounded by ghosts, not just that of Hamlet's father, but of all the other productions I had seen, acted in and directed. Burton was unhappy in Elizabethan clothes and so I thought of modern dress, of staging the play as if it were a rehearsal. I conceived a very interesting set, modeled on Craig's description of the Lyceum at rehearsal time, a tree from *The Bells*, a tombstone used in *Eugene Aram*, a great sledge and a gabled housefront from *Faust*, all huddled at the sides of the empty stage. I discovered, however, that an American audience would not understand such a set, as their theatres are stripped completely after every production and need new scenery and lighting installed for every play. So I decided the cast should wear perfectly ordinary street clothes and play as if it were a rehearsal, using a wig-stick or umbrella as a sword, an overcoat to represent a cape and so on. They all spent fortunes on buying new clothes, but none of them seemed right. The King brought different costumes to rehearsal — panama hats, blazers, slacks — and the Queen brought a mink coat which did not look right either. The set, although it was rather impressive, was bare and bleak, and the audience had no idea what we were getting at. It was too theatrical an idea to succeed in the theatre! I played the Ghost myself. I recorded the speeches and projected a huge shadow on the stage which I thought was the only really effective idea in the whole production.

The American cast did not appear to understand very much of what I was trying to do. All they wanted was motivation. Unfortunately, the Method does not work for Shakespeare. In 'intellectual' drama, Ibsen and Shaw for instance, a character's intentions are motivated very clearly, and his background too. There is a story of Barrie or Pinero saying at rehearsal, 'Now remember, you have an aunt in Surbiton who wears grey felt bonnets.' In Shakespeare's plays, characters like Rosencrantz and Gui!denstern, Salarino, and all those lords in the historical plays, are not developed individually but can be turned into effective cameos if clever actors play them. In America I was attacked after every rehearsal by desperate actors asking 'What is this character *about?*' I fear that, in the end, my ill-tempered reply would be 'It's about being a good feed for Hamlet.' In England a young, ambitious actor takes these minor parts in his stride. He plays Oliver in *As You Like It* or Salarino in *The Merchant of Venice* or any of those supporting roles, and tries to find something to do with them, while waiting for the time when he will be allowed to play Orlando or Shylock.

The last time I ever played Hamlet was in the Cairo Opera House. It was a school matinée, packed with children, and as we started the play I thought 'Well, this is the last time I shall ever play this wonderful part. I'm forty-five and it's quite time to give it up.' Early on in the performance the unfortunate man who played Horatio fell into my arms in an epileptic fit on the line 'My Lord, I think I saw him yesternight.' The audience was bewildered as I shouted to the prompt corner, rather crossly, 'Drop the curtain. Put something between his teeth. Fetch the understudy.' The understudy came, rescued from the bowels of the theatre where he was making up for Guildenstern, and did not know a line. When he pointed to the Ghost and said, 'Look my Lord it comes,' I said, 'No, you fool, the other way!' or words to that effect. Fortunately, the epileptic Horatio recovered the next day, but I could never quite forgive him for ruining my final performance of Hamlet!

Miss Baylis asked me to return to the Vic for the 1930 season at £20 a week. I was much impressed, knowing what an agony it was for her to increase a salary. Between the two Vic seasons Playfair asked me to go to the Lyric, Hammersmith, and play John Worthing in *The Importance of Being Earnest* with my aunt Mabel Terry-Lewis as Lady Bracknell, Anthony Ireland as Algy and Jean Cadell as Miss Prism. The production was entirely in black and white in the manner of

Beardsley drawings and was a great success. It could have run longer
if I had not had to go back to the Vic. We played it all through that
very hot summer. One day, at a matinée, we were trying to play the
muffins scene when I glanced at the audience and saw about six old
ladies in different parts of the stalls all hanging over their seats fast
asleep. I became quite hysterical and Tony Ireland and I were nearly
sacked because we giggled so disgracefully.

In my second season at the Vic we were joined by Ralph Richard-
son.⁵ I had seen Ralph quite often on the stage before I got to know
him and work with him for the first time. He had been in a number
of productions for Barry Jackson and was a friend of Frank Vosper,
who was also a friend of mine.

Ralph was a remarkable man, shrewd, observant, warm and gen-
erous-hearted, once you get to know him. He was also reserved and
cautious, never making a swift decision about anything. He did, however, make a very swift decision about me at our first meeting. He
thought that I was affected and conceited and wore unsuitably dandy
clothes. Gradually, however, we found we had a lot of interests in
common, and one day when we were rehearsing *The Tempest* — he
was playing Caliban and I was playing Prospero — he suddenly decided that I knew what I was talking about and that he liked my acting, and we remained the most devoted friends ever after.

We were both in *Henry IV Part I* with which the 1930 season
opened. Ralph hated the fighting and I did not like it much either.
During the battle of Shrewsbury Ralph used to shout 'Left ... right ...
now you hit me, Cocky ... now I hit you' — I was sure the audience
could hear him. He was not particularly happy as Prince Hal, but absolutely superb as Caliban and, later in the same season, as Enobarbus and Kent. In fact, I cannot imagine anybody playing them so
well. He always took great pains with his make-up, for which he
would make elaborate drawings beforehand. He and Olivier vied
with each other in the construction of putty noses. I always implored
him to revive his Falstaff which he played in 1945 at the New Theatre, and which was, to my mind, a definitive performance. What a
magnificent Peer Gynt he was in the same season and how unforget-
tably good in Priestley's *Johnson over Jordan* and *Eden End*, and, of
course, in so many successes since.

Ralph and I always got on extremely well whenever I acted with him or directed him. He knew that out of twelve suggestions I make two will be some good and the rest can be thrown in the dustbin. We were neither of us wildly intellectual but Ralph had a far wider range of interests than I do. He followed history and poetics, he read voraciously. He knew about clocks and furniture and china and motor cars and all things mechanical. He had endless hobbies. He was far less frivolous, theatrically, than I am. I have always adored the 'cheap' side of the theatre, the billing, the advertisements, the queues, the fan-letters and the somewhat unbalanced adulation of certain people whose admiration is extravagant and often insincere. Ralph, like Edith Evans, had enormous dignity and reserve where the public was concerned. Both were far more exercised about the quality of a performance than its effect upon an audience, whereas I am inclined to think to myself 'A jolly good house today, went marvellously and I made a lot of stunning effects, must try to remember to put them in again tomorrow night.' That was not the way of Ralph and Edith, both of them selective and economical in their work. (Oddly enough, when they played together, there was no great rapport — Ralph admired Edith, but I suspect that she found him too eccentric.) Realistic actors, like Ralph, labour to find the core of a character. Until they have had time to study a role they do not want to be looked at or even criticized. By contrast, I am rather conceitedly ready to jump in and take a wild dash at a part at the first rehearsals. I find it difficult to work by myself at home. I develop a part during rehearsals with the company, make mad suggestions, throw them out and try some more. I am featherheaded and not really thorough. Now and again my method appears to work — so long as my fellow players are prepared to put up with it.

During those two seasons at the Old Vic I learnt a great deal about playing Shakespeare. What was so valuable was the opportunity of getting to know how to act with breadth for an enthusiastic, largely unlettered audience who did not resent us making broad effects. The fact that we worked for such small salaries, which placed restrictions on our social life in our salad days, was very good for us. It was exciting to find that I could do something with a part like Benedick. I was certainly not ideally cast for the role of a bluff soldier, and so I tried to find another way of playing it, as a kind of courtier. It was good experience and led to a good many similar experiments. I even played Antony in *Antony and Cleopatra*, for which I was utterly unsuited, but I padded my doublet and wore a false beard and shouted and boomed, and achieved some sort of result. I remember thinking that I could not learn the words because there were whole speeches I did not understand and there was no time to discuss or analyse them. So I tried a different approach, looking carefully at the punctuation and hoping the sense would in some way emerge. And I found that it seemed to help. Later, in *The Winter's Tale* and *Measure For Measure*, I began to trust to the sweep of a whole speech, concentrating on the commas, full stops and semi-colons. If I kept to them and breathed with them, like an inexperienced swimmer, the verse seemed to hold me up and even disclose its meaning.

In *Macbeth* it was the imaginative side of the character that appealed to me. I knew I would not be able to play the warrior, the giant who cleaves people 'from the nave to the chaps,' but I found a romantic and visionary quality in the character, and a weakness which emerges when his wife urges him to murder Duncan. My interpretation was the absolute opposite of Olivier's which was, to my mind, the definitive Macbeth. Olivier had murder in his heart from the moment he came on the stage.

I thought that Macbeth, when he first comes on, should be what everyone has said he is in the first two scenes, the great warrior chieftain, loyal to Duncan, victorious in battle, flushed with success. Then he meets the witches and afterwards comes home to his wife, and these two meetings, at such a critical moment in his career, suddenly topple him from his nobility. What is so wonderful about Shakespeare is that you can play the parts in many different ways. Olivier convinced me absolutely in his production and so did Ian McKellen in Trevor Nunn's Royal Shakespeare production at the Warehouse in 1977. It is the same with Lear. I tried to play Lear as a very great king who is destroyed. Olivier played him as an eccentric, half-mad before the play begins. All sorts of people have taken different views of the part, as of all the great Shakespearean roles, and if you play them up to the hilt you can be as interesting in one way as you can in another. That is what has given them such enormous appeal for actors over the years.

Chapter Four

1931-1938

Komisarjevsky, Russian director — The Three Sisters *at Barnes* —
Katerina — *Michel St-Denis* — Noah *and* Richard of Bordeaux-
Peggy Ashcroft — Dear Octopus *with Marie Tempest*

The years 1929 and 1930 had been exciting times for me. I was
twenty-six, just the age when a young actor begins to feel his wings
are sprouting. But I was also beginning to long to try my hand at directing, and during the thirties I began to find this ambition. My desire to direct was in a large measure due to the Russian director
Theodore Komisarjevsky.[1]

Komisarjevsky was a fascinating character, who looked like a little monk, completely bald and with the most enchanting smile. He
had an impish, rather wicked humour, but was prone to 'Prussian
moods' when things were not going well, when he would maintain a
grim silence. He loved young people, especially if he thought they
had talent.

In 1925 I had been playing in one of the performances in England of Chekhov's *The Seagull* at the Little Theatre. I played the
young hero Konstantin and, in my black blouse and Russian boots, I
thought I was very romantic and noble, though I was somewhat put
out when the audience laughed loudly as I entered, a gun in one hand
and an obviously stuffed bird in the other. Komisarjevsky came to see
the production and made great fun of it, saying it was quite ridiculous and completely un-Russian. He had not long settled in England
after early years working in Russia, France, Italy and New York. He
was a friend of J. B. Fagan for whom he had designed costumes for
his season at the Court, as well as directing one or two Stage Society
special productions. Although he thought our production was awful,

mired his work so much. When I played Trigorin in *The Seagull* in 1936 I asked Bronson Albery, to whom I was then under contract, to engage Komis to direct the play, and he agreed. Peggy Ashcroft was Nina, Stephen Haggard Konstantin, and Alec Guinness had the tiny part of a workman in the first act. Komis immediately designed a beautiful scene for the first act and boasted to me that the trees were all made of real silk and that the set would cost at least £1,000, an enormous sum in those days. 'Of course,' he remarked, 'Albery is just a tradesman!' At the first reading of the play he delivered a long harangue about how dreadful the English theatre was, with wretched actors, completely lacking in style. Edith Evans, who was to play Arkadina (and was marvellous in the part), sat listening and looking very cross indeed, and I feared she would never get on with him at all. We started rehearsing. Then, in the middle of the first act, when Arkadina stops speaking to listen to the voices of a choir singing on the other side of the lake, Komis said his favourite word, powse, (pause). Edith 'powsed'. She 'powsed' for five minutes, the longest 'powse' I have ever heard, and from that moment she and Komis were delighted with each other.

The Shakespearean productions which he afterwards directed were avant-garde to say the least, though the three he did at Stratford were highly successful, probably because they were largely improvised, with no more than six or seven rehearsals for each play. He did a fine *Lear* with the OUDS at Oxford and afterwards at Stratford with Randle Ayrton. But I did not care for his *Macbeth* at all though there were some thrilling moments in it. The costumes were almost modern dress. The opening scene, dominated by a rusty First War cannon on the stage, was like a deserted battlefield, and the witches crawled about searching for debris. This was most effective, but Fabia Drake, who played Lady Macbeth, wore an unfortunate headdress that looked as if it was made of iron curling-papers. In *The Merchant of Venice* Komis made great use of the trapdoor which had just been installed in the new Memorial Theatre stage. Belmont rose as a little tower through the floor, with Portia and Nerissa sitting on chairs on the roof, to play their first scene. In the trial scene he had a backcloth, like a Longhi picture, with wigged judges, depicted as sheep, painted on it. The actors' heads stuck out through holes. Portia wore spectacles — and a beard.

Some years later, in London, Komis made a disastrous attempt to direct *Antony and Cleopatra* with Eugene Leontovich, who had recently made a great success as a Russian emigré princess in a play called *Tovarich* and did not speak good English. Donald Wolfit was Antony and Leon Quartermaine, as Enobarbus, was quite miscast. Everybody imitated the way Miss Leontovich said 'O weederdee degarlano devar' ('O wither'd is the garland of the war'), as The *Times* critic quoted it. It was the joke of the year. She wore a helmet with Georgian plumes and a dress with a long slit train revealing her bare legs. Komis changed the order of the scenes, opening the play with the soothsayer and Cleopatra's maids. It was a dead failure and ran only three or four days. But Komis thought it was a splendid joke.

In 1931 he did a really beautiful production for me of a play called *Musical Chairs* at the Criterion Theatre by a young and very talented writer, called Ronald MacKenzie who had been a friend of mine at prep school and was doomed to be tragically killed in a car crash just after his play had been running a year.

The last time I met Komis was when I asked him to direct *Crime and Punishment* for me in 1947 in New York, and he behaved in a very strange way. As usual he did not ask a big fee, but he was frightfully rude to any foreigner in the huge crowd who came to the auditions. It was terribly cold weather — a blizzard in fact — and almost a hundred hopefuls stood in a queue outside the theatre, many of them foreigners, because being a Russian play accents did not matter. Whenever a German or a Jew came on to read, Komis turned his back. You never knew when he would become difficult. I remember once, in another play he directed for me, there was an actress he thought was no good. One afternoon she failed to appear and the stage manager said 'Oh, Mr Komisarjevsky, I'm sorry Miss So-and-So couldn't come this afternoon, she has a fitting.' Komis took a photograph of her which was on a table, dashed it to the ground and stamped on it. Yet, in spite of his temperament, Komis contributed a great deal to the theatre in the years he worked in England and had many successes. The stage hands all liked him and worked hard to please him. One of them referred to him as 'Come and Seduce me,' which amused him very much.

He had a very emotional love-life and was always changing partners. I met him once in the country at the house of Constance Spry, the well-known florist. Komis was very taken by a lady novelist who was also staying there. Constance Spry had just designed a lot of costume jewelry and the ladies went upstairs and decked themselves out in some of the necklaces and bracelets and then we all went into dinner at a beautiful table made of alabaster and lit from underneath. It was a summer night. I had seen Komis earlier in the evening sitting under a tree looking rather like Puck and refusing to be drawn into the conversation. After dinner we went into the drawing-room and I played the piano. When I got up to go home and looked round to say goodbye to everyone Komis was nowhere to be seen. Finally I found him sitting under the piano with the lady he fancied, telling her fortune in a pudding-basin filled with candle-grease.

Komis was always moving from one country to another, adopting the new one for a few years and then becoming disillusioned. Finally, he went off to America, married a new wife and started an acting school. He died there a few years later.

Another director I admired greatly in the thirties was the Frenchman, Michel St-Denis.[2] For me, St-Denis's influence was as important as, though very different from, that of Komis. In 1935 St-Denis and his Compagnie des Quinze were giving a season at the Ambassador's Theatre in London. They put on *Noé*, *Le Viol de Lucrece* by the company's resident dramatist, André Obey, and other plays. Like many of my *confrères* in the theatre, I was enormously impressed with these remarkable productions and the small but brilliant team of actors who appeared in them. Noé was simply the story of Noah and the Ark, written and presented in an extremely engaging and stylized way with the animals portrayed by actors in beautifully modelled masks with the effects and sounds done by the company.

In New York, Pierre Fresnay, then a young man of about my own age, who was a great friend of St-Denis, played the part of Noah in English. When I read an account in an English newspaper of his success I suddenly thought how effective and interesting it might be for me to try to play the part in London — a challenging contrast too after the long run of Hamlet. I obtained a translation of the play which had been made for the New York production, but it was a very poor one, and was full of slang phrases like 'Hey, you floozies!' and other regrettable Americanisms. St-Denis agreed to direct the play, but he did not speak English very well as he had only been here for a short time. We found the translation very unwieldy, and I never felt that it achieved the charm of the original. In the end I achieved some personal success in it, although I was never at ease in the part until almost the end of the run, which was only about ten weeks. It was fearfully hot weather and I had enormous quantities of padding, a huge beard and very heavy clothes, so that I was in great discomfort. Physically it was a demanding part, involving a great deal of balancing on planks and climbing ladders, and miming too, which in those days English actors were very rarely asked to attempt.

Michel came to rehearsal every day with complete notes of every movement, every piece of business, every characterization. He was not used to English actors, or to working quickly — we rehearsed only three weeks — and the whole production was somewhat hastily put together. However, I found it a good exercise, and, as has so often happened in my career, I learned a great deal from it. We learn as much, if not more, from our failures as we do from our successes. I tried hard to discipline myself in the technical problems of the part, to make myself believe that, as Noah, I was a practical working man. The play opened with me hammering and measuring the Ark with a ruler, considering its construction with the eye of a carpenter, but I had no idea how to tackle this and Michel had to teach me every move. He demanded great discipline and order from his actors. Komisarjevsky, by contrast, never had notes but would appear to improvise, though I think he had everything very clearly in his head. He was sympathetic to an actor's struggles, mistakes and experiments while St-Denis was something of a martinet, with a very orderly French mind.

My own first West End success as a director came in 1933 with *Richard of Bordeaux*, a new historical play written by Gorton Daviot. Gorton Daviot was a pseudonym for a lady called Elizabeth Mackintosh who came from Inverness and had written several thrillers and novels under various names, including some under the name of Josephine Tey. I thought her script for *Richard of Bordeaux* charmingly written, with vivid characters drawn lightly and without pomposity. The dialogue was simple and colloquial, rather in the manner of Shaw's *Caesar and Cleopatra* — great kings and nobles behaving and talking like modern human beings. The part of Richard was written with a great sense of humour, and was a splendid opportunity — the young, impetuous, highly-strung boy growing into a disillusioned man, his wife dying of the plague, and his best friend betraying him. Shakespeare's Richard, although a wonderful part for an actor, has no humour and can be monotonously lyrical — Daviot's play was amusing and its pacifist angle had a great appeal at the time when it was produced.

'The Motleys' — three talented girls who had trained together at art school — were just beginning then as stage designers. They had a little flat off Kensington High Street, where I used to visit them after they brought me some drawings they had made of me playing various roles at the Old Vic. They devised the clothes and the scenery for *Bordeaux*, simple but elegant, in very pale colours, gold and buff and white. Their decor was exactly right and greatly helped the success of the production. After the first two experimental Sunday nights at the Arts Theatre, Bronson Albery suggested that *Bordeaux* should be put on for a regular run. At first I was reluctant — there were so many things that I had felt were wrong with the play. However, I wrote to Gordon Daviot with some suggestions for changes. A few weeks later she sent me some excellent rewrites, small but infinitely valuable; a new scene for Bolingbroke to strengthen his part towards the end of the play; new lines here and there to improve Gwen Ffrangcon-Davies' part, Anne of Bohemia. In fact the text was so greatly improved that I became enthusiastic about it, especially as, under Albery's management, we could now spread ourselves a little and stage the play more lavishly.

The first night, on 2 February 1933 at the New Theatre, did not seem to be particularly successful, but there was another important opening on the same evening. Then the first matinée was suddenly sold out and the play became a tremendous hit. In fact, I had the greatest 'fan' success of my whole career. Crowds mobbed me at the stage door and often followed me home to my flat nearby, ringing me up, clattering my letter-box and sending me presents. Some of this delighted me, of course. It became somewhat exhausting at times, but now it is a pleasant thing to remember.

Richard of Bordeaux was a big stepping-stone in my career. Gordon Daviot wrote as much in the dedication of the copy of the play she gave me. It was a very much more realistic play than the cloak-and-sword dramas in the days of my Uncle Fred and Matheson Lang, though it had plenty of melodrama and excitement as well as comedy. As a result of its success Albery gave me an extended contract. My first play under his management had been MacKenzie's *Musical Chairs*. I did *The Maitlands*, MacKenzie's last play before he was killed, but it was not a success. Komisarjevsky, for some reason, failed to produce the same magic that had made *Musical Chairs* succeed — and I was myself miscast. However, Albery offered to let me play and direct *Hamlet* in 1934. In 1935 *Romeo and Juliet* followed this production, and then *The Seagull*. The result was that in the many plays that I worked in under the Albery management between 1931 and 1936, I had a wealth of fine opportunities.

After *Bordeaux* I did a lot of directing, my own productions of *Hamlet* and *Romeo and Juliet* as well as plays in which I did not act myself — Rodney Ackland's *Strange Orchestra*, Emlyn Williams' *Spring 1600*, Somerset Maugham's *Sheppey* and Ackland's adaptation of Hugh Walpole's *The Old Ladies*. I greatly enjoyed working with the actors and designers and trying to do justice to the staging of these plays, though I did not presume to interpret them with any marked originality. I merely tried to comply with the demands of the playwright concerned.

The completely original director can hardly be said to exist. Most of his ideas have their origin in memories and impressions of other plays and in experiences in his own life. It is indeed hard to define what 'directing' really is, beyond creating a good atmosphere at rehearsals and knowing, technically, how the actors should be disposed so that the right person is in the proper position at each important moment. Some of our best English actors used to be admirable directors and many of the old actor-managers always directed their own plays. Then came the fashion for non-acting directors like

Komisarjevsky, Peter Hall and Peter Brook. (St-Denis had been an actor, but gave it up, the other three had not.) Actors are often more comfortable with directors who have been actors themselves because they understand the technical problems, but the danger for an actor-director is that he is tempted to impose his own acting style on the cast. An outside director, on the other hand, tends to bring out the individuality of each performer and creates a contrast of personalities rather than an all-over style. The all-over style can, however, if successful, produce an unforgettable effect. Brecht's company, the Berliner Ensemble, for instance, with *Drums and Trumpets*, *The Caucasian Chalk Circle* and *Mother Courage* at the Palace in 1956, impressed audiences with an individual style of playing, broad, defiant, rhetorical, which Brecht had evidently imposed on them.

Any company which has been together a long time creates a recognizable style, like the Compagnie des Quinze, or, in the contemporary theatre, the National and the Royal Shakespeare companies. On the other hand, I have always thought that however good repertory companies are they should be broken up from time to time. My own good fortune has been that, over the years, I have worked with such wonderful companies, afterwards parting from them on excellent terms, and then, a few years later, have come to work with them again. Acting with great artists like Edith Evans or Peggy Ashcroft, Laurence Olivier, Ralph Richardson or Alec Guinness, I find myself so much at home with them on the very first day of rehearsal that I can start work much more quickly than if I have to break the ice with players I do not know at all.

I have had semi-permanent companies several times over the years, once in 1937, once in 1944 and again in 1953. In *Richard of Bordeaux*, in my first years as a director, I was lucky enough to have three or four elderly actors who had been with Tree, Benson, Fagan and Playfair, yet they obeyed me without question and had beautiful manners. At the Haymarket at the end of the war, when I had a very senior company (although, as I discovered afterwards, two or three of them were not very fond of each other) their discipline and good behaviour was unfailing.

In the thirties when Olivier, Peggy Ashcroft and I were just beginning to make our first successes we often found that we would form a solid centre in a company with two sides round us, one a group of very enthusiastic young people, like Anthony Quayle, Glen Byam Shaw, Alec Guinness, Harry Andrews, actors who were just beginning: and another, made up of highly experienced people like Leon Quartermaine, Cecil Trouncer and Leslie Banks. The young people matched with their youthful enthusiasm what the older ones had in experience — an ideal situation, it seems to me.

I first saw Peggy Ashcroft as Desdemona in the Paul Robeson *Othello* at the Savoy Theatre in 1930.³ Ralph Richardson was Roderigo, Sybil Thorndike played Emilia and an actor called Maurice Browne played Iago and co-directed the production. It was a great failure. Robeson, who should have been superb, was not helped by an Elizabethan costume of padded trunks, square shoes and a ruff. It was not until the last scene, when he came on in a white kaftan, that he looked really magnificent. He had a fine singing voice, uniquely gentle and deep, but somehow not suited to blank verse. The scenery was by James Pryde, a very successful painter and a friend of Sickert, Craig and Nicholson in the 1890s. Together they had designed posters for Irving, under the name of the Beggarstaff Brothers, and did a famous one of him as Don Quixote, which I believe was never used. Pryde's scenery was rather impressive, like his pictures: unnaturally high shadowy rooms, a huge bed for Desdemona — but the sets were built too far upstage and they were dimly lit. It was impossible to see what was going on and there was a terrible noise from the scene shifters during the changes. But when Peggy Ashcroft first came on, in her gold dress, in the Senate scene, the audience sat up in their seats. It was as if the sun had come out. In the handkerchief scene she acted so lightly and so touchingly that her performance saved the evening. Soon after that I met her and asked her to play Juliet for me at Oxford with the undergraduates. She akeady had several London successes to her credit, so that when she and Edith Evans both agreed to come it was splendid for me as well as for the undergraduates.

I directed Peggy many times thereafter — in *The Heiress*, the Goetz adaptation of Henry James' *Washington Square*, and Enid Bagnold's *The Chalk Garden*. She was my leading lady at the Queen's

Theatre in 1937 and 1938, playing Portia, Irina, Lady Teazle and the Queen in *Richard II*. We were at Stratford together one whole season in 1950 and toured on the continent together in 1955. Unfortunately I have not worked with her for some years now. I have always loved her acting. She was the most perfect partner and her influence in a company was extraordinary. She helped Peter Hall tremendously during his years at Stratford and gave some wonderful performances for him, particularly in *The Wars of the Roses*, where she played Queen Margaret of Anjou right through from a young girl to an old hag, and her Hedda Gabler I thought was a *tour de force*.

I had done a season of four plays at the Queen's in 1937-38 and I was very tired when, out of the blue, Hugh Beaumont offered me a big salary to take part in a modern play, *Dear Octopus* by Dodie Smith, with Dame Marie Tempest.[4] In those days, except for *Musical Chairs*, I never seemed to be cast in modern dress except to play prigs or bores — and my part in *Dear Octopus*, like that of Inigo in *The Good Companions*, made very few demands. However, I played those two parts in each case for nearly two years. Dodie's play had a very good cast with Angela Baddeley and Valerie Taylor, and Glen Byam Shaw to direct it, and it was fascinating to work with Marie Tempest. She was an enormously skilled little lady with superb technical accomplishments, bright and intelligent in many ways, rather limited in others. I doubt if she had even read the piece when she agreed to appear in it but she trusted Beaumont's judgement implicitly and he was nearly always right. She was getting old and found great difficulty in learning her lines, but she was a rigid disciplinarian and worked like a demon all through rehearsals.

We went on tour for several weeks before opening in London, and Dame Marie would come down to lunch in the hotel dining-room in Newcastle wearing a beautiful hat and white gloves which she turned back at the wrist while she was eating. She would then retire to bed for the afternoon to rest. She did not get on very well with Dodie Smith and on the first night in London, when Dodie came on at the end to take a call with the company, Dame Marie turned her back on her in full view of the audience. To her great embarrassment, when she got home she found a six-page letter from Dodie, written after the dress rehearsal, thanking her and congratulating her and telling her what a genius she was.

The first night was memorable for another reason. It coincided with Munich. I remember at the party afterwards Noël Coward walked in with a grey face, saying that this was the most terrible thing that had ever happened, while we were all waving champagne glasses in honour of Mr Chamberlain's piece of paper. The play ran all through that very nerve-racking year. It was a charming, cosy kind of a play and people loved it. The revival some years ago with Cicely Courtneidge and Jack Hulbert was almost equally successful.

Marie Tempest played herself in every part. She adorned a number of forgotten little comedies at the small theatres that used to begin at 9 p.m. and end at 10:30 p.m., coming on in a series of smart frocks, snapping her fingers and twinkling as she made much play with a little lace handkerchief, and utterly bewitching the audience. Yvonne Arnaud had the same skill. Neither of the ladies could be said to be a great beauty, both were rather short and plump, but they had style. Dame Marie especially wore her beautiful clothes with a great air and knew just how far to go in dressing a la mode. She was always perfectly soignée, with beautiful shoes and crisp little hats.

The first time I ever saw Marie Tempest was in a revival of *Alice Sit-by-the-Fire*. But the part suited her no better than it had suited Ellen Terry for whom Barrie had written it originally. It was a thoroughly sentimental Edwardian piece. Later I saw her in an American farce about amateur theatricals, *The Torchbearers*, where she was extremely funny, and then she had a huge personal success in Coward's *Hay Fever*, in which she was inimitable. At her Jubilee performance at Drury Lane in 1937 she acted with the most extraordinary self-possession in three scenes from plays in which she had triumphed when she was young. At the end, dressed in a pink dress trimmed with ostrich feathers, she was carried on to the stage in a gold chair. All the stars of the London theatre were assembled in a huge group to do her homage, and her chair was put down in the middle of the stage. She curtsied to the Royal Box and made a charming little speech. Her calmness and control on such an emotional occasion was remarkable.

A number of other actresses celebrated in the Edwardian theatre were still active in the late twenties and thirties, notably the Vanbrugh sisters, Irene and Violet, Madge Titheradge and Lillah McCarthy who later became Lady Keeble.

The Vanbrugh sisters were remarkably alike in appearance.[5] Tall and imposing, beautifully spoken, they moved with grace, their feet encased in long pointed shoes. They were elegantly but never ostentatiously dressed, entering and leaving the stage with unerring authority, and always straight-backed when they sat on chairs and sofas. Violet never struck me as a natural comedienne, as Irene was, although she had appeared before my time in a number of comedies by Alfred Sutro and other contemporary authors. I remember her making a most effective entrance in a melodramatic play, *Evensong*, in which Edith Evans was sensationally good as a Prima Donna, a character obviously modelled on Melba.

Though Violet had achieved considerable success at His Majesty's with Tree, playing Lady Macbeth and Katharine of Aragon, I do not think either she or her sister could ever have been at their best in Shakespeare. Both actresses were very much of their own period. When I saw them, quite late on in their careers, playing *Merry Wives* in Regent's Park in 1937 for Sydney Carroll, they seemed to me very much like elegant Edwardian ladies romping about in fancy dress.

The sisters had both been sponsored in their girlhood by Irving and Ellen Terry. Their father was a clergyman, and such distinguished patronage may have been helpful in winning their parents' consent to their going on the stage. Irene was an established star in the early twenties, when first I saw her in three light comedies by A. A. Milne, and I was delighted by her brilliant performances in these pieces which, in her consummately professional hands, seemed much better than they really were. In Milne's *Belinda* she spent the first five minutes of the opening scene deciding how to swing herself into a hammock without showing too much leg (skirts were fairly short in this period) and I can see her now, amid the property hollyhocks and cut-out tree-wings, with Dennis Neilson-Terry as a languid poet in an impeccable grey flannel suit — how I longed to possess one like it — making love to her.

Her husband, Dion Boucicault, often acted with her, and usually directed her as well. A very small man (he was nick-named 'Dot'), he looked delightfully absurd when he took a call with his tall wife at the end of a performance, especially on the huge stage of the Coliseum, where I once saw them in a one-act play of Barrie's called *Half-an-Hour*. Both Violet and Irene often appeared there in playlets which were given top billing in the variety programmes of the time.

Boucicault had the reputation of being a fine though somewhat daunting director and excelled, as Gerald du Maurier did afterwards, in teaching his women stars. Marie Tempest told me that, when she turned to straighter plays after her early successes in light opera and musical comedy, she owed her technique entirely to his teaching. He demanded meticulous pace and timing. Marie Tempest's personality was always crisp and twinkling with mischief, whereas Irene Vanbrugh was graver and more sedate, though equally brilliant in timing and expertise.

Both the Vanbrugh sisters retained their immense popularity to the very end of their careers and Irene's Jubilee, for which Noël Coward wrote a prologue, was a great occasion which I was sad to miss because I was in America. She had been acting just before this time in several small but delightful cameo parts — Lady Markby in *An Ideal Husband* and as the mother of the heroine in Coward's *Operette*. Fritzi Massary, the Viennese star, was also in the Coward piece, and these two veterans stole all the notices though they only appeared in one or two short scenes.

Irene had a very distinctive voice, extremely clear and ringing. In a very dull production of *The Swan* (adapted from Molnar and with a starry but uninspired cast) she appeared in the last act as the Queen Mother of some Ruritanian country. When her voice was suddenly heard behind the scenes just before her entrance the whole audience began to sit up and take notice. And I can see her now in a revival of Maugham's comedy *Caroline*, delivering a long speech in a scene with her doctor as she lay on a sofa and suddenly capping it with a delicious upward inflexion as she looked slyly up at him and remarked 'You're *not* going to charge me a guinea for this, are you?'

Madge Titheradge, known to her friends as 'Midge,' was small and appealing, eager and intense.[6] Her voice was somewhat hoarse but she knew how to adapt it with the utmost skill to the demands of either comedy or drama. Her dark eyes would brim with tears or shine with mischief. I have a recurring image of her in a brown dress with wide lace sleeves hanging loosely from her elbows, her arms flung out at some emotional moment in an attitude of crucifixion.

In the First War comedy *General Post* with Lilian Braithwaite, in which I saw her first, she was as delightfully romantic as she was in a ridiculous melodrama, *Tiger's Cub*, set in a log cabin with a baby in a shawl, Canadian Mounties and husky dogs barking behind the scenes. She was the long-suffering heroine of an adaptation of Robert Hichens' novel *The Garden of Allah* at Drury Lane, an impressive and soul-stirring spectacle featuring real camels and a real sandstorm. Unhappily on the first night the sand blew across the footlights, spraying the orchestra pit and the occupants of the first ten rows of the stalls.

She enchanted me during successive seasons in such different characters as the boulevard heroine of *Bluebeard's Eighth Wife* and as Nora in *A Doll's House*, in which she gave a thrilling performance, especially in the Tarantella scene. One Christmas, during the First War, she was Principal Boy in a Drury Lane pantomime, and recited (in armour, I fancy) a patriotic poem of Alfred Noyes, 'A Song of England,' holding the audience spellbound as she stood alone on the enormous stage.

On only two occasions did she disappoint me; as Desdemona to Godfrey Tearle's Othello and as Beatrice to Henry Ainley's Benedick. Evidently Shakespeare was the only author with whom she was not on easy terms, though before my time she had made a success as the French Princess Katharine to the Henry V of Lewis Waller, the famous Edwardian matinée idol.

In 1924, when Noël Coward achieved his first success with *The Vortex*, managements were eager to stage everything he had written. Madge Titheradge, whom Coward admired as much as I did, was announced as one of the two leading ladies in his *Fallen Angels*, but she did not finally appear in the production. However, she acted in two of his later plays, *Home Chat* (a light comedy which failed to attract the public in spite of her amusing performance) and *The Queen Was in the Parlour*, a Ruritanian melodrama in which she was required to give up her throne in the cause of love — and very movingly she did it. Lady Tree, who also appeared in the play, must have shown her usual good nature in accepting the engagement, since rumour had it that she had been at one time a rival to Madge Titheradge in competing for Lewis Waller's favours. There was even a story that both actresses attended his funeral clad in widow's weeds, though the account was too discreet to mention what Mrs. Waller's reaction may have been.

Madge Titheradge was very emotional both on and off the stage. She came to see *The Constant Nymph* one afternoon and fainted in the dressing room of Edna Best whom she had come to congratulate. Some years later she fainted (on the stage this time) as the curtain fell on the second act of *Theatre Royal* in which she was appearing. However, she recovered almost immediately on realizing that the redoubtable Marie Tempest was about to belabour her with the walking stick she used in the play. She was seldom seen in restaurants or in public, preferring, when she was not acting — which was very seldom — to stay at home and play bridge with her servants.

In 1928 I fulfilled a long-cherished ambition to meet and act with her when I was engaged to appear in New York for the first time. The play was an adaptation of a German costume drama about the murder of Paul I of Russia, played by the veteran actor Lyn Harding. I was the young Tsarevitch and Leslie Faber the principal conspirator, Count Pahlen, with Madge Titheradge as his mistress. I was sent for as a replacement, only arriving from England during the first dress rehearsal, and the play closed disastrously after a few performances. However, I had my first heady experience of speakeasy New York besides the privilege of acting, however briefly, with these three distinguished players. I found Madge Titheradge as fascinating and sympathetic as I had always felt sure she would be, and one evening she gave me a lift in her taxi and played a most affecting farewell scene for my private benefit, telling me she was resolved to leave the stage and marry a rich American. She kissed her hand as she waved goodbye and wished me well in the career that I was beginning, just as she was leaving hers for ever.

Her future was sadly unlucky, as it turned out. Her husband lost his fortune in the Wall Street crash and died not long afterwards and she was forced to return to the theatre after all.

On her return she was equally successful on the London stage for several years and I saw her give a splendid performance in *Promise*, a drama from the French of Henri Bernstein. Besides Edna Best and Ann Todd, the cast included Ralph Richardson, who was as greatly impressed by her artistry as I was.

She was equally effective in *Theatre Royal*, directed by Coward, with Marie Tempest and Laurence Olivier, and her last success was in *Mademoiselle*, another translation of a French play, also directed by Coward, in which she played a repressed governess with Isabel Jeans and Cecil Parker as two delightful comedy characters. But another play, which she had begun to rehearse, failed to come to London after some try-out weeks and she was never able to act again. Stricken with crippling arthritis, she lay bed-ridden for many years. I wrote to her once or twice but did not feel I knew her sufficiently well to ask her to let me go to see her. But I can never forget the pleasure she gave me in so many dazzling performances, and for me she will always epitomize a perfect example of professional expertise combined with unforgettable personal charm.

The first time I saw Lillah McCarthy on the stage she was appearing in a romantic melodrama called *The Wandering Jew* written by a popular novelist of the twenties, E. Temple Thurston, in which Matheson Lang, a fine actor of great power, played the leading part.[7] I had waited for many hours in a long queue to obtain a pit seat for the opening night and was sadly disappointed in the play, though I still remember much of it in some detail. In the opening scene, the procession to Calvary was supposed to pass an open window at the back of the stage, though only the top of the swaying cross was seen by the audience. Then the Jew returned, condemned to eternal reincarnation in different guises through the ages, having reviled Jesus behind the scenes.

The second act, which took place during the Middle Ages, was set in a pavilion (with a tournament supposed to be taking place off-stage) and Lang, in one of his various reincarnations, entered in chain-mail to become speedily involved with a handsome lady in a hectic seduction scene. As she struggled in his embrace, sinking onto a low couch with her back to the audience, her medieval robe was seen to be cut away revealing her in semi-naked splendour.

Why Lillah McCarthy should have bothered to appear in such a play baffled me considerably, for her taste was evidently far above the level of such tushery.

I must have seen her once before this however, in 1913, when she played Helena in the famous *A Midsummer Night's Dream* of Granville-Barker at the Savoy Theatre, but I was still a boy at the time and only have a dim recollection of the production: the gold-painted fairies, the swaying green curtains to suggest the wood, the hanging canopy overhead — a kind of chandelier of white and green — and the slim, tall figure of Oberon, my cousin Dennis Neilson-Terry. I recall also the slightly bewildered reactions of the audience whose older members remained nostalgically loyal to Mendelssohn, picture scenery and real rabbits, and a female Oberon who sang 'I know a bank' in a costume glittering with electric lights, in Tree's production at His Majesty's Theatre only a few seasons before.

Lillah McCarthy had been discovered by William Poel, who cast her as Lady Macbeth in one of his Elizabethan productions, patronized at that time by small but discriminating audiences, and Shaw was one of the first to spy out her talent at this performance. She later married Shaw's great friend and colleague Harley Granville-Barker and, working with them both, acted brilliantly in a wide range of parts in Greek Tragedy and many of the early Shaw plays during the first decade of this century.

She played the leading roles in *The Winter's Tale*, *A Midsummer Night's Dream* and *Twelfth Night*, and went to Amenca to act in some of these productions at the beginning of the First War, but shortly afterwards her marriage to Granville-Barker broke up and she divorced him. Some years later she married again — and was soon to leave the stage for good.

Her second husband, Professor Sir Frederick Keeble, lived at Oxford and they entertained their friends at a house on Boars Hill where Lady Keeble gave occasional poetry recitals to which aspiring undergraduates were often invited. She was also to be seen at first nights in London and at public dinners connected with Shakespeare and poetry. It was on one of these occasions that I met her first, introduced to her, I believe, by Elsie Fogerty, the famous voice coach who was such an invaluable help to so many young players — Laurence Olivier, Peggy Ashcroft and myself. She was one of Lady Keeble's greatest friends.

I was, of course, impressed to meet such a famous actress, though I found her somewhat awe-inspiring and difficult to talk to. But she was still beautiful and distinguished, though I did not dare to ask her questions about Granville-Barker, who had always been one of my greatest heroes, for I knew he had refused to allow either his name or his work to be mentioned in the autobiography she had recently written.

I did not meet her again for some years, until, after a matinée of Christopher Fry's *The Lady's Not for Burning*, in 1949, Lady Keeble came round to my dressing room and congratulated me. But she embarrassed me somewhat by asking that my leading lady, Pamela Brown, should be sent for in order to receive similar congratulations. I could not help thinking this to be rather autocratic behaviour on her part, though perhaps, as she was no longer young, she did not relish the prospect of climbing another flight of stairs.

A good many years later, as I was walking one winter day in Hyde Park, I noticed two elderly ladies, both looking extremely depressed by each other's company, seated on a bench near Rotten Row. Recognizing one of them as Lady Keeble, I thought it only proper to stop for a moment and pay my respects. She seemed delighted to be recognized, and, to my surprise, promptly invited me to come to tea with her at her flat in Gloucester Road on the following Sunday afternoon.

I ascended in a creaky lift to the top floor where the windows of her flat looked out on to a superb view of London, from the Empress Hall on one side to Big Ben and the Abbey on the other, a magnificent panorama of snow-covered roofs and towers.

My hostess greeted me with unexpected warmth and cordiality

and offered me tea, followed by a large whisky and soda. Dressed in an extremely becoming Oriental looking trouser suit, she poured a drink for herself, lit a cigarette and, tucking up her feet on a big divan covered with cushions, began to talk with the greatest freedom and enthusiasm. As before, I felt I should take care not to mention Granville-Barker's name, but to my great astonishment she started to tell me how she had first seen him at Cheltenham, when he was still a boy, dressed in a sailor suit and assisting his Italian mother in a recital, at which he spoke several of the poems himself.

She continued with fascinating reminiscences of their married partnership and of the efforts made by Granville-Barker, with Vedrenne and Bernard Shaw, to start a campaign to find money for an English National Theatre. She told me of a weekend she once spent at the country home of Sir Carl Meyer, a very rich man with a hobby of growing prize carnations in his hothouses. Granville-Barker had urged her to accept the invitation (though he did not go himself) in the hope of winning Meyer's financial help, and Sir Herbert Tree, who had somehow got wind of the party, managed to get himself invited too. As the guests prepared for their departure on Monday morning, Sir Herbert (famous as an enthusiastic ladies' man as well as a superb character-actor and impresario) asked Lillah to share his first-class carriage back to London, though he asked that she would not interrupt his concentration by talking during the journey, as he had to study the script of a play which he had promised to read.

'After a short time,' Lady Keeble told me gravely, 'he threw the manuscript aside, left his seat by the window, crossed the carriage to where I was sitting and attempted to fondle me. Of course, I managed to defend myself successfully, but, in the ensuing struggle, the bouquet of carnations, presented to me by Sir Carl before I left, became severely damaged and the flowers were strewn all over the carriage floor by the time we arrived at Victoria Station. On leaving the platform Sir Herbert bade me a polite farewell, waved me to a cab, and hailed a separate one for himself, remarking that if we should be seen arriving together at the stage door of his "beautiful" theatre, eyebrows might justifiably be raised!'

Enchanted by these fascinating disclosures, I wrote an enthusiastic note of thanks as soon as I got home, only to receive next day a letter in which Lady Keeble said she too had much enjoyed my visit but feared our conversation had been rather too frivolous. She hoped I would call on her another day to discuss the condition of the modern theatre, about which she was seriously disturbed. But, alas, only a few weeks later she was dead.

It must have been some time in 1928 that I met Ruth Draper for the first time at one of Lady Colefax's lunch parties.[8] Sibyl Colefax has been disparaged in recent memoirs, and even during her own lifetime, as a snob and a lion-hunter. Nevertheless I was extremely fond of her and grateful for the wonderful opportunity she gave to young artists like myself to meet many literary, political and theatrical figures of the time whom we should never have had the good fortune to encounter without her hospitable invitations. A few days after the party I went to see Miss Draper's unique one-woman show. She had, of course, been admired in London long before I first saw her — indeed I remember being intrigued as a very young man by the poster she used for the few public recitals she then gave, the famous charcoal sketch which John Sargent drew of her with a shawl draped over her head.

The curtained stage was empty save for a few pieces of essential furniture: a sofa, a couple of chairs and a table. Ruth Draper walked on, a tall, dark-eyed woman in a simple brown dress, beautifully cut, and looked out over the auditorium with grave composure. Her authority and concentration were absolute. How swiftly she transformed that stage into her own extraordinary world, transporting us to other places, other countries — a boudoir, a garden, a church, a customs shed; London, New York, Rome, the coast of Maine — creating in each of those imagined settings a single dominant character and then seeming to surround herself, as and when she needed them, with an attendant crowd of minor figures — children, animals, servants, husbands, lovers. Her wit and imagination could not fail to fascinate and never palled, however often I returned to see her famous monologues.

After the performance I went round to see her in her dressing-room and found her immensely sympathetic and delightful. The trenchant, acid wit which often sharpened many of her stage creations was not in the least evident in talking to her in private life.

I cherish in particular three occasions connected with Ruth. The first was an evening in New York when, at the end of a dinner party, she invited a small group of us back to her flat, and there, in front of the fire, as we all sat around in chairs or on the floor, she acted several of her sketches for us. It was a privilege to observe her at such close quarters and in such intimate surroundings.

The second was an afternoon in London. The great singer Kathleen Ferrier was dying of an incurable disease and some friends of hers, Ruth Draper among them, had taken a beautiful ground-floor flat looking out onto a very pretty garden so that she might recuperate after several weeks in hospital. I was invited to go to see her there and found Ruth standing beside her bed. We all tried to behave quite naturally, talking and laughing as best we could, with Miss Ferrier, radiantly beautiful, sitting up to greet us in a little pink jacket edged with white fur while she held Ruth's hand and waving gallantly to us all as we bade her farewell.

On the third occasion, I had taken an American friend who had never seen her to one of Ruth Draper's last performances at the St James's Theatre in London, and when we went round to her dressing-room she was standing on a white drugget, looking much smaller than I remembered her, greatly aged and a little deaf. Yet only a few moments before I had watched her final sketch — a new one to me — in which she portrayed a temperamental Polish actress full of fire and emotion, speaking at a tremendous pace in an amazing mixture of languages.

During one of her last London seasons she made a few television versions of some of her sketches. These have never been shown, I believe, and I only hope they are somewhere in the archives, preserved for a generation that never had the privilege of seeing this consummate artist.

My first *Hamlet*, at the Old
Vic, 1930. To see a *Hamlet*
of twenty-five was a new
experience then.

Left: Lady Benson as Miranda in *The Tempest*, 1900. I won a scholarship to attend her Drama School in 1921. A very bad actress but a splendid teacher.

Below: My great-aunt Ellen Terry's Jubilee at Drury Lane, 1906. The Masked Dance from *Much Ado about Nothing*, designed by Edward Gordon-Craig. Ellen is standing (centre), flanked by Marion and Kate. In all, twenty-two Terrys appeared in the final Masque.

My grandmother, Kate Terry, *c.* 1865. Kate was the first of the Terrys to make her name on the English stage.

Eleonora Duse. Her acting seemed very, very simple. She had marvellous hands and all her movements were weary and poetic.

Above: 'Golden' Fred Terry with his wife, Julia Neilson, in *The Scarlet Pimpernel*. Fred would be violent about anything in a play that he did not think was manly and noble.

Above: James Bernard Fagan, author and director, Oxford Playhouse, 1924.

Left: Henry Irving and Ellen Terry in *Olivia*, adapted from Goldsmith's *The Vicar of Wakefield*, at the Lyceum Theatre, 1885. He was very slow and she was very swift.

My first *Macbeth*, at the Old Vic, 1930. I knew I would not be able
to play the warrior, but I found a romantic and visionary quality
in the character.

Laurence Olivier (Romeo), Glen Byam Shaw (Benvolio), myself
(Mercutio) and Geoffrey Toone (Tybalt) in the 1935 *Romeo and
Juliet* at the New Theatre.

Hamlet in my own
production, New
Theatre, 1934. This
production ran for 155
performances, beating
all the records for a
Hamlet run since
Henry Irving.

Left: As Hamlet, 1939, at the Lyceum. This was the last stage performance in Henry Irving's famous theatre.

Below: Peggy Ashcroft as Desdemona in the Paul Robeson *Othello*, Savoy, 1930.

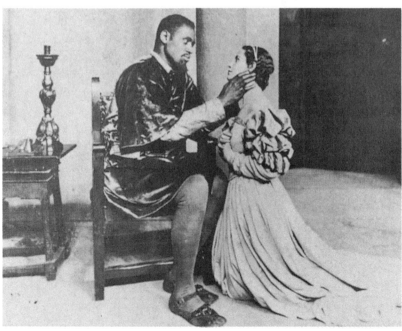

Chapter Five

1939-1945

Mysterious Baroness Blixen — King Lear *with Granville-Barker* —
Revues for troops — *India and the far East* — *Acting in the Blitz* —
The 1944 Haymarket Season and the professors — *George Bernard*
Shaw

In 1939 I went to Elsinore in Denmark to play Hamlet in the courtyard of Kronborg Castle, following the example of Laurence Olivier,
who had inaugurated the Festival two years before. In that production, which Tyrone Guthrie directed, Vivien Leigh played Ophelia
and Lilian Baylis was in attendance to provide sandwiches and en-
couragement, insisting that the courtyard clock should be stopped
from striking because it interfered with the performances.

The outbreak of the War was only two months away when we arrived and we were instantly aware of the tension and mixed feelings
everywhere. Besides this, our performances were marred by cold,
rainy weather and we were not best pleased when, after some rather
poor attendances, one night we saw a group of German sailors from
a battleship occupying the whole of the front row of seats, even
though they proved to be the quickest and most responsive members
of the audience.

The trip did hold one treat for me, however: we were introduced
to the mysterious and fascinating Baroness Blixen who took us all
under her wing and made a moving and splendid speech in English
about Shakespeare at one of the rather tedious lunch parties given in
our honour by the Danes.[1]

It was difficult to tell her age. She had magnificent eyes, heavily
made up, and was rather small in stature, usually wearing black
dresses and small hats with feathers and a veil. Her clothes were elegantly worn but simple, her manner friendly and welcoming in the
extreme. I soon discovered that she was the famous Isaak Dinesen,

author of *Out of Africa* and *Seven Gothic Tales*, though she never seemed to want to discuss her own work. We became friends immediately, and a year later, in 1940, she wrote to me saying she was coming to London where she hoped to find material for some articles she had been commissioned to write by the leading newspaper in Copenhagen, 'documents humains' dealing with all the European countries involved in the War. I arranged to give a party at my house in her honour, but during that very week Denmark was occupied by the Nazis, and she shut herself up in her family home at Rungsted to remain there for the rest of the war and write an anti-Nazi novel under an assumed name.

Karen Blixen had a genius for descriptive conversation. Hearing her talk, in her deep-voiced accent, was like listening to a fascinating short story, whether the subject happened to be Shakespeare, mythology, nights on the African veldt hunting lions, a visit of the Duke of Windsor to her farm in Kenya to see forbidden African dances, a radio appeal she had once made to ask for subscriptions to turn her orchard into a bird sanctuary, or the beauty of the sea sparkling below her house in Denmark, when the yachts were once more able to sail there and she knew the German occupation was over at last.

Ten years or so after the War, when I was in Paris to give a recital of my Shakespeare programme *Ages of Man*, I suddenly came face to face with Karen in the Rue St-Honoré. She was marching along flanked by two apple-cheeked Danish girls, who tactfully immolated themselves against the railings of the church which we were passing as she and I embraced each other in delighted recognition. I found she was staying in the same small hotel as I was, the 'France et Choiseul' (now much grander than it was in those days), with its charming square central courtyard and suites of rickety, plushcovered furniture. We ate ices together at a splendid confectioners, Latinville in the Rue St-Augustin, and that evening she came to hear my recital. We laughed and chatted happily together as if we had known each other all our lives. She was greatly changed in appearance, however, and when I went to Copenhagen to give my recital there some months later she was too ill to see me, only sending me her love and a huge bouquet of roses to my hotel.

But after a while she was a little stronger, and when I was playing in *The Tempest* at Stratford-upon-Avon in the fifties she wrote telling me she was in London and greatly excited at the prospect of coming down to see a matinée. She adored the play but had never seen it performed, and one of the stories in her new collection *Anecdotes of Destiny* had been inspired by reading it. She came on to the stage at the end of the performance but was too frail to climb the stairs so I went down to talk to her and see her safely to her car. She wrote to me afterwards that her day had been perfection. Not only had she seen *The Tempest* and stood on Clopton Bridge to look at Shakespeare's river and the swans, but, on getting into the train at Leamington, she had been asked to mount guard over a number of dogs while their owners, who had been exhibiting them at a Birmingham Dog Show, left for the restaurant car to have their tea. This, she said, was a final delight for her at the end of her unforgettable experience at Stratford.

In 1959 I happened to be working in New York. I had been given an introduction to an elderly lady, a Mrs. Murray Crane, and she had invited me to tea in her spacious and beautiful apartment on Fifth Avenue. The men at the party were mostly fairly young, several of them officials at the Metropolitan and the Museum of Modern Art, and the two most important lady guests were Karen Blixen and Edith Sitwell. I had first met Dame Edith at a luncheon at Sibyl Colefax's in London and had been charmed and surprised to find her so easy to talk to and so ready to make sly remarks about her own strange taste in clothes and jewellery. As a young man I had once been invited to a supper party in a studio near Bond Street and had met her two brothers, Osbert and Sacheverell, who also fascinated me with their brilliant conversational powers. How rare it is to sit at a table with really witty and generous hosts, who can shine spontaneously and rivet one's interest without making one feel totally inadequate oneself.

I discovered that, in New York, Karen Blixen was being fêted by everyone who knew her work. She was speaking in colleges and on the radio and appeared in a television interview. She looked frailer than ever, wearing a black hat like a coal scuttle which almost concealed her face, her body seemed shrunken and her wrists and ankles pitifully thin. But she was still able to hold her own with Edith Sitwell and the intellectual young men in Mrs. Crane's apartment, amid the silver trays and cakestands, like a scene from a novel by Henry James.

I saw her once more after this, in 1962, not long before she died. I lunched with her at her charming house near Copenhagen with its porcelain stoves and long *broderie anglaise* curtains trailing on the polished floor. There she sat at the head of her table, surrounded by young people, tasting a few oysters and a glass of champagne, the only food and drink she was still able to swallow. Before I left she walked with me round her rambling garden, leaning heavily on my arm. 'That is where I want to be buried,' she said, pointing to a knoll at the top of the hill, 'but I mustn't tell the priest because my favourite dog is already buried there and I'm sure he wouldn't approve.' Then, as we turned the corner and saw the white sails of the yachts skimming over the water below, she spoke of the Nazis leaving and her unhappy time during the occupation. When I kissed her goodbye and drove away I knew I would never see her again.

The outbreak of the Second War naturally transformed everything in the theatre. I was extremely lucky not to be called up, the authorities taking the view that I could do a better job by staying in the theatre. I found myself living, somewhat precariously, from one production to another.

I remember that on the day war broke out I had started rehearsals for *Rebecca*, Daphne du Maurier's play, in which I was to star with Celia Johnson. Michel St-Denis was next door at the Queen's Theatre rehearsing *The Cherry Orchard*, with Edith Evans and Ronald Squire, and we all met in the pub during the lunch break. I had decided not to go on with *Rebecca* and I told them why: 'It's a commercial play, very good for peacetime, but I don't think it's the right thing to do now. Perhaps I can go back to the Old Vic for a bit and do something classical.' It was Guthrie, I think, who suggested that we should do *Lear*. He and Lewis Casson remembered that Harley Granville-Barker had written a fine preface to the play and thought he might be persuaded to help us. And so we wrote and asked him and he agreed.

Granville-Barker had become disillusioned with the theatre after the break-up of his first marriage to Lillah McCarthy. He had fallen madly in love with a rich American lady called Mrs. Huntingdon who disliked the theatre and treated it as a kind of disagreeable mistress. Whenever Granville-Barker attempted to come back to the theatre she encouraged him to forget it and to live a pseudo-aristocratic life. For a time they had a large country house in England and attempted the roles of Lord and Lady of the Manor but it did not last long. In London they always stayed in a suite at the Ritz and Granville-Barker would never meet the press and only very few people in the theatre. He broke with Shaw altogether, though he remained devoted to Barrie. He lived in Paris during his last years, where he had a beautiful house and entertained all the eminent people, lecturing at the Sorbonne as well as working on his brilliant prefaces to Shakespeare. This was all very different from the young genius, eating nuts and wearing sandals, acting and directing in London, intensely violent and passionate about everything. He was to become one of my greatest heroes and the letters he wrote me over the years are among my treasured possessions.

When he first came to work with us on *Lear* in 1940, he had not been in the theatre as a director for many years. He did not know any of the younger actors and kept suggesting that Nicholas Hannen and Lewis Casson should play some of the young parts, not realizing that they were twenty or thirty years older than when they had all worked together as young men. But, of course, he was delighted to meet them again and when he began to work with younger people like myself he was able to sum us up in a very short time, knowing exactly which of us was worth taking trouble over.

I had worked with him once before, when we did *Hamlet* in 1939 at Elsinore. Before going to Denmark we had a try-out for a week at the Lyceum, which was about to be pulled down. This was in fact the last time it was used as a theatre. I heard that Barker was going to be in London and wrote to him. He agreed to come to a run-through on condition that 'there won't be any press or publicity — my name is not to be used in any way'. We acted the whole play for him and next morning he sent for me at the Ritz. I had the great distraction of keeping Mrs. Granville-Barker out of the room for three hours — though she kept trying to get her husband away to go to a lunch. He sat on the sofa with a new edition of *Hamlet* in his hand, cutting the pages with a paper-knife as he went along and giving me notes at a great rate. I scribbled away with all my might, determined not to let him get away until he had finished. Then I rushed off and rang the theatre where the company was waiting and said, 'I've had three hours with Granville-Barker, he has told me wonderful things about the production that can improve it. Would you be willing to rehearse again tomorrow [a Sunday] to try to put them in?' and they all agreed.

Working with Granville-Barker on *Lear* in 1940 was one of the great experiences of my career. He came down every morning, Irish red eyebrows shooting out like Shaw's, wearing a bowler hat and a business suit, and we hung on his every word. He never praised you and he never tore you to pieces. He was quite impersonal, calling everybody by the name of their part or by their own surnames — none of the 'dears' and 'darlings' in which we are apt to indulge in the theatre. He was determined not to get caught up in any sort of publicity nonsense, interviews or photographs. He had laid down his terms clearly enough: 'I will come for those ten days for you only if nothing is said to the press.' Of course the news got out in the end and he left before the first dress rehearsal, which was terribly disappointing.

Tyrone Guthrie and Lewis Casson had been preparing the play for two weeks before he came, but when he arrived he changed everything they had done. He had previously come to London for one day to let me read over the part with him, and at the end of the reading he said to me 'Well, you've got two lines right. Of course, you are an ash and this part demands an oak, but we'll see what can be done,' which I thought was pretty shrewd. He knew exactly what he wanted to say and do. He would take infinite pains to achieve what he thought necessary yet was always prepared to give an actor a certain amount of latitude. He was no sergeant-major, forcing us to adopt his own tones and inflections; somehow he *implied* what he wanted. He was wonderfully perceptive musically; he knew just where the voice should rise, just where it should be sustained or dropped.

To me he was like a masseur who forces you to discover and use muscles you never knew you possessed. I remember rehearsing the last scene of *Lear* one night very late and he stopped me on every two words to give me inflections and tones. And I thought that at any moment he would say, 'Now don't act any more, we'll work it out technically.' But he never did. So I thought I had better stick it out and keep going if I could with full emotion. By the time I looked at my watch we had been at it for forty-five minutes and I had never stopped weeping and ranting, but he found me a way to do the speech that night which I have never varied since.

Someone afterwards said that Granville-Barker spoiled my first entrance in *Lear* by ignoring the convention that the leading character should always come on from the centre. But in *Lear* the throne has to be in the centre for the opening scene. Irving got round the problem by coming down a great staircase at the side of the throne, but I've seen a drawing showing that he also sat at one side of the stage. Granville-Barker put the throne dead centre, with the six seats, for the other principal characters, placed three on each side of Lear, and the whole scene worked out in an absolutely symmetrical way. He declared that the much-held view that the first act of *Lear* is impossible, that Shakespeare wrote a ridiculous story, was nonsense. He told us to think of it as something from the Old Testament or one of the great fairy stories — 'Once upon a time there was an old king with three daughters' — and it illuminated it for us all.

I do not remember Granville-Barker saying much about the characters of Goneril — played in this production by Cathleen Nesbitt — and Regan — played by Fay Compton. He had worked with Cathleen Nesbitt years before, when she had played Perdita in his *The Winter's Tale*, but it was the first time that he had worked with Fay Compton. She realized at once what a fine director he was, and although so many of her successes had been in sentimental and sympathetic parts — in *Mary Rose* and *Quality Street*, for instance — in *Lear* she played Regan as a kind of cold pussy-cat, a wonderful conception. I remember Granville-Barker invented a tiny piece of business for her in her short scene with Oswald, after the blinding of Gloucester and the death of Cornwall. He had her making up her face, dressed in widow's weeds, with a mirror in her hand.

After rehearsal, Granville-Barker would say, 'You did some very good things today, I hope you know what they were,' and would then produce a page of shattering, critical notes, which I wrote down at the time. I once asked him about the scene when Goneril is cursed by Lear and he leaves the stage on a very high note. A few lines later he returns in a totally different mood, in tears. 'What! fifty of my followers at a clap, Within a fortnight?' I asked Granville-Barker how Lear knows about the dismissal of his followers. Who told him? Granville-Barker replied that it does not matter. There is, he said, no off-stage time in Shakespeare: it did not come in until Ibsen, Pinero, Galsworthy and Shaw. In their plays you leave the stage to write a letter, stay off the stage for exactly the ten minutes it takes to write the letter and then come back. But Shakespeare knew how to convey an effect of time passing without realism. In this particular case the audience accepts the fact at once that somebody has told Lear the news off-stage. In the same way Macbeth and Hamlet become older during the course of the plays, but we are not sure of their exact ages — whether Hamlet is very young, or thirty, as the grave-digger says — or of the actual lapse of time, though it is obvious in *Hamlet* that a considerable time passes during the action. In *Macbeth*, also, the last act is usually played as if months, or possibly a year or two, have passed. Shakespeare does it in a very simple way, knowing that the audience will not be aware of such exact details while they are watching, whereas critics, students and experts have spent years trying to work out the niceties of time — whether Cassio could actually have had time to seduce Desdemona, and so on.

For this privileged production we had a splendid cast — Fay Compton, Jessica Tandy, Cathleen Nesbitt, Robert Harris, Jack Hawkins, Stephen Haggard — and there was a tremendous feeling of urgency and excitement. It seemed to take our minds off the awful things that were happening in France. When people used to come round I would say, 'How can you stand seeing so agonizing a play when such terrible things are going on in the world?' and they would answer that it gave them a kind of courage. It was a catharsis; you felt at the end of the play that the old man had learnt something from all the ghastly things that had happened to him, and the glory of the play and its magnificent poetry took you out of yourself. Shakespeare has always had that extraordinary appeal for every kind of audience. I felt it again when I played Prospero, and again when I played Hamlet abroad to the troops at the end of the War.

One of the earlier and most successful of my wartime productions was *The Importance of Being Earnest*, which we toured all over the country and then brought back to London, where we had first launched it for a few special matinées in 1939. After one of the performances Lord Alfred Douglas came round to see me, and soon after I met him again at a friend's house in the country. I had a cottage at Finchingfield in Essex in those days and one of my neighbours was A. J. A. Symons, who founded the Wine and Food Society and wrote a clever book on Frederick Rolfe, called *The Quest for Corvo*. At the time he was also trying to write a life of Wilde but was to die before he finished it. I went in one night and had drinks with Symons on the terrace of the house when Douglas was staying with him. They were a somewhat sinister pair and I was very disappointed in Douglas. Not only had he no longer a trace of his famous good looks but he was not very interesting to talk to either. He started on Wilde almost before I got through the door — Wilde was obviously his 'King Charles' head. I asked him a lot of pertinent questions about the original production of *The Importance of Being Earnest*, but all he could say was 'Oh, I stood at Oscar's shoulder all the time when he was writing the play at Worthing.' He could tell me nothing of the way in which it had been originally played; how much it was caricatured, all the nuances which I longed to discuss with him. Presumably he was not really interested in the theatre at all. I felt it must have been tragic for him to lose his beauty.

In 1942 I was asked to arrange a Christmas revue for the troops in Gibraltar. I commissioned various people to write sketches and collected a brilliant company which included Edith Evans, Beatrice Lillie, Michael Wilding, Elizabeth Welch and Phyllis Stanley. We were not quite sure what Edith Evans would want to do. Suddenly I remembered a benefit in which Edith and I had appeared at the beginning of the War. We had performed the great courtship scene between Mirabell and Millamant from Congreve's *The Way of the World*, one of Edith's most brilliant early successes. So I suggested that we should get somebody to write a little poem which Edith could recite in her Millamant dress, to open our revue. I commissioned a very nice woman, the wife of an actor, who composed satirical poems for the *New Statesman* under the name of Sagittarius. It was a very simple poem: 'We thought of you when to and fro/We wandered in the streets you know,/And as we acted in a play...' and so on. I showed it to Edith and she liked it very much. However, she thought there was one verse too many and in rehearsal cut the last verse. On the first night in the charming little theatre in Gibraltar the men were wild with excitement. They had seen no kind of live entertainment for two or three years and they knew there were some famous names on the bill. I went to the back of the auditorium to see the opening. The lights went up on Edith, dressed in her beautiful eighteenth century Millamant costume, with beauty spots on her face and a white wig. To my horror, there was a most enormous laugh from the audience. I thought 'My God, they've never seen a woman dressed like this before and they think she's a Pantomime dame.' Edith stood her ground. She spoke her three verses perfectly — not the fourth, which she had been clever enough to cut — stood quite still for a moment and then swept off the stage. The house came down. She received a tremendous ovation. Her coolness and authority had completely conquered the audience. It was very moving, and at subsequent performances they never laughed again.

The man responsible for all such entertainments for the troops during the War was, of course, Basil Dean, head of ENSA. Nobody thought he was particularly good at it and he was certainly fairly unpopular. I remember him once suggesting to me that I should take a play called *Diplomacy* to the troops. I had heard of this famous piece (a great standby of the Bancrofts and the Kendals and revived as late as 1934 by du Maurier with great success), but I had never seen it. So I took a copy into St James's Park and read it. I was absolutely dismayed. It was a wildly old-fashioned melodrama about a female spy, whose identity is betrayed by her scented gloves, and an innocent heroine who crucifies herself against a door. Four remarkably elaborate sets are needed, and the elaborate costumes of the 1880s. It would have been quite impossible to stage and I am sure the troops would have found it utterly ridiculous.

Dean had worked with a number of the best actors in his company before the First War at Liverpool. He had brought some of them to London backed by Alec Rea, a rich shipping magnate, and established himself in a series of productions at the newly-built St Martin's Theatre. After the First War, the men who came back, like Leslie Banks, were longing of course to start acting again and Dean was clever enough to collect fine companies round him. He still called himself Captain Basil Dean for long after the First War was over and went on behaving rather as if he was still a soldier, ordering everybody about. However, he chose good contemporary authors — Galsworthy, Masefield, Lonsdale — and had a sensitive feeling for poetry and spectacle and romantic theatre. James Elroy Flecker's *Hassan*, Dean's most cherished project, looked very handsome. The sets were by George Harris, his favourite designer and great friend.

When Harris died, Dean was shattered. This, and the death of Meggie Albanesi, a young actress whom he had discovered and who made an enormous success in several of his productions in the early 1920s, was a great grief to Dean and I doubt if he ever recovered afterwards. He certainly had a flair for casting and in rehearsal he was meticulous and extremely efficient. The only play in which I worked for him was Margaret Kennedy's *The Constant Nymph*, in which he was rather unkind to me, but I did appreciate how well he had arranged the play. I think he was too cold a personality to inspire actors to poetic work, good though he was for realistic stuff; his production of Galsworthy's *Loyalties*, for instance, could not have been better. When he directed *An Inspector Calls* by J. B. Priestley I was quite surprised to hear that both Alec Guinness and Ralph Richardson worked under him with the greatest respect and admiration. He certainly mellowed considerably as he got older.

In 1945, again under the auspices of ENSA, I made a five-month tour of India and the Far East, playing *Hamlet* and *Blithe Spirit* alternately for the troops. The first stop in our itinerary was a disused cinema in Bombay. We had a company of about twenty and brought our London costumes — which proved unwise as they were hot and cumbersome — and a minimum of scenery and lighting.

I was given a large bedroom at the Taj Mahal, a somewhat bleak but fairly luxurious hotel, sticky and clammy except for the dining room where the air conditioning and whirling fans suddenly struck one with a chilly blast. We rehearsed all day in the open-air cinema, sweating and cursing, while children swarmed outside, banging the walls with sticks, throwing pebbles and occasionally managing to sneak under a gate into the auditorium to peer and giggle at us as we worked. At the end of the exhausting afternoon I called the company on stage for notes, hastily taking off my doublet and shirt and putting on a very old, thin, white dressing-gown. Standing with my back to the auditorium, I was holding forth to the actors when I suddenly heard peals of laughter from the intruding children and, feeling something must be amiss, clapped my hands to my backside' to find that the dressing gown had a gaping hole in the seat through which my black tights were plainly visible.

We were supposed to perform only for troops in uniform, but as the performance started that evening we saw that the front rows were occupied by turbaned Indians, several of them accompanied by saried ladies, who proved to be an admirably attentive and enthusiastic audience. The soldiers had evidently realized that intellectual Indians are devoted to Shakespeare and had flogged their tickets to advantage.

A night or two later we were all invited to a party at an Indian film studio and accepted without realizing that it was more than an hour's journey outside the city. We drove along apparently empty streets which seemed to be white with discarded newspapers. I was horrified to see these pale shapes materialize into beggars and vagrants, clad in dirty white rags which scarcely covered them. They rose from where they were lying and scattered in all directions as the car approached. When we finally reached the studio we were ushered, to our dismay, into a small projection-room where we had to endure three-quarters of an hour of an excruciatingly boring Indian film musical — mermaid princesses reclining on rocks in subaquatic settings and princes, with bows and arrows slung on their backs, diving to encounter them in amorous pursuit. Emerging from this exhausting spectacle, we found a huge buffet laid out and so much strong drink (which, of course, after wartime conditions in England and our recent hard night's work we could hardly wait to sample) that several members of the company collapsed immediately in a drunken stupor.

On the following afternoon I was lying naked on my bed in the hotel, trying to rest before my performance, when the telephone rang. A lady wished to see me urgently. I made excuses and declined politely but two minutes later my bedroom door was flung open by the manager with his pass-key and a voluminous female in purple muslin marched up to my bed as I hastily covered myself with the adjacent counterpane. 'I am Mrs. Sabawala,' she announced. 'My house on Malabar Hill is a sermon in stone. You must lunch with me tomorrow. My car will call for you at one o'clock.' And she was gone without giving me time to protest

Reluctantly, but secretly rather fascinated, I climbed into the car when it arrived next morning. Mrs. Sabawala's house was large and imposing, with a crescent moon in cardboard attached to the front gate. There was a small party already assembled. The chairs were of black teak, without cushions, and consequently very hard to sit on. A small pool with a couple of rather sad lilies floating about in it occupied the centre of the room and I nearly tripped and fell into it as I retreated from a gentleman who rushed up to me to recite, at uncomfortably close quarters, a poem he had composed in my honour.

Mrs. Sabawala turned out to be a very enthusiastic and successful amateur actress. She had lately scored a triumph as Madame Arcati in a local performance of *Blithe Spirit*. Her ambitions led her to hope she might come to England and try her fortunes on our stage — Equity, of course, permitting. She was extremely amiable and remorselessly pressing in her attempts to make me a party to her ambitions but I was not to be so easily persuaded. I never heard from her again.

In Bangalore we experienced charming hospitality from Ram Gopal, the famous dancer. He knew London well as he had given some seasons there before the War and now came several times to see our *Hamlet*, sitting among the troops in his beautiful brocade coats of red or green. We were invited to his house — called 'Torquay Castle' — where statues of various Indian gods shared the place of honour with a large engraving of a Madonna bearing a bleeding heart. Mounting a steep outside staircase, he bade us remove our shoes as the room we were to visit was sacred to his mother. Here one of his aunts was sitting on the floor playing a large lute-like instrument and we listened politely, not quite knowing when the piece had finished or the appropriate moment at which we should be expected to applaud. On another evening, when we asked Gopal if he would not dance for us, he declined firmly but said his Guru would perform instead. We took our seats in a rather drafty courtyard with white walls and benches, rather like a fives court, where an orchestra of about eight persons, all of different ages, was already playing. A rather sinister figure was walking about behind the players drawing patterns on the floor in coloured chalks, reminding me forcibly of the vagrant who wanders in during the second act of *The Cherry Orchard*. Some time passed as the orchestra continued to play spasmodically. Then a very old gentleman, his body smeared with white streaks of paint and naked except for a loincloth, appeared and began to dance. We were told he was miming the god Shiva coming down from heaven and stealing the clothes of three maidens while they were bathing. We were duly impressed, though it was a cold night and we could not help wondering if the veteran performer managed to keep his circulation going more successfully than we did.

On another night at his house, Gopal at last consented to dance for us and retired to don his elaborate make-up and costume. He was away so long that most of the party had left before he finally appeared to delight the few of us who remained. The servants, who had hidden under the table-cloths, suddenly emerged to swell his rather scanty but enthusiastic audience.

A few days later Gopal kindly offered to take a group of us to Mysore in three cars and off we set, with Ram chattering gaily all the way, full of gossip about the London Theatre, which seemed unbelievably far off in such surroundings. The Mysore Palace was impressively elegant and massive, though somewhat unsuitably garnished with strings of coloured-glass lights left over from a recent festival. We became slightly hysterical when, as we were led to a fenced enclosure to admire a group of magnificent sacred elephants, they all greeted our approach by getting erections and then urinating for several minutes in splashing streams.

In Madras, the theatre was a kind of Senate House with tiers of seats ascending to the roof in a semi-circle and an enormously wide orchestra pit between auditorium and stage. There was a monsoon raging outside and the rain lashed down so fiercely that we could hardly hear each others' voices as we tried to arrange the scenery and lighting. I realized immediately that we could never succeed in communicating *Hamlet* under such circumstances and, in a desperate flash of inspiration, enquired if the orchestra pit could not perhaps be boarded over. This was quite quickly done and I supervised a hasty rehearsal, moving all the action in front of the proscenium. The result was a very exciting performance. I was able to speak my soliloquies quite close to the audience, and made several effective entrances and exits through the gangways between the seats.

In Rangoon we played in a converted chapel with only a single row in the small gallery reserved for officers, and it was wonderful to find the non-commissioned audience so attentive and enthusiastic. I had feared they would want the conventional kind of troop entertainment, girls with concertinas, music and jolly jokes, but even if their initial motive for coming in was to take the weight off their feet, the entrance of the Ghost in the first scene of *Hamlet* seemed to awaken an interest which never faltered, even in the fairly long version which we played. It was well worth the trouble we had taken with our black curtains and simple but effective lighting; and our costumes were certainly impressive and decorative, however uncomfortable to wear in such a climate. I besought the actress who was playing Gertrude not to fling her heavy train to one side in the final scene, as clouds of dust flew up to choke me as I lay on the floor in the throes of approaching death. 'Oh, dear,' she said, 'I don't really feel like a Queen unless I can fling my train!'

One day we visited the Shwe Dagon Pagoda, a famous landmark of great antiquity and veneration. The central shrine was a huge copper dome within a railing, surrounded by a stone pavement and approached by a most imposing flight of steps. On each side of the stairs were stalls and shops with men in bowler hats and sarongs, some with cigars in their mouths, squabbling and bargaining and spitting scarlet betel juice in all directions, while mongrel dogs barked and copulated and chased each other all over the shrine.

Singapore was dank and humid with forbidding Victorian archi-

tecture and statues. Staying at the famous Raffles Hotel, lately occupied by the Japanese who had left it in a state of considerable squalor,
I woke in the middle of the night to find myself covered with strange
white bites which had disappeared mysteriously by the time I woke
up next morning. The theatre was large with good acoustics, but as
the windows had all been knocked out, the swifts, attracted by the
lights, whirred noisily in and out all through the performances. The
concert hall next door where the pianist Solomon was giving recitals
was equally windowless, so that applause or reactions in either auditorium disturbed any possibility of complete concentration in the
other, though the enthusiastic audiences did not seem to mind as
much as I did.

One night when I was not acting I went to the concert hall and
stood at the back of the packed house to listen to an orchestra of soldiers recently released from prison camps, who were learning to recover their skills in playing instruments that they had not been able
to touch for years. Behind me, in the harbour, was a line of dark bat-
tleships spread out under the night sky. It was extraordinary to hear
a Beethoven symphony performed so movingly under such strange
conditions.

The atmosphere of the Second War in London was a complete contrast to that of the First, when a tremendous number of revues were
put on and *Chu-Chin-Chow* ran for years to an audience packed with
khaki. In the Second War, with the Blitz and then the V1s and V2s,
it was amazing that audiences came to the theatre at all, but there was
a feeling of grim determination. I remember going to see *Swan Lake*
at the Sadler's Wells Ballet one afternoon and watching the little
swans doing their very intricate dance, crossing their feet, when suddenly a V1 went over. They tried not to look up into the air and we
all held our breaths till the bomb burst somewhere on the other side
of London. I remember lying on the stage, 'dead' in *Hamlet*, when a
bomb was dropped into the Thames near the Savoy Hotel. Our
scene-dock doors at the Haymarket Theatre in Suffolk Street burst
open with a crash and a huge draft blew in. I thought 'Now we're really going to get it!' We felt that at any moment there might be fearful chaos in the theatre and people would be killed, but the audiences
took it with amazing calm. There was no need for the sort of action

urally. He began to look very sleepy and soon after he and his wife left in a taxi. About a week later he wrote me a charming letter in which he said some very nice things about my Hamlet; but he would never have been late for the first act of *Hamlet* in the old days.

Chapter Six

1946-1954

Importance *in America* — The Lady's Not for Burning — *Eliot* — Much Ado — *Peter Brook at Stratford* — Twelfth Night *with Olivier* — Macbeth *with Richardson* — *The last-minute* Heiress

By the end of the War I was pretty well tired out. I had fulfilled so many of my youthful ambitions that I did not know where to go. I had a fairly bad patch for a few years when I did not choose plays particularly well and my luck seemed to have run out. I did a version of *Crime and Punishment* in 1946, for instance, that was fairly interesting, but I was really too old for Raskolnikov. Many times in my career I have been bothered about the question of age, though I cannot help admiring old actors who can still give an impression of youth. Leon Quartermaine, for example, who became a great friend of mine and was a most beautiful artist, acted with me in Congreve's *Love for Love* when he was nearly seventy and hardly used any make-up at all. He played the part of a young rake with such charm and style that you never noticed that he was much too old for it. On the other hand I think it is dangerous to encourage very young people to rush into parts like Romeo and Juliet just because they are in fact thirteen and fourteen. Of course my own first Romeo, at nineteen, had been more or less a disaster!

Just after the War, in 1947, I went to the States with *The Importance of Being Earnest* and *Love for Love*. *Importance* was an enormous success but the Americans did not take to *Love for Love* at all. It was not perhaps as well played as in London. We had been acting it for a long time in England and I think I had become stale. The same thing happened later with *Much Ado* which I had done three times in England before I took it to New York. *Importance* stood up to new rehearsals, but *Love for Love* did not. I think, too, that Americans find it difficult to accept the sort of debauched aristocratic society that Congreve draws so well. They also find the very long sentences and archaic language difficult to understand. The Victorian era of *Importance* is much more familiar; Wilde did, after all, go to America himself on lecture tours and his play has always been a success there.

I take some pride in the fact that, after our revival with Edith Evans as Lady Bracknell at the beginning of the War, nobody put on *Importance* for some ten years. That is one of the tests of a successful production. It shows that you have made a definitive mark with a certain play. The same thing happened with *Much Ado* and it gave me much satisfaction.

The Importance of Being Earnest has to be played very strictly; it is like chamber music. You must not indulge yourself, or caricature. You must play it with your tongue in your cheek, like a solemn charade. The muffin scene, for instance, very easily degenerates into a knockabout. I discovered this years after I thought I had finished with the play for ever. Robert Flemyng and I were asked to do the second act at a benefit in Oxford. We rehearsed it again and I said, 'I believe I've been wrong about this scene whenever I have played it. I think it must be acted very slowly.' We began rehearsing it at half the pace and got many, many more laughs out of it by eating the muffins with real solemnity. Edith Evans always played Lady Bracknell in a very deliberate manner without any sense of urgency or crisis. My mother once said to me, 'Your generation will never understand the meaning of leisure. We used to spend whole afternoons driving round the park, leaving cards turned down at the edges on people we'd had dinner with the week before.' Even in my own youth there seemed to be so much more time for everything although, of course, many things took much longer. Love affairs carried on during the afternoon must have been more than usually time-consuming when you think of the amount of clothes that had to be taken off and put on again before the participants could reappear downstairs for their five-course dinner.

I remember doing pieces of Sheridan and Congreve at my drama schools and finding the plays very difficult to read. When we came to revive *Love for Love* I discovered that I remembered some of the lines from 1924 when I had played Valentine at Oxford. I had seen one revival of the play by Guthrie, with Charles Laughton and Athene Seyler, at Sadler's Wells in 1934, and I remembered that Valentine's mad scene was fun to play.

When I suggested doing it to Binkie Beaumont in 1943, he rather jumped at the idea. Beaumont was a very clever man. At a dress rehearsal he knew exactly what to say. Although Shakespeare and Congreve were not really up his street — he was a modern man with no pretensions to education at all and no knowledge except what he had learnt as he became successful — he immediately put his finger on what was wrong, advising us on cuts and all sorts of other details that were admirably constructive and not in the least discouraging. I always trusted his judgement. He would leave me alone until a very late stage in production and would then say just two or three things at the last moment which were extremely helpful.

The great exponent of Restoration comedy was Edith Evans. Nobody could touch her in parts like Millamant in *The Way of the World*. This is a cumbrous and difficult play — Millamant really has only three good scenes in it — and while Lady Wishfort is fun, the plot is a frightful bore. In *Love for Love*, the balance is more attractive. There are about eight good parts in it, whereas in *The Way of the World* the majority of the parts, except for Millamant and Lady Wishfort, are feeble and by no means easy to cast. I had a wonderful team when we performed *Love for Love* — Yvonne Arnaud, Cecil Trouncer, Miles Malleson, Leon Quartermaine and Leslie Banks, all dyed-in-the-wool professionals who had been in the theatre for so many years that they brought great experience to the work. But in *The School for Scandal*, which I directed many years later, the cast was far less evenly balanced. The difficulty is to find the actors to play Charles and Joseph Surface. Also, the action is divided all through into different sections which the director must try to weld together somehow.

When I came back from the 1947 tour of America, I was told about a play called *The Lady's Not for Burning* which had been done in my absence by Alec Clunes at the Arts Theatre. I found out that Clunes, who was running the theatre at that time, had paid Christopher Fry a bursary for a year to write the play for him. Clunes had acted in it and directed it but nobody could decide whether it had any sort of chance with an ordinary public. After its short run at the Arts Theatre, where it had had encouraging notices, Clunes suddenly decided to sell the play, and I was asked if I would be interested to which I replied that I had not even read it yet. I was going down to see some play at Cambridge with Binkie Beaumont and I read the first act in the train. I threw it across to Beaumont and said 'I must do this play. You must get it for me.' And he did.

We took nearly a year to put it on because Pamela Brown was not available. Fry had worked a great deal with her at Oxford during the War — where she had made great successes as Hedda and in various other parts — and he was determined that she should play the part of Jennet, the supposed witch. When it came to casting the boy, Beaumont had no doubts: 'We must have Richard Burton, of course.' I said 'Who's he?'

Richard had just made a great success in Emlyn Williams' *The Druid's Rest*. He turned up at rehearsal the next day and I realized that he was perfect for the part. I never had to tell him anything at all, except not to yawn so much when he wanted his lunch.

Esmé Percy played the tinker who had one scene in the last act. He was a delightful man.[1] He had played nearly all the big Shaw parts, touring for years with the MacDona Company. He had been very handsome until one of his eyes was bitten out by a dog and his nose was disfigured in another accident. He was odd-looking when I knew him, short and rather stout, but he had the most entrancing generosity and sweetness and was a very clever, volatile actor. I asked him to help me direct *The Lady's Not for Burning*, which he did, and he was very good in his one scene at the end, though he used to amuse himself with all sorts of business and antics. He had worked with Bernhardt as a young man, and he told me that he had to leave her company because she said he was getting too much like her! Indeed, he could imitate her brilliantly and told wonderful stories about her. He was the actor who, in the heyday of his good looks, was asked by Herbert Tree to supper one night after the play by himself. Lady Tree is said to have looked in at the door and said: 'The port's on the sideboard, Herbert, and remember it's adultery just the same!' One night during his big scene in *The Lady* his glass eye fell out. We were all transfixed with horror but Richard Leech, who was a doctor as well as acting in the play, had the presence of mind to step forward and pick it up. Esmé was saying under his breath, 'Oh, do be careful, don't tread on it, they cost £8 each.' After that I persuaded him to wear a patch, which he did rather reluctantly.

He was very much the old-fashioned English gentleman. When we were on tour in America — he was then in his seventies — he used to ring me up at nine in the morning and tell me he had been made an honorary member of some distinguished club in Boston or Washington, and he would invite me to lunch and then have some famous house opened specially for us to go to see. We used to go down to Greenwich Village after the theatre and he would have lots of young people sitting round him at supper listening to his stories. He still loved ammals, particularly dogs, in spite of his accident, and when he died, the night before he was to have opened in a play in Brighton, they found him in his hotel, dead in bed, with his last dog lying on his lap.

I managed to persuade Christopher Fry to make a few minor changes and cuts in the play and clarify some lines while we were on tour. In rehearsal I would go out front to watch my understudy walking my part so that I could see where I had to be in a scene — and very often I would find I had put myself in the wrong place and would have to change things round. We rehearsed the play most thoroughly and when we opened in London it became a huge success and ran for a year. When we took it to America it was equally successful — the text was still in the best-seller list of *The New York Times* the week our production closed.

After the long years of the war it was curious how T. S. Eliot and Fry both had a few years of great theatrical success with modern verse plays. People seemed to long to hear modern verse spoken again on the stage.

The audiences liked the romance and colour of *The Lady's Not for Burning*; there had not been a costume play in London for a long time and Oliver Messel had done a most beautiful décor for it — a little too beautiful I thought afterwards. I had an idea that if it had been staged in modern dress perhaps the meaning of the play would have been clearer. Christopher Fry had been a conscientious objec-

tor and his views were reflected in the character I played, a soldier returning from the war, wanting to be hanged in his disillusionment. I
thought that if he had come back in battle-dress, the disowned son of
a gentleman who had joined up in the ranks, the message might have
been clearer.

I got on better with Christopher Fry than I did with T. S.
Eliot. In some way I seemed to alarm him. In 1939 I had intended
to direct and act the leading part in *The Family Reunion*, which had
intrigued me, though I did not understand it very well. I had lined
up a wonderful cast — Dame May Whitty, Sybil Thorndike, Martita Hunt — and had scheduled the play for matinées at the Globe
Theatre. I was then asked to go to meet Eliot for the first time at
the Reform Club. To my surprise he was a rather sober-looking
gentleman in a black coat and striped trousers. We had oysters, I
remember, and it was very formal. I was rather nervous and began
to draw patterns on the table cloth. 'Should the set be like this?' I
asked him. 'The French windows, should they be there?' and
'How do you want the Eumenides to be seen? Or should they be
invisible, or perhaps in masks?' The more I talked, the more silent
Eliot became. However, I left thinking that I had created quite a
good impression. I continued to think so until, a few days later, I
met Sybil Thorndike who said 'You know, Eliot's not going to let
you have his play — he says you have no faith.' Evidently he feared
I was going to turn it into a fashionable Shaftesbury Avenue comedy though he never wrote to me to explain his decision.

Many years later I went to Marrakesh for a holiday and found
that Eliot was staying in the same hotel with his second wife. He was
already ill — it was not long before his death. I spoke to him and said
how sorry I was I had not done *Family Reunion*, but he still did not
reveal what he had felt about me or why he had turned me down. I
said I had played in it on the radio with some success and had made
a recording of his *Journey of the Magi* which people liked. He asked
me to send it to him, and he wrote me a very nice letter about it. I am

sure that, over *The Family Reunion*, he had found me over-assertive — perhaps he was right.

My 1949 production of *Much Ado*, at Stratford-upon-Avon, with Anthony Quayle and Diana Wynyard as Benedick and Beatrice, was very successful indeed. The whole cast worked wonderfully together and I engaged an enchanting designer called Mariano Andreu, a Spaniard, whom I discovered more or less by accident. I had been to see a ballet by Michel Fokine at the old Alhambra Theatre in Leicester Square, and had never forgotten the marvellous sets. There were white curtains with black and red motifs on them, rather like an Aubrey Beardsley. Four women, who looked enormously tall, came on and drew the curtains aside to reveal beautiful insets of palaces and gardens. When it came to *Much Ado* I thought that I must find the same designer. Somebody told me that he had recently designed a one-act play by Montherlant called *Le Maître de Santiago* in Paris. I rushed over to Paris, but in the lobby of the hotel where I was staying there was a poster advertising *Le Maître de Santiago* and, pasted over it, a slip saying the performances were cancelled because the leading man was ill, so I never saw Andreu's scenery for this play, but I did discover the man himself in the end. He came over to England and we worked together happily on *Much Ado* and, later, *The Trojans* at Covent Garden. He was an elderly man, sixty I suppose, very amusing, but speaking little English. We had endless discussions with diagrams and pantomime and he produced wonderful designs for *Much Ado*. I had always been obsessed by the photographs of Christian Bérard's designs for Louis Jouvet's production of Molière's *L'Ecole des Femmes*, in which a series of walls showed the street outside and then opened out like screens to show the garden. Mariano saw just what I meant at once and he devised for me a kind of picture-book garden setting for *Much Ado*, very simple though extremely decorative. Eight pages came on at the end of the scenes and mined the walls and the garden became a ballroom and, later on, a church.

Much Ado was interesting for me for another reason. I have acted Benedick with three different Beatrices. At Stratford in 1950, Peggy Ashcroft played the part and in the London production Diana Wyn-

yard took it on. I was afraid Peggy would be disappointed, but fortunately she and Diana were great friends and there was no awkward-
ness. I played it again with Peggy a few years later, and when I took
the play to America in 1959 Margaret Leighton was Beatrice — and
absolutely enchanting too. But by that time I thought my production
had become rather old-fashioned. They reproduced the scenery
poorly and it was not well lit. It looked like a Soho trattoria and
lacked the lovely classical Italian quality that it had in England.

Peggy Ashcroft's Beatrice was most original. Diana Wynyard
played it much more on the lines that I imagine Ellen Terry did —
the great lady, sweeping about in beautiful clothes. When Peggy
started rehearsing, she rather jibbed at all that and said 'I'm not going
to wear those dresses, they're too grand for me.' She evolved her own
approach to the character, just as good as Diana's but totally different
— almost with a touch of Beatrice Lillie. She wore much simpler
dresses and created a cheeky character who means well but seems to
drop bricks all the time (perhaps she got it from me). Everybody
thinks Beatrice will never marry because she is too free with her
tongue and is rather impertinent to people without intending any
rudeness.

As far as my own performance was concerned over the years I
kept trying to make Benedick into more of a soldier. At first Mariano
encouraged me to be a dandy, wearing comic hats, one like a blanc-
mange, another with a round brim trimmed with feathers. The hats
used to get laughs the moment I came on in them. I decided that this
had not much to do with Shakespeare's play, so I gradually discarded
them and wore leather doublets and thigh boots and became less of
the courtier. I tried to inject a good deal more bluffness and strength
into the part. Benedick ought to be an uncouth soldier, a tough mis-
anthrope, who wears a beard and probably smells to high heaven.
When this went against the grain I tried to console myself with the
idea that Irving must have been more of the courtier too, but of
course I never saw his performance. I saw the play once with my
uncle Fred as Benedick, but by then he was too old for it and he did
comic tricks like hiding in a tree in the orchard scene and falling out
of it. He was very fat and a bit more like Falstaff than Benedick,

though he was, as always, wonderful in the love scenes with his tenderness and his lovely voice.

Much Ado has been an enormous success in very varied productions since the 1950s. There was the Zeffirelli version with statues that came to life and Albert Finney in a Mexican get-up smoking a cigar, and one with an Indian setting with Judi Dench and Donald Sinden. Michael Redgrave and Googie Withers played it at Stratford in Victorian clothes, which Edith Evans assured me was brilliant. But I have never wanted to see *Much Ado* in Victorian or Edwardian costume, because I do not think those fashions can ever suit a play which is so full of Elizabethan sex jokes. The jokes are hardly credible when set in a period in which everybody was ashamed to show so much as an ankle.

Personally, I do not like Shakespeare to be acted in any period later than Jacobean, because it seems to me that if you are playing in Restoration costume with big wigs, or in eighteenth-century dresses with white wigs and high heels, or in Victorian strapped trousers and frock coats, you cannot sit or stand appropriately to match the text. You can, of course, avoid costume altogether and use modern dress, but I find it confusing. Guthrie did Edwardian productions of *All's Well that Ends Well*, *Hamlet* and *Troilus and Cressida*. I was unfamiliar with *Troilus* and could not follow the play properly, being unable to distinguish between the Greeks and the Trojans. Of course, *Antony and Cleopatra*, and the other Roman plays, and even *Macbeth*, were originally done in Elizabethan clothes with a few extra touches to give an idea of period. Probably the Elizabethan audience would have accepted very simple suggestions — a Roman helmet or a toga thrown over a doublet — enough to give a feeling of ancient Rome or Egypt. I was once very rash when I asked Noguchi to design *King Lear* for me in 1955. His Japanese costumes killed all our efforts to act in them. There were very interesting things about the production, but it was hopeless from the costume point of view, and I remember saying at the dress rehearsal to George Devine, who was directing it with me, 'Can't we scrap all the costumes and just have rubber sheets with holes for our heads?'

Costumes in correct period can be a problem for an actor. But designers are determined to have their own way and they are quite right. I remember in *Love for Love* I had the luck to persuade Rex Whistler, who was to be killed so tragically in France on D-Day, to do the scenery. He was training in the Guards and could not get much time off, so he was unable to design the costumes and I therefore engaged a wonderful elderly lady called Jeanetta Cochrane. (The theatre at the Central School of Art and Design in Holborn is named after her.) She was rather jolly and red-faced, like an admiral's daughter, and when we went for the first fittings to Simmonds the costumiers, who were supposed to be the best in London, she said, 'Oh, that coat is not cut right at all, the shoulders shouldn't be like that, they shouldn't be padded, that's not in my design.' The cutter was furious and said, 'How dare you speak to me like that? I have just done 350 dresses for Mr Ivor Novello and he was delighted with them.' 'Well,' Miss Cochrane replied, 'old Monsieur Leloi trained me and I happen to know that the shoulders should be this way.' 'Monsieur Leloi! He is my god,' cried the cutter, and Miss Cochrane had her way.

If given a chance, costumiers will often take short cuts, and actors and actresses too can be very difficult about their costumes. The high heels and heavy coats for men in eighteenth-century plays alter your balance, and actresses used to be very reluctant to wear tight corsets, although the young actresses today seem to be very good about it all. I have noticed in the last few years how they all wear the correct corsets and petticoats, perhaps because television and films insist on greater accuracy. Edith Evans was exceptional, as she always said she could not play a costume part unless she was dressed absolutely in the right period, right down to the underclothes. Nowadays, directors are also anxious that the actors and actresses should have some rough idea of what they are going to wear at rehearsal so that they can get used to it.

In 1950 I had what amounted to a fresh start in a glorious season at Stratford, playing four parts — Angelo, Cassius, Benedick and King Lear. It was meeting Peter Brook at Stratford and doing *Measure for Measure* with him that really started me off on this new line of work. I had seen *Measure for Measure* with Charles Laughton in the early thirties at the Old Vic in a production with Flora Robson and James Mason that Guthrie had done. It was the best production of that season. Most of the other plays were less successful because Laughton was not really very good in any of them. But he was wonderful as Angelo and I remember thinking that this highly unsympathetic character, a self-righteous prig, was one I could play — perhaps there was a bit of my own nature in it. Angelo, and afterwards Leontes (in which Peter Brook directed me too) were great challenges for me, though I have always thought I was rather good in unsympathetic parts — in *The Circle*, for instance, as the husband who likes the antique furniture better than his young wife, and in *A Day by the Sea*, in which I was the dreary son of the house who is an ineffectual civil servant. If you play someone who is not very agreeable, you do not try to make him sympathetic, but you do try to make him amusing and interesting. Bores, after all, are interesting phenomena in that they themselves do not think that they are bores at all.

Peter Brook has become something of a legend now, but in the 1950s at Stratford he was still very young, approachable and jolly.[2] Like Komisarjevsky he did everything himself, designed the scenery, found the music, controlled the lighting. His *A Midsummer Night's Dream* was extraordinary, I thought. He is also an enchanting companion and we have always liked each other. Some actors find him unsympathetic, even somewhat severe, but I would do anything he asked me. I trust him entirely for his beautiful taste and marvellous imagination.

Peter has great respect for the text, especially in Shakespeare, though lately he seems to have worked more enthusiastically with improvised texts or even (as Craig used to suggest as an ideal) with no text at all. He does not mess about with the lines, and he does try to work with his actors. I used to stop in the middle of rehearsing Leontes or Angelo and say 'I don't understand this speech at all, Peter,' and he would break off the rehearsal and go into a corner to discuss it with me for ten minutes. He is enormously thorough and full of inspiration.

He and I did the Seneca *Oedipus* together at the National Theatre in 1968 and had an exhausting time preparing it. Nowadays, Peter will not even design the set until he has started work with the actors. In *Oedipus* the management was very upset because he would not decide what we were to wear or what scenery was to be built. Peter enjoys his authority: he would walk into the rehearsal room and say curtly 'No newspapers!' and every morning the whole cast had to do exercises. It was rather like being in the Army and I dreaded it; but at the same time I knew I wanted to be a part of such an experiment. Peter Brook battered me down to my lowest ebb during the rehearsals, saying 'You can't do that, it's awfully false and theatrical,' and giving me extraordinarily difficult things to do. In the big scene, when I discovered what had happened — that I had killed my father and married my mother — I had to deliver a highly emotional speech kneeling on the ground, then get up quietly and go to sit at the side of the stage on a stool with the chorus, quite impassively, while the messenger came on and described me putting my eyes out. At the end of his ten-minute monologue, I had to get up from my stool (I was dressed in slacks and a jersey) and go into the voice and manner of the blinded Oedipus, trying to produce my voice in a strange strangled tone which Peter had invented at rehearsal with endless experiment. Technically, that was one of the most difficult things that I have ever done in my life — very good, I suppose, for my ego.

I have always been sorry that there was no record of *Oedipus*, either on disc or film, because not only the look, but the sound of it was so impressive. The chorus was disposed in the most original way, with some of the actors tied to posts around the pillars of the auditorium. (Latecomers were sometimes known to ask them for programmes.) There was one chorus, when Icarus falls from the sky, where the voices came from high up in the top gallery, passed down the circles and then were taken up by the actors on stage. The effect was like the great picture by Brueghel with the boy falling into the water.

After Stratford I worked with Peter again in my own season at the Lyric Theatre, Hammersmith in the year I was knighted, 1953. We had opened with *Richard II*. I decided I was too old to play Richard myself and rather regretted it afterwards — and followed with *The Way of the World* and Otway's *Venice Preserv'd*, which Peter was to direct. I directed *The Way of the World* and *Richard II* in which Paul Scofield gave a fine performance, though I do not think I helped him very much. I was too aware that I had played the part myself and that I was not giving him a sufficiently free hand to develop it along his own lines. He is a very individual actor in that he seldom feels really confident in his performance until just before the first night. Peter Brook, who has worked with him a great deal, told me that in *The Power and the Glory*, in which he was to give such a superb performance, he came to life only at the last dress rehearsal when everybody was in complete despair and thought the play was going to be a failure.

In *The Way of the World* I could not find much to do with Mirabell and was haunted by the memory of Edith Evans' performance as Millamant, which was perhaps why I failed to help Pamela Brown, whom I loved and who had made such a great success with me in *The Lady's Not for Burning*. The success of the production was chiefly due to Margaret Rutherford's splendid Lady Wishfort. The charming décor was designed by James Bailey and I managed to arrange the text a little better than usual to simplify the rather boring complications.

I had read *Venice Preserv'd* some years before and felt there was something strikingly effective in the play, and Peter Brook agreed. Nobody had done it since the eighteenth century, when all the great actors and actresses had played it, but it seemed tailor-made for me and Scofield — one of the few plays, like *Othello*, which has two magnificent leading parts for men. Beaumont liked it but we both realized it needed a certain amount of doctoring. So Peter Brook and I did a little work on the text. Leslie Hurry was engaged to do the décor, which was beautiful, very simple. The cast included Eileen Herlie, Pamela Brown, Scofield, myself and Herbert Lomas, a fine old character actor. It was really a great success all round though, oddly enough, of the three productions that season it was the only one that lost money.[3]

Later in 1953, I decided to take the production of *Richard II* to Bulawayo, where I had been asked to appear at the Rhodes Festival. I thought it would be an opportunity to play Richard for the last time, out of London. We took the play out with the scenery we had used at Hammersmith, little realizing that when we got to Bulawayo we would have to perform it in a vast theatre, part of a huge exhibition built on a windswept plain. The stage was enormously wide and when we put up our poor little scenery from the Lyric it looked like a child's plaything. It was July, but freezing cold, and the audience sat with rugs over them. Fortunately, our costumes were fairly thick. Very few people came to the Festival, everything was very expensive, the hotel was horrible — only two spoons to be found in the whole establishment. After the show we had to eat in the streets, hot dogs by the light of paraffin lamps, because nobody would stay up to give us any supper when we got back and the night club was too expensive. At the end of the four week run I went off to the game reserves for a holiday. I shall never forget the Victoria Falls, especially from the air, as our plane flew over them, and Rhodes' impressive tomb, hidden away in the depths of the country.

In 1955 I directed *Twelfth Night* at Stratford with Vivien Leigh as Viola and Laurence Olivier as Malvolio. Somehow the production did not work; I do not know why. *Twelfth Night* must be one of the most difficult plays to direct, though it is one of my favourites. I have seen so many bad productions and never a perfect one. I would give anything to have seen Granville-Barker's. In the first one I ever saw — Fagan's at the Court many years ago — the only memorable performance was by Arthur Whitby, a splendid actor, now forgotten, who played Sir Toby Belch. I acted Malvolio once at Sadler's Wells with Ralph Richardson as Sir Toby and enjoyed it, though that production was not very good either. It is so difficult to combine the romance of the play with the cruelty of the jokes against Malvolio, jokes which are in any case archaic and difficult. The different elements in the play are hard to balance properly. At Stratford I know that the actors were not very happy with my production, partly because of the scenery, which was too far up-stage. I thought Vivien Leigh was enchanting — though the critics did not care for her very much — but she was torn between what I was trying to make her do and what Olivier thought she should do, while Olivier was set on playing Malvolio in his own particular, rather extravagant way. He was extremely moving at the end, but he played the earlier scenes like a Jewish hairdresser, with a lisp and an extraordinary accent, and he insisted on falling backwards off a bench in the garden scene, though I begged him not to do it. I had not directed him since the days we had done *Romeo and Juliet* together and he was inclined to be obstinate. But then Malvolio is a very difficult part. The problem is to combine the dignity of the character with the fun and to make the tragic end, when he is put in the madhouse, succeed.

In 1952, I had directed Ralph Richardson in *Macbeth* but that too was not at all a success. I enjoyed the production if only because I also designed the scenery which I thought was pretty effective, though rather obvious too, consisting mostly of black velvet. This worked much better than the Arthurian medieval scenery I had used in my own production in 1942, which was picturesque but did not help the play very much. At Stratford I had a pitch-dark stage with very strong lights on the actors and the scene of Birnam Wood coming to Dunsinane worked rather well, as did the apparitions. On the whole, however, the production was a great disappointment both for Ralph and myself. I was sorry I had not managed to make it a success; perhaps *Macbeth* really is an ill-fated play. When I did it in the War three people died during the tour. There must be something in the legend of the curse.

I would like to have been clever enough to design more productions myself. I have always had a very strong feeling for the space on the stage, and I found that when I came to work as a director with designers it was fascinating to see how quickly the good ones recognized areas of the stage which could be used in different scenes to break up the monotony of a conventional square scene. At Barnes when I worked with Komisarjevsky on a tiny cinema-type stage he did some brilliantly inventive sets for *Three Sisters* and *Katerina*. In the latter play he broke up the stage space and cut a trapdoor in the middle of the floor, through which we made our entrances in the studio scene. The furniture was angled obliquely from the audience and I realized the possibilities open to a clever director for interesting grouping, how the actors can be raised at some points and lowered at others.

Then I went through a period of wanting pretty picture scenery, and the productions I did at the Queen's Theatre in 1937 were fairly decorative, though simple and not spectacular. They were an attempt to give the Motleys, who did *Bordeaux* for me so beautifully, a chance to develop their gifts. In the late 1940s there was a period of elaborate scenery at Stratford and James Bailey, Leslie Hurry and a number of delightful designers did beautiful décors at different times. I do not think now they would suit the feeling of the theatre today. John Bury has lately produced quite different kinds of settings for the classics though, of course, even he owes something to some of the best designers of the past — Lovat Fraser, Gordon Craig, even Bibiena.

In the past ten years the designers have been experimenting a great deal with the floors of their settings. I think a sloped stage can often be very effective though it can also be very awkward for the actors. When I was young a lot of the stages were already raked — the Haymarket, for instance. In Peter Hall's production of *The Tempest* at the Old Vic by John Bury, the rake was so steep that I could hardly keep my balance on it. It is difficult to realize, unless you have been an actor for many years, particularly in Shakespeare, how important it is to have a firm floor under your feet to keep your balance. When I played Hamlet in America I was given a beautiful set with two flights of steps; but there were so many that I spent my whole time with one foot up and the other down, which was terribly tiring. When you are speaking very long, elaborate speeches, it is vital to be comfortably balanced, especially in the classics, where so much is spoken standing. Marie Tempest always insisted, even in a modern play, that every sofa she acted on had boards under the cushions. She would never have a soft piece of furniture to sit on because it was not possible to keep a dignified stance — she was very small — and push her voice out.

One designer who always fascinated me from boyhood was Edward Gordon Craig, the illegitimate son of Ellen Terry and the architect and designer Edward Godwin. He wanted not only to conceive the production and to design the scenery, but also to do the lighting, cast the play and direct everybody. I suppose the fact that he himself had failed as an actor made him contemptuous of the way the London theatre was run commercially. He used his mother very unintelligently when she offered to back him at the Imperial Theatre in 1901. He persuaded her to do Ibsen's *The Vikings of Heligoland* and play a part quite unsuited to her, and she had to put on a revival of *Much Ado* to replace it. Craig exhausted all the money she had saved to put it on.

His strongest influence, undoubtedly, has been by proxy, in the effect he has had on other designers and directors; and I think he knew it. He was a jealous, slightly bitter man and yet very funny. He inherited Ellen Terry's sense of humour which made him very amusing company, although he did not seem to have a grain of humour in his love affairs — especially the famous episode with Isadora Duncan. He treated women in a cavalier fashion, deserting them when they found themselves inconveniently pregnant. He had various children all over Europe and was very strict with them when they lived with him, getting them up at five in the morning to clean his brushes and sweep his studio. When I knew him he was a very old man but still in wonderful spirits. He had no teeth but ate enormous meals and chattered away, looking picturesquely sly and coy and nodding, like an old raven, with his head on one side. He refused to learn any languages; though he lived in Italy and France most of his life, he went on speaking English and managed to make himself understood somehow.

He was surprisingly knowledgeable about what was going on in the theatre all over Europe. He went to see Olivier in *Richard III* in Paris and admired him greatly. The only time he visited England in my day was in 1930, at the invitation of C. B. Cochran, the great British impresario, just after I had made my first success at the Old Vic.

He was rather patronizing when we lunched together and I found him a disappointment. He did no work at all, left unpaid bills behind and really behaved, as usual, pretty badly. He was irresistible all the same. I could understand why Ellen Terry worshipped him. How she must have longed to help him, knowing his ideas were thrilling and before their time. She would have liked to help him to make a financial success out of them. She also sympathized with all his discarded lovers — she had been unlucky in love herself after all — and always kept in touch with them, giving them money for themselves and their children. Craig became more and more a crackety, curious genius, a sort of scandal to the whole of Europe. He enjoyed becoming a legend, but he was too suspicious to let anybody manage him or help him to carry out his ideas and to solidify the promise of his drawings and essays.

There are times when I think I have made a reasonable success as a director. I would not want to direct Shakespeare now because I think my methods are probably out of date. I would perhaps be adequate to direct a perfectly straight play, knowing how to group the people and put over the points correctly; but as a director I have never, I think, been able to put any great personal stamp on a play.

It is difficult to tell exactly what the director does unless you have been at every rehearsal. Ordinary playgoers do not appreciate the amount of compromise, the coaxing, the occasional ill-feeling and the numerous changes of direction which a play may take in the course of rehearsals. The actors are the only ones who really know what the director has contributed to a play. For many years I thought that the director's business was not to be noticed either by the critics or the public, though I have often been impressed by directors who do obviously manipulate their actors. I remember seeing Granville-Barker's production of *The Madras House* in the twenties at the Ambassador's Theatre and being bowled over by his skill, the movement and the shape of the production, especially in the elaborate first act, though everything seemed quite spontaneous.

My greatest satisfaction as a director was in 1949 when I was asked, at the eleventh hour, to direct *The Heiress*. I was acting in a play called *The Return of the Prodigal* at the Globe Theatre with Sybil Thorndike and was preparing to act in and direct Fry's play, *The Lady's Not for Burning*. Oliver Messel, who was to design it, arranged to show me the model for the set. We had been discussing it for nearly a year and I was very excited to see it. Beaumont and I drove down to Messel's studio one evening after my performance and he suddenly said to me: 'There's a terrible crisis about *The Heiress* — we've had to get rid of the director. Could you take over?' And I said, 'When is it to open?' And he replied, 'Monday week.'

Luckily, I had seen the play in America about six months before, with Wendy Hiller and Basil Rathbone, and liked it very much, so I knew what it was about. I told Beaumont I would do my best.

al for only half an hour and went away. Four weeks later, when
ere finishing rehearsals, I was told that the music was ready and
be recorded. I thought it was extraordinary and feared it would
t properly, so I went up to the big recording studio in Maida
and there was a huge orchestra, about fifty pieces. I found that
e witches' scenes had been perfectly timed, exactly to the
m of the words, just as I had sketched them out. It took many
s to record — far too long — and, with three hours extra time to
r, I found myself signing cheques like Ludwig of Bavaria. How-
the music was most effective and we took it on tour and used it
wards for six months in London. I was not so pleased, however,
ear it again some years later, in a production of Thornton
er's *The Skin of our Teeth*. As the records belonged to the man-
ent, Beaumont had decided to make use of them again.

I enquired about the scenery and Beaumont told me it was being
built in a carpenter's shop in Waterloo. I went down and examined
the set carefully in the morning before I met the company. At the
theatre I found James Donald, who was playing the juvenile lead, sitting gloomily on the empty stage saying, 'I've offended Sir Ralph.'
Everyone, it seemed, was at daggers drawn, the play was not ready,
but nobody wanted me to take over the direction, fearing that I
would immediately try to rearrange everything and the result would
be chaos. Even my friends in the cast had doubts about accepting me
to direct the play, because I have such a reputation for changing
things at every rehearsal. I do it because I believe actors have to try
things and then discard them and try others. I am very restless as a
director and very apt to change my mind. I expect the actors to sift
the wheat from the chaff, and know when I suggest good ideas and
how to discard the bad ones.

The next night, after my own performance in *The Prodigal*, we
had a rehearsal and I asked to be shown one of the scenes that had already been prepared. The stage manager, the management, the casting director and the authors, Mrs. Goetz and her husband who had
adapted the play from Henry James' novel, *Washington Square*, collected in the auditorium and the actors began to rehearse a few
scenes. They had all learned their lines, they were all very well cast.
Little by little, over the next hour or so, they began to gain confidence in what I rather timidly suggested. I said a few things that were
right and I suddenly realized that I had won over the confidence of
the company. I found that no props had been arranged, no noises off-
stage of carriages driving up, people were without muffs or fans (it
was a Victorian play) — all the details had been completely neglected.
So naturally, when I began to pay attention to all those things, it
seemed to come together quite easily. We rehearsed about seven or
eight days and opened at Brighton to an enormous success.

Directing opera is a different kind of challenge, which I have several times had the opportunity of taking up, with varying success. I
did *Don Giovanni* at the opening of the Coliseum when the opera
moved there from Sadler's Wells in 1968, and it was a terrible failure
for which I know I was greatly to blame. The conditions with opera
are very difficult. You are presented with a cast you know nothing

about (unless you are a singer yourself) and you have got to learn the opera by heart from records. Before that, in 1957, I had directed *The Trojans* and spent about a year beforehand studying it and it came out reasonably well. Then I did Benjamin Britten's *A Midsummer Night's Dream* and knowing the play so well of course was a great help. I did *The Beggar's Opera* at the Haymarket during the War with Michael Redgrave, but I tried to be too clever and do it in the Regency style. I had happened to see a statuette in Edinburgh of a Regency actor playing Macbeth and I thought we would not copy Nigel Playfair and do an eighteenth-century *Beggar's Opera*, but try a nineteenth-century approach. It was not a good idea. It changed the colour of the play and gave it a Dickensian atmosphere.

I was greatly helped in *The Trojans* by Sir David Webster, who was a great friend of mine and saw me through all the hard times with the chorus, which numbered no less than 120. We rehearsed for an extra week in Chenies Street and I was bewildered by the volume of noise. I did not know how to stop them, and when I succeeded at last, could not get them started again. They all seemed to do knitting in their half-hour breaks. However, I was very fortunate because for the first production of *The Trojans* I had Blanche Thebom from America and for the second Kirsten Meyer, both of whom played Dido beautifully and were excellent actresses as well, which solved a lot of my problems. Miss Thebom was nevertheless rather autocratic about her clothes. I was sitting next to the designer, Mariano Andreu, on the first night and he said, 'My God, she's cut off half her train.' And then she came on in a wonderful gold peplum which he had designed for her big aria in the last act, and she had put a belt round it to show off her beautiful figure. One of the things that amazed me was that singers never seemed to wait for notes. We would have a dress rehearsal and they would all be gone by the time I got up to the stage at the end. They expected to have notes given by my secretary. I had no secretary, but it was some kind of etiquette in the opera world.

Of course I loved working with the music, and I was fortunate with that too, because Rafael Kubelik conducted *The Trojans* in the first year and Georg Solti in the second, and they both seemed very sympathetic to my efforts. I quickly came to realize that the moment the conductor comes onto the scene, he really is the boss. The cho-

rus master is an important overseer too, and liab cancel all one's carefully prepared groupings by voices must be in the place demanded to achieve the music, and with a direct view of the conduct it very bewildering when I had arranged this hu groups that I thought were quite effective with up their heights and sizes, and then suddenly the cl say, 'You can't have your tenor there, the tenor gether on this side' or 'the altos have to be some hearsals at Covent Garden they have a long brid on one side of it, that crosses the orchestra pit, w used to run from the very back of the auditorium, leading to the rickety bridge onto the stage, seize rus round the waist and move her from one group t would go on singing and not take the slightest not explain the scenes they did not seem to find it ve you had to do a lot of coaxing and try to remembe take trouble not to treat them like a lot of cattle.

I have, of course, used music in many of my s We had very pretty music in *Much Ado* and also in *T dal*. It is a pity we do not have live orchestras any days, if the play was not very successful or was rat chestral interludes brightened things up a little, alth somewhat grim, with an awful chamber orchestra sa a lot of imitation palm leaves, playing tea-shop mu acts.

One of the innovations that is not so successful, really understand why, is taped sound effects. In *No* of wild animals and birds were performed by the act and it was splendid. I have never seen the storm in *L* erly done, though with recorded sound one might ex spectacularly effective, and yet controlled.

One of my great satisfactions in the war years w William Walton to do the music for *Macbeth*. Natura done on records. Walton came to the first rehearsal w ing to do the scene with the witches, getting them to rhythm in the doggerel they have to speak. He lister

hear
we w
coul
not
Vale
all
rhyt
hou
pay
eve
afte
to
Wil
age

Chapter Seven

1955-1978

The Secret Agent — *Marlon Brando* — *Lord Raglan* —
Providence, *the avant-garde with a vengeance* — Chimes at
Midnight — The Tempest: *'You ought to look like Dante'* — Home
and No Man's Land

The past two decades have brought me two rewarding new forms of acting. I found, somewhat to my surprise, that I enjoyed working in films; and I had several parts in exciting modern plays, very different from anything I had done before.

I had tended to avoid making films. In the days of the silent film and the early talkies, I made *The Good Companions* with Victor Saville in 1931, and *The Secret Agent* with Alfred Hitchcock in 1935, but since I was always acting in the theatre at night, I found filming terribly exhausting. I had to get up very early in the morning and was always fidgeting to get away by five or six for the evening performance, so I grew to dislike working for the cinema. Of course, I was paid more money than in the theatre, but I had a feeling that no one thought I was sufficiently good-looking to be very successful. I was happy working with stars like Jessie Matthews and Madeleine Carroll, who were both delightful, but the directors were naturally inclined to give them the best advantage of the camera, while I was seen mostly from the back of my head — which fortunately had some hair on it in those days. In *The Secret Agent* I played with Peter Lorre, the very striking German actor who played 'M' for Fritz Lang. He was a morphine addict and an expert in stealing scenes by putting in extra unrehearsed business at the take. Lilli Palmer made her first appearance in *The Secret Agent*, in just one scene. I enjoyed working with Hitchcock; he was a great joker, but I did not have much confidence in my talent as a film actor and I thought when I saw the film that I was rather poor. In the three or four silent films I made I knew I had been perfectly ridiculous, over-acting grotesquely.

Joseph Mankiewicz's *Julius Caesar*, made in 1952, was the first film I really enjoyed making. The producers wanted to emphasize the political side of the play and Caesar was played as a Tammany boss, so it was said, though I did not see much sign of it. One or two effective scenes in the play were left out, such as the 'Cinna the poet' scene and the scene when Portia sends the boy to the Senate House, but the film was made with sincerity and was quite well mounted, except for the battle scenes, which were done in a great hurry in the Hollywood Bowl on the last day of shooting, when I was nearly killed by a horse leaping on top of me. The set for Caesar's house appeared to be so full of gongs and statues and elephants' tusks that you could hardly move, so I plucked up my courage and said to Mankiewicz: 'I don't think Roman rooms were quite so full of clutter as this,' and he had a lot of it taken away. The big set for the opening scene had been built for *Ben Hur* in Italy and then transferred to Hollywood and re-erected. But when I took a very erudite friend to see the Forum set one day he remarked, 'This is quite good, but all the statues are of Emperors who haven't been born yet.'

Brutus was played by James Mason and I very much enjoyed working with him and thought his performance underrated by the critics, since Brutus is certainly the most difficult part in the play. He was extremely kind and generous to me. I was the only Englishman out there (of course Mason was English too, but he had not been in England for a long time) and I was afraid the Americans would think I was the star actor from London who had come over to teach them how to play Shakespeare. So I kept my mouth shut as much as possible and we all got on very well together. I got the part of Cassius almost by accident. Mankiewicz had come to London to get Paul Scofield to play Mark Antony. He saw me as Benedick (Paul was playing Don Pedro in my production) and engaged me for Cassius. But when Brando's tests for Antony arrived they were so successful that he was engaged and Scofield never even made the test.

I was amused to find that the huge crowd of extras were all paid different salaries. The ones in the front row who had the most striking faces were the highest paid, next came those who were only vaguely seen, and the ones at the back of the crowd who were not seen at all were the lowest paid but were able to keep their trousers on under their togas. One of my favourite moments was when a whole menagerie of animals, sheep, dogs and pigeons, was brought in to make the streets of Rome look more lively. The pigeons were put on the statues and plinths and I could not understand why they did not fly away. I was told later that their wings were clipped. Next day, I was waiting to go on the set when one of the pigeons, which had been perched on a pillar, jumped off and began walking about on the floor of the studio. A hefty cowboy, who evidently looked after all the animals, dashed up and yelled at the bird, 'Get back, get back, don't you want to work tomorrow?' I was told by a friend who acted in a film with Lassie, the star dog, that every day they used to bring an entire wagonful of Lassies to the studio: the smiling Lassie, the scowling Lassie, the gloomy Lassie and so on, and there was a great argument when she won an Academy prize as to which Lassie should appear at the dinner to collect the coveted award.

I was surprised to find that I did not have to alter my stage per-formance for the film to any great extent, and my knowledge of the play was a great help. Marlon Brando, on the other hand, was greatly hampered by the fact that he did not know how the scenes were placed by Shakespeare or how they progressed from one climax to another. They would photograph him for a couple of days in the tax-ing speeches of the Forum scene, and then he would lose his voice and be unable to work. They would fill in time by filming the extras, taking a lot of shots of faces in the crowd responding, then Brando would recover and come down to the studio to do another speech. I imagine that the director hoped he could put it all together in the cutting-room, but Shakespeare is too big for that.

Brando was very self-conscious and modest, it seemed to me. He would come on to the set in his fine, tomato-coloured toga, his hair cropped in a straight fringe, and would look around nervously, ex-pecting to find someone making fun of his appearance. Then he would take out a cigarette and stick it behind his ear. He told me that he was so well-off that he sent all his money home to his father and that he really had no need to work at all. I begged him to play Hamlet, and said that I would like to direct him if he did, but he said he never wanted to go back to the theatre.

I had only one scene with him in the film. 'We went through the speeches in the morning and he asked me 'What did you think of the way I did those speeches?' So I went through them with him and made some suggestions. He thanked me very politely and went away. The next morning, when we shot the scene, I found that he had taken note of everything I had said and spoke the lines exactly as I had suggested.

The next time I came down to shoot, Mankiewicz said 'Oh, Marlon's done the great speech over the body absolutely marvellously,' and asked me to see the rushes, which I did not like very much. I thought he was giving a bad imitation of Olivier, but it was hardly my place to say so. I never met Brando again, which was a pity because I felt that he was enormously responsive. The very first day I was introduced to him he said, 'You must come and do a speech for me — one of my Antony speeches. I've got a tape recorder in my dressing-room.' He had tapes of Maurice Evans and John Barrymore and three or four other actors and listened to them every day to improve his diction. I thought he would have made a wonderful Oedipus.

After *Caesar*, I had no film offers until I did Clarence for Olivier in *Richard III*, which involved only a few short scenes. Then Tony Richardson asked me to go to Hollywood to play in *The Loved One* from the Evelyn Waugh novel. We became good friends at once, and in 1967 he asked me to play Lord Raglan in *The Charge of the Light Brigade*, a most amusingly written part.

We went to Turkey for twelve weeks with a huge cast and lived most of the time in a hotel in Ankara, driving out to the Crimean plains at half past five every morning, with marvellous spreads of food under canvas twice a day. I cannot think how it was done. A charming actor called Mark Dignam was with me in most of my scenes and we spent weeks in terrific heat, sitting on horseback side by side. I dread horses and cannot ride at all, and since I had to have one arm tucked inside my overcoat — Lord Raglan lost one in the Battle of Waterloo — balancing on horseback was rather difficult. The first time I went for a riding lesson in Turkey, the horse just threw me off, lay down and kicked its legs in the air. I had to remount the wretched animal at once and pretend I loved it. I was terrified that the horse would bolt and I would not know how to stop it. There was one scene involving an enormous procession of horses and marching troops. Hundreds of actors assembled on the top of a ridge and I was right out in front with two men on each side of my horse to prevent it from suddenly bolting. There was a very long take, and I remember thinking that if the horse did decide to bolt, it would ruin the whole set-up, which had taken hours to get ready. Fortunately, the animal behaved rather well.

The principal players were each supposed to have individual horses. However, soldiers from the Turkish Army were also being employed and when we were not there they would borrow the horses to ride themselves, so that when we got them back, they did not know us any more. The Turks were very tough with us, did not care for us at all and made things as difficult as they could for Tony Richardson.

I am, I suppose, lucky in that the physical discomforts of filming do not worry me unduly. I am no longer troubled by getting up early, sitting about for hours, and coping with the make-up and continuity departments, which can be tedious and exhausting. I find now that I am rather good at quietly doing my crossword and watching other people's scenes. One does, after all, have plenty of spare time to think about one's part, gossip with one's colleagues and have fun. The routine and discipline of filming are quite different from those of the theatre — occasionally one even has an evening off, and one lives more luxuriously, unless the location is particularly difficult. In the theatre you can digest a scene over two or three weeks of rehearsal and experiment; in films you only rehearse five or six times before the scene is shot. It is no good being hysterical or highly-strung in movies. At the same time you have got to have all the energy ready coiled up inside you.

There are drawbacks of course. It is usually fearfully hot under the lights; a tight or uncomfortable costume can be very tiring to wear all day. The severest torture in film-making, however, is dubbing, which I really hate. Nowadays it is used a great deal, especially with films made abroad. You have to go into a horrid little room and see yourself fifty times over, saying the same line or two with a guide strip going over your face to tell you exactly the moment to speak.

You think 'Oh, I'll say that line better now, I'm sure,' but you cannot, because if you change it it does not match your lip movements, so you end by giving, with great difficulty, a cold-blooded imitation of something you did more or less spontaneously the first time.

By far the most exciting film I have ever made was Alain Resnais's *Providence*. I was very impressed by David Mercer's script. My own part was fascinating, if somewhat alarming; a very tough, Augustus John kind of character, drunk half the time, lying in bed drinking white wine and throwing bottles about, and roaring a lot of very coarse dialogue. He is an old man trying to finish a novel and at the same time dying of cancer and confusing the novel with his own past life. His wife has killed herself by cutting her wrists in a bath and he feels he may have been responsible. He has never got on well with his son and daughter-in-law. He keeps inventing scenes for the novel which involve them in various situations, settings and contexts. He has curious nightmares about werewolves and people being hunted in forests and herded into stadiums. Finally in the last part of the film, there is a beautiful scene on the old man's seventy-eighth birthday, when he gives a lunch party in his garden for his family. His son arrives with his wife, and his illegitimate son too, and they all get on very well, drink his health and leave him with the empty garden in the sunshine. A touching end to a somewhat macabre story.

The whole structure of the film was rather oblique and as it came at the same time as I was playing Pinter's *No Man's Land*, I felt I was in the avant-garde with a vengeance. The director, Alain Resnais, had never done a film with English dialogue before, except for *Stavisky* which he made in America. He does not speak English very well, but was at the time married to the daughter of the late André Malraux, who speaks perfect English and is always there, working at his side — a delightful woman. I took an enormous liking to Resnais the moment I met him and he seemed to like me too.[1]

The part seemed to have wonderful opportunities, though I was afraid that I would not be sufficiently craggy for it. However, Resnais seemed to have confidence in me, and I threw myself into the work, acting scenes that would have embarrassed me dreadfully on the stage. At one point I was asked to put suppositories up my bottom under the bedclothes and play a scene in the lavatory which I confess I found somewhat intimate.

Resnais was wonderful to work with, so beautifully impassive, always the same whether it was fine or wet, hot or cold. We had very tricky times with the weather. We were near Limoges, in a beautiful park, where we played the last scene, with the crew in windcheaters and parka hoods, stamping their feet to keep warm, while I lay in a tropical Palm Beach suit, on a *chaise longue*, trying to pretend it was lovely weather. Resnais interrupted very little. I used to say, 'Is that scene all right?' and he would say, 'Well, it amused me.' I had splendid actors to work with. There were only five of us, very strongly contrasted: Dirk Bogarde, whom I have known for many years, but only worked with once before; and David Warner, Elaine Stritch and Ellen Burstyn.

It was fascinating to see how *Providence* evolved in the rushes. I remember going along to see one scene in which I did not appear. In the scene a man is being hunted down in a wood. Five men with rifles come out of the bushes and move in for the kill. I suppose I saw twelve takes of this scene, yet each time I saw it, though I knew the men were going to come out of those bushes, I became terrified as they emerged. It showed how wonderfully it was grouped and photographed.

Resnais has a genius for individual grouping. In *Marienbad* it was rather like watching a chess game — all those people in the palace gardens standing in set attitudes. In *Providence* there is a fine shot of the static scene at the lunch table, at the end of the film. A camera on an enormous crane focused on us all as we began our meal, sitting round the table with the servants, and the big dogs sitting nearby. Then the camera went up into the air over an enormous expanse of trees and sky, and did a complete semi-circle. As it slowly came down again the servants were seen clearing away the lunch. It was a most beautiful shot and took a long time both to act and to photograph. We had to keep still for about four minutes before the camera came back to us again. Everything, every camera movement, detail, piece of furniture, was carefully thought out by Resnais beforehand.

Many people found it difficult to distinguish reality from fantasy in *Providence*. I think that, with a film of such complexity, you have to make your own judgement about what is reality and what is not. Some of the people who did not understand it in America said that the last scene, the reconciliation, should have come first, and then all the early part would have been clear. But the structure is deliberately created by Mercer and Resnais to fascinate and intrigue the audience. It makes the film almost like a thriller. You cannot think what is going to happen next when you see a man with hair on his hands being chased through a forest by riflemen. There are scenes in a law court, others in a rather chic flat, and yet more in my Victorian bedroom, with the rain pelting down outside, and the old man knocking back another drink and trying to create another scene for his novel. It is enormously varied, there is no chance of getting bored.

When I made films in the thirties I always felt that I had to be careful exactly how I looked, and this made me camera-shy. Now, when I play character parts and it does not matter how hideous I look, I lose my desire to exhibit and try to live inside the part. When I was doing *Caesar* in Hollywood I observed James Mason's technique, particularly in close-ups, and saw how brilliantly he expressed a character's thoughts without making faces or grimacing. I began to watch films with a different attitude — studying the way actors restrained their facial play so effectively.

One of the oddest films I have ever made was *The Prime Minister*, in which I played Disraeli. Possibly because I have a big nose, some people think that I have Jewish blood and am perfect for Jewish parts. I always rather hoped this was so because so many of the best actors in the world are Jewish. But I asked my father and he assured me that there is no Jewish blood in our family at all.

I have never had much luck with Jewish characters. I had no success as Shylock, though Olivier was kind enough to say it was one of the best things he had ever seen me do. I tried to play him as a little monster, shabby and dirty, with a foreign accent. However, it was in 1938 when the Nazis were in power and I think that the public in England would have preferred to see a more sympathetic, heroic Shylock, which is what they expected from me as a romantic actor.

The War was a year old when I came to play the screen Disraeli and air raids were taking place every night. The extras used to get very cross if I fluffed my lines and prevented them from getting home before the blackout. The script showed Disraeli 'from the cradle to the grave' and I had a very enterprising make-up man to create whatever age was necessary. I would play a scene in the morning as the old Disraeli, covered with fish skin (which gave me impetigo) and then they would scrape it all off so that I could do an earlier scene as the overdressed young dandy in the afternoon. The film was made on a shoestring at Teddington and, soon after, the studios were bombed and one of the managers was killed.

I had one scene in which I sat in a low chair by a fire reading through some old love-letters from my recently dead wife. I had no words to say and it was the only scene that turned out well. For the first time I realized that filming must be treated as if it were silent, and that although the dialogue must be studied and put over as it would be in the theatre, there must be more spontaneity and less emphasis. On the stage I have always had a tendency to make faces — what my intimate friends call my 'Shylock' face. I screw up my eyes and pull my mouth down and look very peculiar. I try very hard not to do that on the screen and, in watching the rushes, I am always on the look-out for unfortunate mannerisms.

I have always wanted to play the old King in *Henry IV* and when the National Theatre was about to open I implored Ralph Richardson to play Falstaff again, with me as the old King and perhaps Finney and Scofield for the younger parts, but Ralph would not do it. I was therefore delighted to have the chance to play the King in Orson Welles' *Chimes at Midnight*, even though it did not turn out a great success. Like most of Orson's films it was full of very fascinating things but it did not work as a whole, though it did have a real Shakespearean feeling.

Orson Welles was splendid to work with, although he was always pressed for money and usually in poor health.[2] He engaged a very fine company but he could not afford to keep us all permanently employed. I went over for a week's shooting in Spain, then Margaret Rutherford went over for a week, then Jeanne Moreau, and Orson, who was playing Falstaff, had still not done any of his own scenes. By the time he got round to them he was tired out and there was nobody left for him to act with. I never even saw him made up as Falstaff until I watched the film in the cinema. He had found a marvellous setting for the court scenes, a great empty building in the hills above Barcelona, which had been a prison at one time and had a huge hall with a stone floor. However there was no glass in the windows and the cold November air poured in. I was wearing tights and a dressing gown and practically nothing else for my death scene. I would sit on my throne with a tiny electric fire to warm my feet while Orson spent his last pesetas sending out to buy brandy to keep me going.

I had first met Orson with the Oliviers. We were due to stay with them in the country and went down with them in their car. Orson sat in front and I leaned forward and said, 'What are you doing here?'

'I'm going to play Othello.'

'On the stage — in London?' I asked with rather tactless incredulity and he was not at all pleased. Next day we all got up rather early but Orson had already disappeared. He left word that he had a business appointment in London and I thought perhaps he had been very offended by me. At about nine o'clock that night the bell suddenly rang and he came in. The servants had gone to bed and Vivien Leigh went off and made scrambled eggs for him in the kitchen. I asked Orson if he had had a good day in London. 'Not at all,' he said, 'she cried the whole time.'

We once had a hilarious day making recordings of an episode of a Sherlock Holmes series for the radio. I was Sherlock Holmes, Ralph Richardson was Dr. Watson and Orson came over to play Moriarty. We all went to lunch at the Éitoile in Charlotte Street and Orson shouted and drew so much attention to us that everyone in the restaurant began staring. Ralph and I felt like two little boys from Eton who had been taken out at half-term by a benevolent uncle.

I have always wanted to make a film of *The Tempest*. Prospero has been a favourite part of mine and it would be a wonderful thing to do at the end of one's career, because it is so obviously Shakespeare's last work — the end of his career.

My first Prospero was in 1930 at the Old Vic with Harcourt Williams. Leslie French was very charming as Ariel, singing beautifully, and naked except for a loin-cloth. It was seeing his performance that is supposed to have inspired Eric Gill to create the statue in the front of Broadcasting House.

In all four productions of the play I have acted in over the years, with Harcourt Williams, George Devine, Peter Brook and Peter Hall, I was consistent in one thing — I never looked at Ariel. He was always behind me or above me, never in front of me. I tried to see him in my mind's eye, never looking at him physically. It heightened the impression of Ariel as a spirit.

In directing the play in 1957 for Stratford, and afterwards for Drury Lane, Peter Brook conceived the last scene in the play as the great triumph for Prospero returning home to accept the dukedom; I had a beautiful blue robe with a coronet which I placed on my head as Ariel dressed me. At the end, as I moved to the back of the stage, some ropes fell from above, the other characters turned their backs to the audience and the scene changed and became a ship sailing away, then I turned and came down to the front to speak the Epilogue. But in 1974 Peter Hall wanted me to play Prospero as a disillusioned man who had kept his old court suit in his cave for twenty years and got it out very reluctantly. He felt that Prospero did not want his dukedom back and resented having to leave his island. My reading of the Epilogue thus became quite different, more humble and not as grandiloquent as in the Peter Brook version.

Komisarjevsky, curiously enough, told me back in the twenties that I ought to play Prospero without a beard. He said, 'You ought to look like Dante!' and that is how I tried to look in the Vic production, clean shaven, with a turban.' Peter Hall, in contrast, insisted on my putting on a pointed grey beard. He wanted me to look like the Elizabethan wizard Doctor John Dee, and he and John Bury designed a costume and make-up with which I was never very happy. In Peter Brook's production I had invented my own costume with his help, and tried to look like a figure from an El Greco painting, half naked above the waist and wearing sandals to give me the look of a hermit. At the Vic, in 1940, when George Devine directed me in the play, I had a small grey beard and spectacles. It was interesting playing the part in these different ways and I found effective things in all of them.

Caliban is always a difficult part to cast in *The Tempest*. He must be a tragic figure as well as providing comic relief. In 1930, Ralph Richardson contrived to combine both these qualities to perfection. I remember seeing one production with an actor called Louis Calvert, who wore an animal skin and walked about on all fours like a pantomime bear and was perfectly ridiculous. Benson used to play Caliban hanging from a tree, eating a fish, while Tree arranged a final tableau for the end of the play, with Caliban stretched out on a headland, lonely and forlorn, and a model ship moving away in the distance.

The first time I ever appeared in the play, as a very young man, I was asked to play Ferdinand for a few matinées with an actor called Henry Baynton who was starring as Caliban. The scenery, with a lot of potted palms, was old and dreadful and the cast was dressed in terrible hired clothes and wigs. Baynton prefaced his entrance with tremendous roars offstage and then emerged from a cave in the centre of the stage in a splendid, specially designed costume. He was an extraordinary performer who would play Caliban one night and Hamlet the next. At the end of Lear he would whip off his make-up and come on in a smart dressing gown to take the calls. He played Hamlet with a string of pearls round his neck which I thought was going rather too far.

I think *The Tempest* would make a wonderful film and have my own ideas about how it could be done. The play has to be set in several, unidentifiable, locations: marshes one minute, cornfields the next, then cliffs and sea, and finally sands. Japan would be marvellous for this, remembering the beautiful effects of *Rashomon*. I once asked Benjamin Britten if he would compose the music for such a film and he agreed. He suggested that the earlier parts should have an ordinary soundtrack, but when the scene moved to the island there should be no noises, only music.

In more recent years I have found myself appearing more and more in modern plays, notably Alan Bennett's *40 Years On*, Edward Bond's *Bingo*, Charles Wood's *Veterans*, David Storey's *Home* and Harold Pinter's *No Man's Land*. I am proud and thrilled to feel that in the latter two plays I have had not only a personal success but also a wonderful partnership with Ralph Richardson.

I read *No Man's Land* in forty minutes and knew instantly that I must play the part of Spooner. Peter Hall had sent the script to me expecting that I would want to play the 'posh' part of Hirst, because it was more the kind of role I had done in the past. I told him, 'Don't be silly. The other part is infinitely more what I want to play.' The part of Spooner was a complete impersonation, such as I had never had a chance to do in the theatre. It was very exciting to have a chance of doing it, and I was quick in finding a way to look and to dress. The moment I read the play I saw Spooner clearly, which was rare for me. I remember saying to Harold Pinter, 'I think Auden, don't you? Do you think sandals and socks?' and he jumped at the idea. Then I said, 'Do you think we should add spectacles?' and he liked that too. About a week after we started rehearsal I came on the stage with the wig, the suit and the spectacles and everybody said, 'It's exactly right, perfect!' And I said, 'Yes, and now I must find a performance to go inside it!'

It took longer to find a voice for Spooner. I did not want anything too affected. I eventually found it by throwing back to my eldest brother's generation. I had a very brilliant brother, Lewis, who was something of a poet. He was badly wounded in the First War, and lived abroad most of his life. When I was a boy I visited him once or twice at Oxford — he was at Magdalen after the First War. He was a great friend of Aldous Huxley, the Haldanes and all the intellectual Oxford people who afterwards joined the Bloomsbury Group. Many of them had a curious drawl which I remembered vividly, and I adopted it for Spooner. I also had in mind the bookshops in the Charing Cross Road where I used to buy cutouts of the ballet. They were run by Bohemian semi-failures who were very much the kind of man Spooner seemed to be.

One reason I so enjoy working with Ralph Richardson is that we are old friends and we laugh a lot and seem to balance each other's style in a very happy way. It is wonderful to play with somebody who is so absolutely opposed to you in temperament: we are a tremendous contrast in personality. Now, after so many performances and interviews together, we say we are becoming like the broker's men in *Cin-*

derella. People even mix us up and greet us by each other's names, particularly in America, where titles often confuse the public. When we first read the plays neither of us was quite sure whether we dared to undertake them, fearing we might make fools of ourselves, but we were very fortunate in our directors, Lindsay Anderson and Peter Hall. Both of them had enormous feeling for the plays and we felt they would not have wanted us to play in them unless they were confident that we were the right men for the parts. There was no question of being engaged because we were stars, as sometimes is the case in more commercial plays.

In *No Man's Land* lots of people came round after every performance, both in London and America, complaining that they did not understand the play. 'What does it mean?' they would ask. Why should the play 'mean' anything if the audience was held the whole time and was never bored? That is surely the important thing. I do not think *No Man's Land* has any deep social significance. Pinter is a marvellous writer of character and suspense and, although people tried to make out that the play was about God, the decline of England or any number of other symbolic things, it was enough for me that the audience was fascinated and mystified. Certainly a few people walked out, but that is true of any play, and the general appreciation of it both here and in America was extraordinary.

Unhappily George Devine had died by the time Ralph and I did *Home* at the Royal Court. Irving Wardle has written a splendid book about him — one of the best stage biographies I have ever read. He interviewed me while he was writing it and I felt as we talked that I had been ungenerous to George. All the people who worked with him at the Court, like Tony Richardson, Anthony Page and Peggy Ashcroft, were devoted to him. He and I had rather an awkward relationship because I had known him from the very beginning when he was my undergraduate Mercutio at Oxford. Then he was with me for a number of years in my seasons in the 1930s and was excellent in many small but difficult parts. He went to India to fight in the war and came back to take over at the Court in the 1950s. He and I directed Lear together in 1955, the Noguchi Lear in London, which was rather a disaster. He had become tremendously fond of Michel St-Denis and had been one of the founders of his schools at Islington and the Old Vic with Glen Byam Shaw. I suppose I felt slightly jealous because he and Glen (and the Motleys) had been with me so long, and then left me to work with Michel. Devine did once ask me to play at the Court in Beckett's *Endgame*, which I did not like at all (he played it himself afterwards) and he also asked me to be in John Osborne's *A Patriot For Me*, in a part which I did not care for. I did not see much of him in his last years. I am very sorry now; I am sure I missed a lot by not allowing him to influence me in his enthusiasm for new writers of the avant-garde, but he and Michel were always tremendously taken with Brecht and Beckett, with neither of whom I have been able to find much sympathy.

One of the hardest things I ever tackled was to direct myself and perform solo in the Shakespeare recital, *Ages of Man*, which I toured for many years. When I opened in New York I nearly missed the first night as a result of going to Havana for a weekend just before Christmas. The hotel where I stayed seemed curiously empty and the next day the revolution broke out. I spent the whole day in the American-Consul's office trying to get a visa back to New York, and I arrived back only a few hours before I was due to open. On top of that, there had been a newspaper strike in America and I was the first actor to get a notice for six weeks.

The only time the *Ages of Man* recital was not a success was when Beaumont suggested that, since I had had such success in the provinces before the War, I should take it to Edinburgh, Liverpool, Cambridge and Brighton. At Liverpool no one would come near it and Edinburgh was very hard. In Brighton it was so badly attended for the first three nights that Alan Melville and Godfrey Winn both wrote letters to the *Sussex Gazette* and said it was an outrage that it was not a success. The theatre was packed for the rest of the week. I had to write to thank them, which I found somewhat humiliating. The audience seemed to be suspicious of a one-man show, perhaps because they felt they would not get their money's worth. I toured *Ages of Man* for so many years that I feared I would be out of practice when it came to acting again with other people. Also, eight perfor-

mances a week all by myself, and sitting alone in a dressing-room between the acts, was a very lonely and sometimes depressing business.

Chapter Eight

Impressions of America

Arrival — Guthrie McClintic — Alexander Woollcott — The Lunts — Ages of Man — U.S. television

I have always looked on New York as something of a second home. I have been unusually lucky in my work here, and have made many friends both in the theatre and outside it. I have watched the city grow and change ever since my first sight of it all those years ago and looked forward ever since to the many opportunities of returning here. To me, Fifth Avenue, from St Patrick's Cathedral to the Plaza, is one of the finest and most elegant streets in the world, and the towers of Central Park South, twinkling with their myriad lights as dusk begins to fall, are for me among the most magical and romantic sights imaginable. Even the extremes of climate, the crumbling pavements, insistent traffic, the extraordinary mixture of luxury and squalor — all these contrasting elements never fail to absorb and excite me. I work well, eat and sleep well and look forward with liveliest expectation to whatever the following day may chance to bring.

My first impression of New York was as long ago as 1928. I was engaged by Gilbert Miller in London to play the young Tsarevitch in a play called *The Patriot*, adapted from the German by Ashley Dukes, about the murder of Tsar Paul I. I was told I must leave immediately and learn my part on the boat. It was not a very long part. The actor originally cast had been sacked and I was to arrive in time for the first dress rehearsal. I sailed on a German ship with only one or two people speaking English, so of course I was very nervous. When we docked in New York I was met by a tall black man from Miller's office and driven straight to the theatre where the dress rehearsal was already in progress. In London I had been told that I would be paid a certain salary and given a six weeks' guarantee. At the theatre there was an army of stage hands pulling the sets on trucks from one side of the stage to the other, and Gilbert Miller, various assistants and Norman Bel-Geddes (a famous architect who had designed the scenery) were all arguing loudly with each other. Behind the scenes Lyn Harding, a fine old English actor, was sitting dressed in uniform in his dressing-room with a large plate of oysters on his knee. He invited me to share them and we went through our lines together. Then I was dressed in a very fine costume with a powdered wig and flowing cloak. The next night we opened.

Leslie Faber and Lyn Harding were both skilled players, as was Madge Titheradge whom I had always greatly admired but had never met before. We went to a big party afterwards where I noticed that Faber seemed very depressed. The next morning the notices said that he looked like George Washington (he did resemble him a little), and the play was not admired at all. Still, allowing for the lack of vocal response from cheaper parts of the house, which of course I had always been used to expect in London, I thought things had gone quite well. I did not know that half the audience had walked out before the end. As the play had already been sold to Paramount for a film Miller did not mind losing the big money that had been spent on the stage production, and it closed after only a few days.

Of course I had not had time to do anything about my contract, and when I went down to the office the morning after the first night and asked about the six weeks' guarantee, they said that Mr. Miller had gone to London and that they knew nothing about it. I had not the sense to make a fuss, so I hung about New York for a few days and saw as many plays as I could and had a very fascinating time. I was interviewed by one or two managers, including one from the Theatre Guild, which was going to do a very interesting play called *Wings over Europe*, about splitting the atom (rather extraordinarily prophetic in 1928). This had the part of a young genius scientist in it which I might perhaps have been engaged to play if I had been able to stay in New York, but I could not afford to, and eventually the play was not a success either in New York or London.

Meanwhile I saw the first production of *Showboat*, standing at the back of the newly-built Ziegfeld Theatre (now pulled down), with a wonderful cast, including Helen Morgan — a famous torch singer who sang 'My Man' sitting on a piano with a long handkerchief dangling from her wrist. She had a wonderful tragic quality. And Helen Hayes was making one of her first big successes in *Coquette* in which her acting charmed me greatly. Judith Anderson was appearing in *Behold the Bridegroom*, rather a clever play in which a woman fell so desperately in love with a man who lived next door that she was pining to death.[1] The man was brought to her bedside, very embarrassed since he had no idea that the woman had been in love with him for years. I thought her beautiful then but I did not meet her until she played the Queen in *Hamlet* with me in 1936 on my second visit to New York.

That first time when I arrived at my hotel, the black man who brought me from the dock was not allowed to share the lift, which embarrassed me very much. But I went to Harlem several times to clubs to see the wonderful dancing — Bill Robinson and Cab Calloway. I remember the elevated railway on Third Avenue being very noisy, rushing past the houses on the same level as the first floor windows, and Faber took me to see Radio City and the Roxy Cinema, and Grand Central Station with its wonderful ceiling newly painted with a constellation. It was speakeasy time. I used to venture out with Emlyn Williams, who was playing next door in *And So To Bed* (brought over from England — a play about Pepys — with Edmund Gwenn and Yvonne Arnaud) and we used to tap at doors with gratings and wonder if we were likely to be blinded by bath-tub gin once we got inside. I was also somewhat dismayed by the spitting in the streets in the very windy weather. There were spittoons in the hotels and the men all seemed to chew rather wet cigars.

I never cared for ships (or indeed the sea) but there was a certain splendour and excitement about arriving at the Statue of Liberty in those days. And when English actors left New York at the end of the season there would be telegrams and flowers and parties held in the cabins. In America everybody seemed to send telegrams a great deal. In England, where they were pretty rare, they usually came to announce somebody was dead or something dreadful had happened. But in New York (especially in the *Hamlet* time when I was being very much fêted) they would arrive continually, inviting one to lunch on

Thursday week or saying how much they had liked the play. But of course in those days telegrams were very cheap.

I never liked the big ocean liners much because the people I wanted to meet always seemed to stay in their cabins through the voyage, and the ones I did not care to know would attach themselves to me instead. On the last day they used to clear all the big lounges and you had to stand in a long queue to have your passport signed.

On my second visit, in 1936, I had become an established actor in England but I had already refused one or two American offers. I was approached about playing Romeo in a film with Norma Shearer, a part eventually played by Leslie Howard, and once, when Charles Laughton was in a temperamental mood and threatened to walk out of *The Hunchback of Notre Dame*, I was suggested as a possible re-placement.

I was approached by the manager Guthrie McClintic about coming to New York in *Hamlet* and I was interviewed by him at the Ritz in London. He said he wanted to direct the production himself. Unfortunately he had seen my production in Edinburgh when we were on tour after the long London run, but it was getting very shabby by that time and we had lost some of the best actors who had been in it in London. I was rather disappointed he had seen it not at its best, so when he said he could give me a much better production (lighting, scenery and so on) I was a bit nettled, but thought perhaps it would be better for me to work under someone else's direction in New York. Some weeks later Guthrie came down to the South of France, where I had a villa for my summer holiday, with Jo Mielziner, his very fine scenic designer, to discuss the decor. I said I did not want to wear mediaeval clothes, but an Elizabethan or Jacobean costume as I had in London, and Mielziner said, 'We are going to do it Van Dyck.' I paused a moment and said, 'But why not Rembrandt?' but he did not understand what I meant. The finished designs were rather too domesticated, I felt, though very beautiful—elegant satins and velvets—but Van Dyck is a court painter, whereas Rembrandt, with his soldiers and courtiers in fur and armour, would, I thought, have given the Nordic feeling better.

Naturally I did not want to interfere too much as it was not my production, but when he said he was going to have Lillian Gish for Ophelia I said, 'Isn't she too old?' Of course I had seen Lillian in films several times when I was a boy. Then, a few weeks later, when I was acting in London, the Stage Door Keeper announced there was a lady to see me, and a little head came round the door wearing a white straw hat with velvet ribbons hanging down the back. She said that she was Lillian Gish, and asked 'Am I too old for Ophelia?' This won my heart of course and we became devoted friends, as we have been ever since. Lillian and Judith Anderson, who was playing Gertrude, spoiled and encouraged me in every possible way.

We went to Toronto and played a week there. Then we moved to Rochester, just for two performances, and I was amazed at the efficiency of the staff with the elaborate set and hundreds of light cues to manoeuvre, managing them without a single mistake. We opened in New York at the old Empire Theatre, where we had very good notices and a wonderful reception on the first night. Still, I had a feeling that the production was not going to be a lasting success. But it was a fearfully exciting time for me and I went to parties and met celebrities and was showered with presents and letters. I was much amused by the *Variety* notice of the Toronto opening which was headed 'Well known British Thesp makes good.'

Everything has changed tremendously on Broadway since I first remember it in the *Hamlet* time. Helen Hayes was at the theatre opposite on 45th Street, playing in *Victoria Regina*, and when I was packing my things to move to another theatre several streets away, someone came in carrying a great tray with champagne and glasses, sent over by Helen with a message to say how sorry she was that we were leaving—such a charming, courteous thing to do.[2]

On another occasion I had a page-long telegram from John Barrymore (known to his friends as Jack), saying how amusing and complicated the part of Hamlet was and how delighted he was I had made a success of it. I had seen him play the part in London in 1926 and thought him splendid in it, though he was already forty-five, and afterwards, when I saw him as a guest of honour at some dinner on a Sunday night, I thought he was looking terribly ravaged, with pouches under his eyes. It was said he had to be woken up with black coffee and dragged to the theatre, and often used to get into black rages and strike the young actors who played Laertes in the duelling scene, so that they had to be replaced every few weeks. I never met him, alas, but I did meet Ethel Barrymore once in London, when she was a bit suspicious of me because of my success in *Hamlet* (of course she thought John was the only Hamlet), though when I met her in Hollywood many years later as an old lady at George Cukor's house, she was enormously distinguished, and very courteous.

Diana Wynyard once told me that when she was engaged to play the *ingénue* part in a film about Rasputin and the Tsar and Tsarina, made by MGM, she arrived on the first day of shooting in full court dress, with a train, long white gloves and a tiara, and walked across the enormous studio. At the other end the Barrymores were standing (the three of them—Lionel, Jack and Ethel), all glowering in their magnificent costumes, and an assistant studio manager came across to Diana and said: 'With compliments from the Barrymores, you are not allowed to leave your car on that side of the parking lot.' And she had to go down in all her splendour and move it herself.

Towards the end of the run of *Hamlet* I begged McClintic to let me do *Richard II* to follow. I thought I was better in that title part than I was in *Hamlet* and the play was not well known in America and might cause a lot of interest. But he said, 'Oh, a Pansy King, that will never do in America. No, no, you must go on the road and play Hamlet for another six weeks and get some of the money back.' So we went to Washington and Boston and had a great success. In fact I think we gave nine performances, including an extra one for a Flood Relief in Boston, which I found extremely hard work.

Maurice Evans had telephoned me before I went on tour. He had heard I was not going to do *Richard II* and asked if I minded if he staged a production of it. He had played the part in London at the Old Vic. Of course I told him to go ahead. So he got Margaret Webster, who was an old friend of mine, over from England to direct it and another friend, David Ffolkes, to design it, and when I got back to New York, just before my return to England, I found that Maurice as Richard was the toast of the town. My nose was rather out of joint, of course, but I crept into his theatre and saw his last act of *Richard* played to a huge cheering audience. I was always sorry that I never had a chance to play the part in New York, but it was wonderful for him. Afterwards he did *Hamlet* and later *Henry IV*, also with Margaret Webster directing, and those productions led to great things for them both.

One Sunday night in New York during *Hamlet* I had an invitation from Alexander Woollcott, the famous critic. He had been to one of our rehearsals and had afterwards given a very enthusiastic radio talk about it. He asked me to dinner one Sunday night in a private room at a restaurant and I stupidly misread the invitation and was three-quarters of an hour late. When I arrived I found to my horror that the whole party had been waiting for me—Lillian Gish, Alexander Woollcott, Thornton Wilder and Ruth Gordon. Woollcott was famous for his rages if people were unpunctual, so all the others were trembling at what he would say when I finally arrived. But I was so remorseful at being late that he forgave me and we had a fascinating dinner. Thornton Wilder was very silent till suddenly, towards the end of the meal, he burst like a soda-water syphon, discussing Shakespeare and all sorts of other things with enormous zest. Afterwards I asked him why he had been so quiet at first, and he said Woollcott had told them all that they must none of them speak because he was going to write an article about me and they must let me do all the talking. Not difficult of course, because I usually talk too much. Woollcott was always kind as far as I was concerned, though he was often said to be venomous and unpredictable, and when he was enthusiastic he could write most vividly and his radio talks were enormously popular.

The last time I saw him was in 1942 when he came to London just before he died. He invited me to breakfast, which is a great thing in America but has never been a favourite time for me, and he met me in his suite at the Dorchester Hotel in his pyjamas. I was planning to do *Macbeth* and Woollcott told me that the Lunts had always wanted to produce the play.[3] 'Lynn has a wonderful idea,' he said. 'She will go naked to murder Duncan.' I thought it was not a bad idea, but enquired how she proposed to do it. 'Oh,' said Woollcott, 'there will be a very high parapet between her and the audience, and she will keep her pudenda strictly for Alfred.'

The Lunts were always adored by their companies; though they worked them so hard and were never satisfied either with their own performances or anybody else's, they were wonderfully appreciative as an audience. There is a story that Alfred Lunt, with only two nights left at the end of a long run, called everybody back for a rehearsal. And in *The Visit* he invented some business of finding a pebble in his shoe and said to Peter Brook, who was directing the play, 'Do you think it would be better if there were two pebbles?'—and produced a second one which he had picked up in Central Park that afternoon. I imagine the Lunts never stopped thinking about the theatre from the moment they woke up in the morning till the moment they went to bed at night. (One felt sure they rehearsed in bed too.)

I implored them in their late years to make some records. After all, there would be no need for them to memorize the lines or even to be seen in person, but a few scenes from some of their great successes would have been preserved to show something in years to come of the techniques of their long and brilliant partnership. But they would never agree to do it. All they left behind were a couple of television films (*The Magnificent Yankee* was one) and a print of their film of Molnar's *The Guardsman*.

Before I ever thought of giving *Ages of Man* in New York I had done a thirteen-week tour right across Canada and America with it, beginning in Stratford, Ontario, and ending in Tallahassee, Florida, and I motored and flew everywhere in small cars and aeroplanes, never knowing, from one day to another, whether I was going to appear in auditoria, chapels or schools, or if the audience would be 2,000 or 600. I never had the chance of staying more than one or two days in each place, so I saw the whole of America but have little recollection of anything I saw. It was all motels and travelling.

I do remember staying at the Brown Palace in Denver and meeting Gina Bachauer, the Greek pianist, with her husband, and sharing our experiences of what a lonely life we found it. I realized then that being a pianist practising in trains with a dumb piano, doing endless tours, and playing with different orchestras and conductors, must be even more exhausting than touring is for an actor. Of course I enjoyed working on my performance, although I had no real plan then of doing it either in New York or London, but towards the end of the tour the recital began to be such a success that I felt I had found the way to present it, at last, in its best possible shape. I certainly owed the eventual success of the recital to that tour.

The 46th Street Theatre in New York seemed, I feared, to be much too big, but to my amazement *Ages of Man* was sold out after the first night, and I had to play two more weeks than was announced. On the first night Marlene Dietrich, Lauren Bacall, Lillian Gish and two or three other big stars all sat on the steps at the back of the auditorium, cheering and shouting and coming round to see me afterwards. A 'standing ovation' was something quite new to me, and enormously gratifying of course.

When Emlyn Williams and I met again just after I had done the recital in New York, I was a bit embarrassed at first because, as a solo performer, he had made such a success himself for several years with his Charles Dickens and Dylan Thomas programmes. I said rather shyly, 'Isn't the traffic awful in New York, with the fire-engines and ambulances going by—don't you find that you always hear them about two blocks away and you know that on your quietest line they are going to pass your theatre?' And he looked at me very slyly and said, 'Yes, and of course you can't hurry up your speech so that it will come on Peggy Ashcroft's lines.'

I had my first experience of television in New York. *The Browning Version* was originally written for me by Terence Rattigan in 1948. I did not see much of him in his last years, though we were great friends in London in the thirties and forties. He wrote *The Browning Version* and a play called *Harlequinade* to be done in a double bill. Hugh Beaumont was my manager at the time and was rather dubious about the idea of a double bill—such a programme had never been very successful in the West End. He and I were both enthusiastic about *The Browning Version*, but he would not even show me *Harle-quinade*, which was a kind of skit on the Lunts (who had recently been acting in a play Rattigan wrote called *O Mistress Mine*) and on me. Years before, in 1932 (the first time I had ever directed—at Oxford with the OUDS), Terry Rattigan had walked on as one of the musicians in *Romeo and Juliet*, and in *Harlequinade* there is a joke about the director who is always changing the flowerpot from one side to the other, and who has various other tricks and mannerisms of mine, as well as some of the unusual mannerisms of Alfred Lunt. Beaumont thought the Lunts would not care for that so he persuaded me to turn down both the plays and Rattigan, naturally rather disappointed, took them to Stephen Mitchell, who promptly bought them, and they were finally produced with Eric Portman and Mary Ellis in the leading parts, with great success. (They were revived in London in 1980 at the National Theatre with Alec McCowen and Geraldine McEwan.)

I was sorry that I had not created the wonderful part of the schoolmaster in *The Browning Version*, so when I was asked to play it much later in New York for television—in 1959—I jumped at the opportunity, especially as the medium was new to me. The other actors were Robert Stephens, Margaret Leighton and Cecil Parker, and we were directed by John Frankenheimer, who was very excitable and used to sit practically between my legs while the cameras were running, making faces and gesticulating.

I was also amused at doing a pilot film in 1966 with Alan Arkin, who was playing the part of a taxi-driver in a series called *The Love Song of Barney Kempinski*, which never got made, in which I was supposed to be a drunken stockbroker. We filmed on location, also a fairly new experience for me. We went down to lower New York on a very hot day, and there I had to play a scene in a taxi. They took out one side of the cab, and the cameraman was with us on the floor, pointing the camera up at me, and we had to keep going round and round the fishmarket, which smelt to high heaven. In the next scene I had to climb onto the roof of another taxi, still very drunk, carrying a briefcase and umbrella and wearing a bowler hat and city suit, and harangue the crowd. We were shooting in the middle of a very busy street and opposite was a girls' school, with all the girls hanging out of the windows. I had never had to work in public like that in my life before, but I was determined not to be put off and somehow ignored all the interruptions. It was a very good experience and helped me to learn not to be embarrassed by the onlookers on location.

I am surprised to find, looking back, how many times over the years I have acted and directed in New York working on modern scripts, as well as the classical revivals I brought over from London at various times, and the two avant-garde plays *Home* in 1970 and *No Man's Land* in 1976, which were appreciated as warmly as they were in England in recent years.

Medea was a triumph for Judith Anderson in 1947, of course, though I was not much satisfied by my direction of it nor with my performance as Jason, a part she persuaded me to accept with some reluctance. But *Big Fish, Little Fish* by Hugh Wheeler (1961)—one of my greatest friends, who has since been so successfully associated with the great musicals of Hal Prince and Stephen Sondheim—was, I thought, a most rewarding piece of work for me as a director, greatly helped by Jason Robards, Hume Cronyn, Martin Gabel and George Grizzard, with a brilliant performance by Ruth White, whose death soon afterwards saddened me very much. Sadly, Wheeler himself died in 1987.

Tiny Alice, by Edward Albee, was an extremely taxing experience in 1964, but I loved acting with Irene Worth, that splendid actress with whom I had played several times before in London, and whose enthusiasm and loyalty is now so greatly missed in the English theatre, which she adored.[4] Now that America has claimed her back, she is again adding to her laurels—in her own country, but I only hope I may one day have the joy of appearing with her again.

All Over, which Albee generously invited me to direct in 1971, was unhappily a failure in New York, though I had enormous pleasure working on it with a fine company (Jessica Tandy, Colleen Dewhurst and Hume Cronyn), but the following year my only attempt to direct a musical—*Irene*—resulted in my being replaced (with huge subsequent success) by Gower Champion, and I realized the painful truth propounded by the experts, that choreographers—Jerome Robbins, Bob Fosse, Michael Bennett—are the only people with the all-round expertise to tackle the immensely complicated demands of the American Musical.

Angelo in *Measure for Measure*, at Stratford, 1950, directed by Peter Brook.

Cassius in *Julius Caesar*,
Stratford, 1950, directed
by Anthony Quayle
and Michael Langham.

The Ages of Man
Shakespeare recital,
New York, 1959.

Prospero in Peter Brook's
production at Stratford and
Drury Lane, 1957.

Prospero in *The Tempest* in Peter Hall's production at the
National Theatre, 1974.

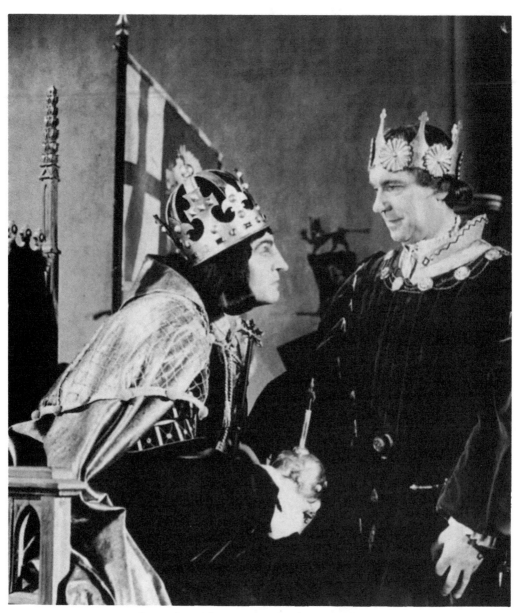

Laurence Olivier as *Richard III*, in his 1955 film,
with Ralph Richardson as Buckingham.

Louis Calhern as Caesar with Marlon Brando as Mark Antony,
Greer Garson as Calpurnia and Deborah Kerr as Portia in the
1953 film of *Julius Caesar*.

As King Henry IV in *Chimes at Midnight*, directed by Orson
Welles, with Keith Baxter as Prince Hal, 1964.

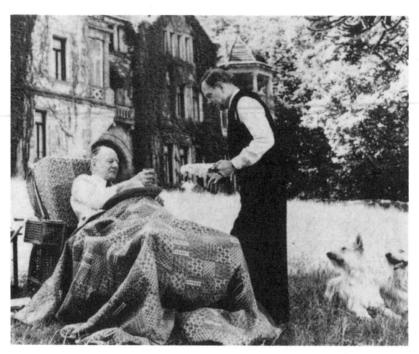

In Alain Resnais's *Providence*, 1977. Probably my best film.

With Dudley Moore in *Arthur*, 1981. The Oscar came
as a complete surprise.

Chapter Nine

1979-1989

Acting for the camera—Caligula—War and Remembrance—
Wagner and Richard Burton

I have had a surprisingly varied screen career, dating back to the
twenties, when I actually made two silent films, and continuing in the
thirties with *The Good Companions*—with Victor Saville and Jessie
Matthews—and *The Secret Agent* with Alfred Hitchcock. I was very
busy in the theatre in those days, and much disliked the long hours
and untidy atmosphere of film studios, and I only worked in a film
for the first time without being distracted by my acting and directing
for the stage when I was engaged to play Cassius, in 1952, in the
Joseph Mankiewicz *Julias Caesar*, with Marlon Brando and James
Mason.[1] The latter was afterwards to become a most valued friend
and colleague, and I acted with him in several subsequent films right
up to his untimely death, with continued pleasure and admiration.

Back in 1934, Alexander Korda had approached me about filming
Hamlet, in which I had been acting in London in a production directed by myself.[2] I was highhanded enough to veto the idea, saying
I did not think Shakespeare a good idea for the screen, and of course
he never asked me to work with him again—a lost opportunity which
I always regretted afterwards, when so many of my most gifted contemporaries, Charles Laughton, Flora Robson, Emlyn Williams,
Vivien Leigh, Ralph Richardson and Laurence Olivier, were all to be
given rewarding contracts to work under him during succeeding
years.

It was not until 1965, when I was persuaded by Tony Richardson
to play a not very good part in his film *The Loved One*, and his enthusiasm and charm encouraged me, that I managed to enjoy a sec-

ond visit to Hollywood. Then in 1968 he asked me to play Lord Raglan in *The Charge of the Light Brigade*. This turned out to be quite a thrilling experience, and I began to lose some of my former self-consciousness before the camera and enjoy the work for the first time.

In films you never know when you are suddenly going to be given a day off, or asked to stop in the middle of a sequence, or if you are going to have to begin very early next morning with some highly emotional scene. You have to be prepared for any emergency, whereas in the theatre there is a certain ordered routine—rehearsals, learning the lines, dress rehearsals, the opening, run, matinée days—everything more or less in order, while in films and television everything is out of sequence and apt to be confusing.

On the other hand, the fact that you have not prepared everything properly beforehand can be of value on the screen, because sometimes you spontaneously do things that are very instinctive and very natural. But so much else is not natural—keeping in the right angle, keeping your head in the right place, moving on your marks to a certain place. In Hollywood, when I was playing Cassius' first scene, with James Mason as Brutus, I remarked to one of the crew, 'It's so difficult for me, after my years in the theatre, having to do a scene when I have to walk up steps, stop on the fourth step without looking at it, four more steps and then deliver another speech. I would be able to work this out in the theatre over several weeks, and I would find it quite easy with lots of practice, but it's a very difficult thing to do quickly and not to make mistakes.' And the man said, 'Well, you know the great exponent of this kind of work is Tyrone Power. He can be asleep in bed in a scene, and the camera comes down from the roof of the studio, and swoops right down over him, and he can wake up, yawn, stretch, jump out of bed and hit his marks!' He thought Power was the ideal film star.

In the theatre, rehearsals allow one to experiment and develop. Years ago Sybil Thorndike came to the RADA when I was a student there and rehearsed us in *Medea*. I was playing Jason. She said, 'Don't imagine this man is a hero, he is the most terrible prig and a cad, and you must play him that way.' Her great enthusiasm would enable her to let herself go, even to go overboard, in an emotional scene, and she also told me, 'Do everything at rehearsal. Let yourself go, make a fool of yourself, go to any lengths, and then learn how to control yourself in performance and do much less.'

In films this experimental acting is seldom possible. On a few lucky occasions I have been able to rehearse quite thoroughly. The whole cast rehearsed for *Julius Caesar* in Hollywood for three weeks in the skeleton sets, which was a great help. But very often, when I have played cameo parts, there have been no rehearsals at all, and in films like *Plenty* (when I was greatly charmed and impressed by the brilliant acting of Meryl Streep), *The Shooting Party* and *Gandhi* I was only called for a few weeks, or sometimes for only a few days, so I just fitted in as best I could. Rather an alarming prospect when you do not know the director or most of the rest of the cast, and have little idea how you are to fit in to the other scenes and the general style and atmosphere of the whole film.

The screen is really the director's medium, and you hope that if he does not tell you much he must be fairly satisfied. One of the things that frightens me, now that I am old and fairly well respected, is that people may not have the courage to tell me when I am not good, when I am boring or using old tricks left over from other performances. But on the whole I have been very fortunate with the film directors for whom I have worked. In *Arthur* and *Plenty*, for instance, the directors, Steve Gordon and Fred Schepisi, were quite strangers to me, but in a very short time we seemed to gain confidence in each other. When I worked in Poland in *Dyrygent (The Conductor)* with Andrzej Wajda, and with Alain Resnais in *Providence* in France, I had a feeling that if they did not like something they would honestly say so although they hardly spoke any English. I am not too grand to resent criticism, but it is always only too easy to give the wrong impression and to appear to be distant or resentful. And of course it is important to listen to film directors, and to try and make them talk constructively, though they are often too busy and mainly concerned with all their own complicated technical problems. For example, the director of *War and Remembrance*, Dan Curtis, is a remarkable man, with an amazing organizing and staying power (we travelled to locations all over Europe), but he tells the actors practically nothing.

The only time I worked in a film in Hollywood for a number of

weeks was in an unfortunate remake of *Lost Horizon* in 1973. I was
very happy living in a friend's home on Pacific Palisades—a long bun-
galow with a rose garden, a small swimming pool and a view over the
golf-links (where I was much amused to see that nowadays none of
the players seemed to walk at all, but were driven round in little
carts). Peter Finch and Liv Ullman were both delightful company,
and the weather unfailingly brilliant. But the film itself was a disaster, though not without its humorous side. The snow-covered peaks
of Tibet were contrived by spreading huge sheets over the verdure of
a park in Los Angeles (the shrubs and small trees were not allowed to
be uprooted). It was high summer and we sweltered in mountain-
climbing gear for a week or more pretending to be freezingly cold. I
was given several idiotic hats as a lama in a monastery (which I should
have firmly refused to wear but did not like to make a fuss) and
ridiculous lines to speak. Later we moved to another location, the
Fox Ranch, with junks, water buffaloes and hordes of natives of various nationalities, and one morning I was staggered to behold a mass
of workmen actually painting flowers in the grass to provide a more
glamorous display of preRaphaelite detail to the scene.

I had a small part in another film, *Sphinx*, in 1981, as an Egypt-
ian curio dealer; I had to be slashed in the throat by a thug with a
scimitar, and stood by while my hefty stand-in, dressed in my costume, was pinned down in my shop, smashing the glass-covered
showcase against which I had been pushed by my assailant. On the
next day I walked through a Cairo slum with my neck painted realis-
tically to simulate the wound I had apparently received in my shop
the day before, and ended lying on a very dirty staircase, upside
down, bleeding to death. Some other scenes on the same film were
shot, for economic reasons it seems, in Budapest.

Travelling for films is always something of a nightmare, though
one gets used, after years of location work, to the hurly-burly of air-
ports, endless trudges along footways, escalators and staircases,
strange hotels and languages, and anxieties about exchanges and
packing, to say nothing of the hand-luggage and bags of duty-free
goods.

I shall never forget the alarming experience of arriving in Libya
(where I went to play an Arab Sheik with a Father Christmas beard

and appallingly hot garments which shrouded me completely). At the airport an enormous crowd of natives greeted us with clenched fists and yells of derision, sneering at the photographs as they inspected our passports, and keeping us standing in the midst of the hostile throng for half an hour at least in blazing heat.

In India, when I arrived at 1:30 in the morning at Delhi airport, to play an English colonel in the television film *The Far Pavilions* in 1984, the reception was hardly less alarming, only equalled by a similarly disagreeable departure some weeks later, when the plane took off round about 4:00 a.m. These little things are sent to try us.

Arthur was a complete surprise to me as I had twice refused the script thinking it was unnecessarily vulgar. But the charm of the author-director, Steve Gordon, who very sadly died of a sudden heart attack only a few weeks after the triumphant reception of his film in 1981, and the charm and expertise of Dudley Moore and Liza Minnelli, compensated most agreeably for the laborious days of a New York summer heat wave. My opening day of shooting was scheduled for 4:45 a.m. at Bergdoff Goodman's and we worked there until 9 o'clock, when the store opened, and emerged into the full glare of Fifth Avenue, where we proceeded to film for a full week just in front of the Plaza Hotel. I suffered considerably in my black business suit, and tried not to be too greatly abashed as we were watched by a great queue of passersby, held valiantly at bay by wooden barriers and determined assistant directors. Some weeks later I had a scene to play with Dudley Moore on a racetrack several miles from New York. A small racing-car arrived in which we were both supposed to drive together, only to find that the vehicle—specially built at considerable cost—held only one occupant. So we had to rewrite and rehearse the whole scene *in situ*, which luckily seemed to turn out very well.

In television I have had some good parts and pleasant experiences. I was very happy to work with the brilliant Elisabeth Bergner, whom I had long admired, and who was also an enchanting friend as well as a superb actress. This was in Shaw's play *In Good King Charles's Golden Days* (1970), when she played Charles' Queen, Catherine of Braganza. I was in several *Tales of the Unexpected*, working happily with Joan Collins on one occasion, and with Bernard Miles on another. As well as these, I had splendid parts in *Brideshead Revisited*

(1981), *Time After Time* (1986) (from the novel by my old friend Molly Keane) and *Quartermaine's Terms* (1987).

Probably my weirdest experience in films was *Caligula*. I was acting in *No Man's Land* when I suddenly received a script. I had met Gore Vidal years before with Tennessee Williams.[3] He now sent me a very flattering letter saying, 'We're going to do this marvellous film, *My Caligula*, and want you to play Tiberius, the Emperor.' It had '*Gore Vidal's Caligula*' in gold lettering on the script, so I took it home and read it that same night in some excitement. Then I rang my agent in the morning and said, 'I am not going to play this part. The whole film is pure pornography. My first appearance is coming out of a swimming pool with a little boy and a little girl emerging from under my tunic.' So I turned it down. Then I got a very rude letter from Vidal saying, 'I suppose you've never read Suetonius. All these things really happened. If you knew what Tennessee Williams and Edward Albee think of you you'd be more careful of the way you behave.'

Then I went off to France to do the Alain Resnais film of *Providence*, and while I was there my agent phoned me up to say they had offered me another part in *Caligula*. I could hardly believe it. He said, 'It's quite a small part in the beginning, just three or four scenes, there are no dirty bits in it, and you kill yourself by opening your veins in a bath.' Of course I felt a bit ashamed in accepting the engagement, and somewhat embarrassed when I got on the plane to go to Rome, to find Peter O'Toole sitting next to me having accepted the part of the Emperor. I did not know whether he knew I had been offered it first and turned it down, and I said, 'Peter, are you really going to do all these disgraceful things?' He said, 'Oh well, I'll just be old Father Christmas, it doesn't matter to me.'

When the time came I had three terrible days cutting my veins in a great bath which stood in the middle of a huge set like Waterloo Station. It was filled with warm water, and I was dressed in a kind of shift and nothing else, and a little chair was put inside the bath for me to sit on, and there I had to stay for hours while the electricians lit the scene. Every few hours the water would get cold, and they would take me out and some alarming old ladies would rub me down and give me a fresh shift, and then I would go back into the water, which had been warmed up again. The director, Tinto Brass, did not seem to bother about the acting at all. We just said our lines, five television cameras were ranged up in front of the set, and we kept on playing the scene over and over again. I did not know what on earth the result was going to be like until I saw it years afterwards in New York and thought it was pretty boring. But it ran successfully all summer at 8 dollars a ticket, and a blue-rinsed lady, who was just in front of me as we came out, announced to her husband, 'Well, all I can say is it was worth every penny!'

The director was a very peculiar man, and there were actors of every nationality. Nobody seemed to speak the same language, and one actress walked out because she said her dress was indecent. I was an onlooker in the swimming pool scene when Tiberius climbed out of the pool with the little boy and girl, and there were about twenty more girls and boys splashing about, very good looking all of them (the girls shaved to make them look younger), and all stark naked. Then, the moment the bell rang for lunch, they all put their hands in front of their genitals and rushed out to have pizza with their families, who were waiting in the corridor with lunch-baskets.

I find it hard to believe that I have acted in so many films over the last twenty years or more, and I can scarcely remember many of the directors for whom I worked or the different range of parts I acted for them. I was beginning to think I had appeared in too many small parts (cameo roles, as they are called in the film world) and I feared that both the critics and public would become tired of seeing my face popping up for a few minutes in so many different contexts, though I had some lucky scenes in *The Shooting Party*, *Gandhi* and *Plenty*, as well as some very indifferent parts in a number of very indifferent films. So when I was offered a long and complicated part in the epic television production of *War and Remembrance* some years ago, I felt I should not miss the opportunity of trying to create a new character with many fine scenes and a variety of poignant situations, though I could not help wondering if I should be able to stay the course and what would happen if I died or had to be replaced before the work was finished. The film, made for American television, has been adapted from Herman Wouk's novel, the sequel to *The Winds of War*, and covers the whole period of the Second World War. It was a mammoth undertaking, and was finally shown in nine three-hour episodes—twenty-seven hours of viewing—and is said to have cost over a hundred million dollars, taking over three years to complete. It was a very taxing and exciting time, but I would not have missed it, in spite of rigorous hours and weather and locations of all kinds.

In my last scenes I had to go into the gas chamber and be burnt alive. Although a very expensive dummy had been made for the occasion, they finally found they could not use it, so I had to do it myself, putting my feet into the oven, which I did not like very much. And on the previous day we had all been marched into the gas chamber together, a hundred naked men. Later that week, a strange man came up to me in the hotel and said, 'I don't suppose you recognize me with my clothes on.' But one had to joke, because these crematorium scenes were a really searing experience. We had filmed for weeks before this near Zagreb in Yugoslavia, in sets which represented the concentration camp at Theresienstadt, with all the wretched prisoners grubbing in the streets, and hearses going by with corpses on them and pits being dug for the dead. The director liked us to see the rushes, and after working all day in this rather depressing atmosphere we would have to watch two hours of rushes at night before we had any dinner, which made rather a long day. But I did manage to complete the work, and I have a very fine part which I only hope may have turned out well.

My character is a rather obstinate old Jewish-American writer living in Siena. As he has been a Catholic in his youth, and has the papers to prove it, he thinks that the Germans will not pursue *him*, but he is betrayed to the Nazis by an ex-pupil and is hunted all over Europe. The Nazis capture him and his niece (played by Jane Seymour) who has come to Europe to try and persuade him to go back to America with her and her young child, who has to grow up from two to five years old. (This part involved five different child actors from an orphanage in Yugoslavia who caused endless delays and complications.) Finally we are all put into a concentration camp. Then I become a Jew again and am made Head of the Elders among the

bistro run by a Czech. We had about eight bottles of champagne and then a very good supper. But when we came out, at two in the morning, there were more than a hundred people in the snow waiting to see the Burtons. The next day when I went back to pay the bill they would not give me one. I said, 'Well at least let me tip the waiters,' and they said, 'Oh no, our boss did that last night. It's been such a good advertisement for the restaurant.' So it was the cheapest entertaining I ever did in my life. Elizabeth Taylor came to the first night of *Hamlet* in Toronto and unfortunately disrupted the proceedings because the whole audience stood up to look at her. People even stood on their seats (as they say they used to do in London for Lillie Langtry) and some watched her all through the performance, regardless of what was happening on the stage.

Some years later I had an extraordinary day with them both on the yacht they had brought to anchor off the Tower of London. They would not land because of their dogs (all the carpets had to be specially proofed) and they had about fourteen Portuguese sailors running the boat for them. They had asked me to come down to talk about a play called *The Devil and the Good Lord* by Sartre, which Richard had an idea he wanted to do with Elizabeth and me in New York, but I did not think the project was likely to come off. I had taken a whole week just to read it, and it was terribly serious and complicated. They had sent their white Rolls-Royce for me, but unfortunately I arrived when they had just had a row. Elizabeth had locked herself into her cabin with a woman friend, and Richard was having a meeting with all his accountants on deck, so it was not a good moment to appear. Then Ringo Starr arrived with his then wife, Maureen, and I doubted if either of them knew who I was (and I only vaguely knew who they were), so we had a very tricky lunch and of course we did not talk much about the play.

But I went to see them in Hampstead one weekend, when they had slipped away from the Dorchester where they were living officially. There was a scare at the time about kidnapping, but they invited me to go to tea, at a little house they had borrowed for the weekend from Richard's brother, near Hampstead Heath. To my amazement the front door was wide open when I arrived. The secretary was just leaving when I walked in, and Elizabeth said at once,

'You must bring in the dogs,' though they were covered in mud, which did not bother her at all. She had just cooked dinner for Richard, and she had no make-up on. She said, 'Oh, we must show him the ring, the ring, where is it?' And they searched wildly and finally found it on the kitchen table where she had left it while she was washing up. They were both so simple and agreeable. It was one of the nicest afternoons I ever had.

I always felt that Richard was almost as happy talking to friends in a room, or reciting, or telling stories, or sitting in a pub drinking with a lot of chaps, as he ever was in the theatre. In spite of having become such a figure of world importance, it was fascinating to find he still had this strange mixture of naïveté and sophistication, and I do not think he ever quite got used to it.

Epilogue

Shakespeare—Technique and discipline—Tradition and change

People sometimes say that the theatre is not needed, that thousands of people have never seen live theatre at all, and that it will eventually die. If this is true, I can only hope that it does not happen in my lifetime. I do not know whether the theatre is important or not: what art is important? Does it have to be popular to be important? Even if it does, do we perhaps underrate the popular appeal of the theatre? I have always thought it extraordinary that the Elizabethans could understand Shakespeare's very elaborate plays when so many of the ordinary people were entirely uneducated. The dynastic complications of English monarchs from Richard II to Richard III are very involved, yet the public obviously reveled in them and knew about all the great families and their quarrels.

But then Shakespeare is unique in his universal appeal to audiences. In Shakespeare there is sound and fury, tenderness and lyricism, humour and philosophy; and quite a number of platitudes as well! As Shaw pointed out, a great deal of Shakespeare (especially some of the speeches in *Hamlet* and *As You Like It*) contains every simple truism. But they are so wonderfully phrased that you cannot resist quoting them, and it is hardly possible to discuss art or philosophy without Shakespeare very often coming into it, because of the unforgettable things that he has said and the universal types that he has created. People can understand and recognize his characters in any language or culture. When I played *Hamlet* in India, I was amazed to find how familiar many Indians were with the plays. In America, too, I have received wonderful letters about the plays; they are tremendous students of Shakespeare. There are fine collections in most universities, particularly in the Folger Library in Washington, and there is a great tradition of Shakespeare with actors such as John Drew, the Barrymores, Edwin Booth and Richard Mansfield.

There are several Shakespearean parts that have been particularly important to me: Prospero is usually considered such a bore, but I have always found people like me in the part and even seem to like the play better when I have played it. *Lear* has also been an intensely exciting play for me. It is fortunate that these two are the only two big parts that I might still play now. I was amazingly lucky with *Hamlet*. By the time I had finished with it I did not want to read or write about it any more. I had played it many hundreds of times over fifteen years, in six different productions. Shakespeare's Richard II was for many years my favourite, perhaps because I did not play it very often—not as often as I would have liked to when I was young.

It is possible to take one of the great Shakespeare parts and play it in a number of different ways. I was talking to Olivier[1] once about this. When he made his great success as Othello, I was staggered when he came on in the first scene sniffing a rose, as if he were a very vain man. And I then remembered, to my dismay, that early in my rehearsals of *Othello* with Franco Zeffirelli at Stratford (with disastrous results) he had said, 'I believe this man is very vain.' And I had said, 'Oh nonsense, he's the great warrior, whom everybody respects and admires so much,' But Olivier found this flaw in his character, and this was what made his performance so strikingly original. Again, in his *Macbeth* (which I think was definitive) you could see that he had a black soul even in the first scene with the witches, whereas Shakespeare seems to me to make Macbeth a white hero in the beginning, not really tempted to do the murders until he meets the witches and then comes back to his ambitious wife. Olivier made it obvious that he had this black streak in his nature, and this quality coloured the whole of his performance. In a great part there are so many colours and implications, particularly in the great tragic heroes of Shakespeare. I loved playing Macbeth myself and some people thought I was quite good in it (particularly at the Vic when I was only twenty-six), but of course I was never able to achieve convincingly the Great Warrior who cuts people in half and is a ruthless Scottish chieftain, as well as being a great poet. The part of Othello has something of the same difficulty for the actor—the marvellous poetic language spoken by a man with a brutal savage nature.

When I did my Shakespeare recital, *The Ages of Man*, I just threw myself on the verse like a swimmer, marking the punctuation correctly, and found that it seemed to hold me up. I learnt from doing solo speeches without their proper context that in each speech there was an entry, a climax and a fall, and one must find that pattern and deliver it correctly, knowing exactly the phrasing and colour of the words, keeping the whole speech in mind, and then I felt at liberty to put in any amount of variations as a virtuoso can do perhaps in playing Chopin.

When it comes to speaking Shakespeare I have been very lucky, because I have always had easy breath control. Though I have never been able to sing, I have never had difficulty with speaking, except that I tend to gabble. I have often been accused of inaudibility when I drop my voice, just like most other people do, at the end of lines, and in private life both friends and strangers are apt to complain that I talk too fast and am often difficult to understand. But I have a very acute musical ear for phrasing. In modern plays, if there is a line or a speech I cannot speak in the way it is written, I try to persuade the author to change it or I begin improvising until he says, 'I think it's better than mine.' With writers like Edward Albee, Graham Greene, Noël Coward, Bernard Shaw, Harold Pinter or David Storey, of course, it is impossible to change the lines at all. But in the average, colloquial modern play you can make the lines your own in a certain way, and I think you often have to change the phrasing or cut when you feel you cannot make a sentence clearly valid.

I am very keen on pace, and it is, of course, frightfully important to ensure the audience is not bored and that they do not fall asleep or leave the theatre. Shaw always said, 'speak to the lines and with the lines but never in between the lines.'

On the other hand Edith Evans was perfectly right when she said, 'You must control the audience. Never give them too much opportunity for applause and laughter and tears. Don't indulge yourself by showing off; the moment that you begin to find that you can do something well, you must control it and do it more selectively. In a farce you must play as if you have a practical joke inside you but you're not going to let anybody know you think it's funny.'

This dual life that you lead on the stage is a very subtle complicated one—marking your effects, storing them up for the next night, trying to correct what you know is not good and trying to improve on the night before, feeling when the audience encourages you to make some new point, and making yourself so free and familiar with the text that you can do exactly what you want with it without destroying its basic shape for your fellow actors or the original scheme of the director.

When I first worked with Peter Brook I began to take care, once I had got a performance to a certain point, to keep it exactly the same—allowing always, of course, for certain gradations over many performances. There obviously has to be a certain amount of flexibility, but now I am sure it is most important to keep the main lines the same. For many years I had been far too much inclined to make experiments in a part, especially in a long run, and also, of course, in plays which I had also directed myself, so that I was accountable to no one but myself in making changes. Occasionally I would alter things for the better, but it is better discipline to simplify rather than to elaborate.

The discipline of acting in the theatre has changed a lot during my lifetime. It always used to be the custom to take successes on tour to the provinces *after* the London run, though there were also no. 2 (and even no. 3) companies who would tour the provinces playing London successes while the original production would still be playing in London. Young actors and actresses expected to have to learn their business on the road before graduating to the West End. The great Henry Irving played several hundred parts before he ever appeared in London. In the thirties and forties, I always toured after the London runs. Then it became the custom to try out new plays for six or eight weeks in the big provincial towns before opening in London, and the productions would be improved and strengthened during those weeks, even if the audiences were given somewhat tentative performances while we experimented every night.

But a lot of the best West End actors in my early days usually seemed to hate leaving London. Edith Evans always said, 'I never had to go on tour and learn all those bad habits,' although she did tour with us in later years in *Romeo and Juliet* and *The Importance of Being Earnest*. I must say I never much enjoyed touring myself. I hated leaving London, and I hated the discomfort of digs and travelling on Sundays, but touring is very valuable experience, because theatres and audiences vary so much, both in size and responsiveness. Also, if you play a part for a long time you simply have to find a way of keeping it fresh. Sometimes a change of cast, even if it is not quite as good as the original one, is all to the play's advantage, because one is obliged to pull the production together and study scenes again. Most actors nowadays seldom play in very long runs. When I did *Half-Life*, in 1978, we had four different casts in a year, because nobody would stay for more than six or eight weeks. But I think we improved the play: each time we rehearsed we found we did it better; I made alterations and improvements. Actors get annoyed sometimes because I am always changing things all through rehearsals, and even after the play opens, but I am very impatient of a clockwork routine, loss of spontaneity and slavish repetition. In a revival I seldom resort to old prompt-books.

Granville-Barker used to say that productions should be created and kept in the repertoire for ten to twenty years, to which I replied, 'That's all very well if you will promise to come back yourself and direct your work freshly each time.' Actors now hate long runs and demand very short engagements, and they do not want to contract for a long run because of the attraction of films and television. But the advantages of a company working together regularly and knowing each other's potential are of course incalculable. At the National Theatre, the Barbican and Stratford we do have permanent companies now, and plays acted in repertory would seem to be an ideal solution, but it has many disadvantages as well. Rehearsals are called to gabble through the lines on the day of the night on which a play is to be performed after several days or weeks of acting other plays, and these are rarely satisfactory.

If you want to earn your living in the theatre you are bound to be in some failures during your career. All the great people—Edith Evans, Laurence Olivier, Peggy Ashcroft—have had their failures at one time or another. It is very interesting, looking back, to see why certain things went gong. When Beaumont was alive I used sometimes to stay with him at weekends to try to discuss some production in which he was concerned which had failed, but his other friends would say, 'Not to be mentioned in this house. It's dynamite.' It seems to me that when a play is a failure it is fascinating, once the disappointment has worn off, to examine where you went wrong. A play is always a great experiment. The director, the cast, the way that rehearsals proceed, the rows with the designer, the different ways the play goes during a try-out—all these things contribute. It is very important, when it is all over, to look back and see where the mistakes were, because you work just as hard in a failure as in a success.

It is also possible to achieve personal success in a failed play. Laurence Olivier made his name in three plays that failed with the critics and the public—*Beau Geste*, *The Circle of Chalk* with Anna May Wong, and *The Rats of Norway* by Keith Winter. In all three plays he got superb notices personally, so that in a curious way it made his career to be in failures—a comforting thought for young actors!

I am inclined to be rather too impressed by adverse notices and less impressed by good ones. If I am praised too much I think the critics are overdoing it and I cannot be as good as they say. If I am savagely attacked, I think I cannot be quite as bad as all that. But I am inclined to think that one learns more from bad notices than from good ones. If a critic praises a certain detail in your performance it is apt to make you very self-conscious. You go on the next night thinking 'This is the bit they say I do so well'—and find you cannot do it any more. Notices ought to be constructive and I do not like it when they are personal. I was very shocked when two of our important critics criticized a recent play and mentioned by name other actors who, they considered, would have been more suitable for the parts than the actors who played them. I think that is inexcusable, as are remarks about an actor's physical appearance. I could never quite forgive James Agate, who was rather a friend of mine and helped me very much in my early career, for what he said about Dorothy Green. Dorothy, who was then about forty-five and was in *Antony and Cleopatra* with me at the Old Vic, and very effective in the part, had an extremely large nose. In his notice of the production Agate said,

'Miss Green, like a battleship, commands from the bridge' which I thought was cheap and hurtful.

Nor do I like the idea that critics should be invited to watch rehearsals. I think that would be the greatest possible mistake. Too much is known nowadays, both by the critics and the public, about the quarrels of actors and the intimate difficulties of production. In the old days these things were private, closely kept secrets which you did not discuss even among your fellow actors. You should not bite the hand that feeds you and you should not be disloyal to or spiteful about people you may not like. You cannot go through your life without making enemies (and friends too, thank God) but it is difficult to strike exactly the right balance and not to hurt people's feelings at some time or another in the theatre.

Some of our best players hate to feel that they are being showy. The natural dignity and reserve of English people (even of actors) makes them ashamed to think that they may be showing off. Ralph Richardson, for instance, was very aware of this. Edith Evans was never happy even taking a call at the end of a play. She did so only because it was polite and customary. Leon Quartermaine, with whom I played for many years, was an exquisite and delicate actor, and he, too, always seemed to resent the show-off part of the theatre—the advertisements, the gossip, the publicity, the interviews and so on. I have tried to follow their example, though I must admit I do not feel I have always succeeded. If you do not quite receive the respect and appreciation which you know you have earned, it is rather galling and can make you bitter. I am always surprised one does not meet more embittered actors.

Also, one is terribly vulnerable in a dressing-room after a play, longing for people to come around. But if they say something tactless, it can upset one very much. Still, one does not like to have an empty dressing-room after a performance. But at the National Theatre, for instance, the dressing-rooms are so badly designed that I always used to say that when my friends came round I had to line them up against the wall, as if I was going to shoot them, only to find they were standing between me and the cupboards so that I could not get my clothes on.

When I was younger I used to try and see everything in the theatre and the cinema. London was my home for seventy years, and I went to the movies about three times a week, and to the theatre twice or three times if I possibly could. I saw plays that I liked very much many times over, and I knew the names of all the players. So when I came to work in the West End in the thirties, it was a great joy and privilege to work with many splendid actors and actresses, most of whom I had only seen before as a member of the audience. To find that I could meet them on equal terms was very exciting and gratifying. Many of the older players had a great record of work with the older actor-managers, Herbert Tree and George Alexander, Charles Wyndham, and with directors like Harley Granville-Barker and Nigel Playfair. They were punctual, disciplined, and beautifully mannered and did not seem in any way to resent being ordered about by a young actor, as I found to my delight when I began to become a director myself.

One or two actors who had never played in Shakespeare before (Frederick Lloyd and Marjorie Fielding, for instance, both of whom acted with me in *Romeo and Juliet*) brought a very fresh approach to add to their long career of distinction. And they were also very good speakers. It is a pity that many fine actors may often become victims of their personal limitations and, if they have particularly distinctive qualities, they risk becoming type-cast, as Gerald du Maurier and Charles Hawtrey did, for example, not risking failure by having to extend their range. On the other hand, a player who can dare to exceed his apparent limitations, as Olivier did, can sometimes produce performances of genius, as he so often has. Always a superb comedian, he also had a touch of effeminacy, which he uses to great effect in certain parts, so that he can combine his tremendously macho image with a delicate sensitivity—a fascinating combination.

I played a succession of romantic and highly neurotic parts as a young man. I was vain and mannered, though hard-working and ambitious, hoping to succeed on my vocal powers and a certain sense of timing and phrasing, though I think I learnt as much from my failures as I did from my successes. But in certain parts, I always failed completely because I had not the right equipment in various sides of my nature. I think all actors have to measure up to their limitations though on the other hand they must not be afraid of taking risks and trying experiments.

When I am asked what an actor most needs to learn I find it hard to know what to say. I think as a director I was often very harsh on young players when they were beginning. But inaudibility is a terrible fault in the theatre today. The microphone has made things much worse. In the old days music hall singers and performers all had marvellous diction, and in musical comedy and revue people like Cyril Ritchard and Noël Coward were remarkably good speakers. You heard every word of their dialogue and lyrics as you very rarely do today. With amplification, of course, there are further difficulties. You have got to trust somebody to listen and tell you if you are audible, or if you are distorted by the mikes. I once went to see Ethel Merman in *Annie Get Your Gun* in New York and she had to have a bodymike, which seemed to me, with her tremendous voice, a terrible confession of failure on the part of the people who built the theatre.

I believe there is an acting tradition that is passed from one generation to another, though one must not be too much influenced by it. How the next generation will react to it one cannot possibly tell, nor how one might be remembered in the theatre in time to come. It is certainly a great advantage, if one's acting is perhaps to remain in people's memories for maybe fifty years or so, to have been lucky enough to have played the great classics, although so many splendid actors have often played in nothing but comedies or very light plays. Charles Hawtrey and Gerald du Maurier were both of them brilliant artists, as were Yvonne Arnaud and Marie Tempest, but they scarcely ever played very ambitious parts out of their own range, and therefore the public scarcely remembers them now that they are gone. It shocks me to find how quickly they are forgotten. Brendan Gill wrote in the *New Yorker* that he was glad that a rather indifferent book about the Lunts had just been published because America had quite forgotten them. That seems dreadful to me, because they were such great figures all through my career, and only died quite recently. It is amazing to think that, long before television and modern communications, you would find photos of Ellen Terry and Henry Irving in miners' cottages at the turn of the century. They were looked up to as national figures, although there was no publicity as we know it today.

But I do not think we actors should complain. Ours is one of the few creative professions in which artists get a personal reward during their lifetime. If we have a success, we have an audience that applauds and cheers and the critics write nice things about us. We actually have the immediate pleasure of any success we may achieve. One thinks of all the great painters who died penniless, and whose work is now being bought for millions. Of course, one cannot tell how many actors are born to blush unseen. I have always hoped, remembering people like Emlyn Williams and Richard Burton, or Claude Rains, who started as a call-boy at His Majesty's, and Charlie Chaplin, who came from the slums, that if actors have an outstanding talent it is pretty certain to bring them eventual recognition. Yet I wonder how many young people fail through not getting the right part or not being lucky or by having a great failure in some important venture. So much depends, of course, on the material you are given to act, the playwrights, the managers who engage you, the parts you accept or refuse. Some of the great performers of my time were many of them not actors at all. People like Beatrice Lillie, Danny Kaye, and George Robey were absolutely inimitable in their particular fields, and one cannot help envying somebody who can suddenly walk on to the stage quite alone and enrapture an audience by their sheer talent and originality.

I rather deplore the tendency of many modern directors of the classics who feel they have to do something different simply because it will be a break with tradition, but I suppose that is something that the theatre is always trying to do. As one gets older one is inclined to rebel against this. On the other hand I had no opportunity of joining the avant-garde for many years, and yet when I went to the Royal Court and did the David Storey play *Home*, Charles Wood's *Veterans*, Edward Bond's *Bingo* and Harold Pinter's splendid *No Man's Land*, I was surprised and relieved to find that I could apparently do well in some very modern avant-garde plays and came to appreciate and understand them better by acting in them. So it is all largely a question of getting used to a new style.

In one's youth one tried eating oysters for the first time, or drank one's first glass of Guinness, or saw a modern picture by Monet or Picasso, or heard some discordant modern music. When rock-and-roll first came in I simply loathed it (and I have not really got used to it yet) but the fact remains that when I was young, and was mad about Paul Whiteman and the Mount City Blue Blowers and all the gramophone records and music that was so popular at that time, my parents would shrug their shoulders in horror and could not think what the world was coming to. I always remember my father saying to me when he was quite an old man, 'I have just managed to listen to Sibelius, but I don't think I am quite up to Shostakovich.' I suppose in one's old age one is liable to kick against modern innovations of any kind, in clothes, habits, food, recreation, everything.

My own theories about life seem to have become fairly set after all these many years, and yet one must continue to be alive to changes and prepared to compromise with the author, the director, the lighting man. The mystery of the theatre is always bound to be something of a compromise, and it is a kind of miracle when it comes together, like good cooking, and if the right ingredients are there and they all come to the boil at the right moment you suddenly find you have a success. Ours is an extraordinary unpredictable business and there is more luck in it, as well as more hazard perhaps, than in any of the other artistic professions.

I am quite useless at almost everything except where the theatre is concerned and so I have always been completely occupied working there. It has never bothered me that I do not like all the things that occupy most people in their spare time. I am rather solitary in some ways and I prefer to be, though I have had wonderful friendships and associations in the theatre all my life—with painters, designers, musicians and actors — and travelled an enormous amount. What more can one ask?

I am not good at being idle. I have had a few memorable holidays and, of course, in making films one always has a great many days off;

but as I have no family I do not have the urge to take holidays that most people have. I feel useless if I have not got a job and I have been very lucky in being asked to appear in films or on television or make records if I have had no play in mind. Although I live much more inside the walls of a theatre than anywhere else, I still love being out of doors in the country or watching and meeting people in cities. But I have had my share of parties and large gatherings—and no longer crave the excitement I used to feel at being successful. Acting has rid me of my frustrations and satisfied many of my ambitions. It is more than an occupation or a profession; for me it has been a life.

The Gielgud–Terry Family Tree

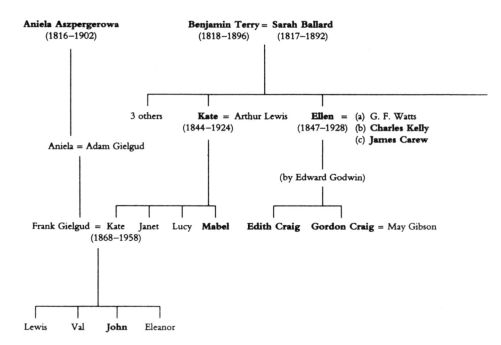

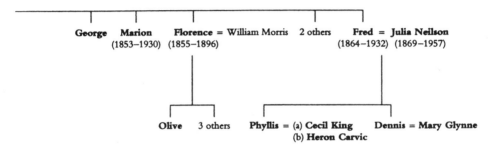

George   **Marion**   **Florence** = William Morris   2 others   **Fred** = **Julia Neilson**
(1853–1930)   (1855–1896)   (1864–1932) (1869–1957)

Olive   3 others   **Phyllis** = (a) **Cecil King**   **Dennis** = **Mary Glynne**
                                       (b) **Heron Carvic**

Names in bold letters indicate members of
the family on, or connected with, the stage

Biographical Notes

by John Miller

Chapter One: 1904-1921

1 The Gielgud-Terry tree. (See previous pages.)

2 **Kate Terry** was the first of the Terrys to make their name famous on the English stage. At the age of eight she had been engaged by Mr and Mrs. Charles Kean to play in pantomime, then Prince Arthur in *King John*, and at the age of fourteen her Cordelia brought her immediate stardom. She continued to attract notice at the Bristol Theatre Royal, acted with the then unknown Henry Irving in Manchester, played Ophelia to Fechter's Hamlet in London, but gave up her brilliant stage career when she married Arthur Lewis. At the Adelphi, London, her farewell as Juliet played to packed houses. When the curtain fell on her Manchester farewell her future husband gave her a gold bracelet, inscribed inside with the names of more than a hundred parts she had played, and outside: 'To Kate Terry on her retirement from the stage, from him for whom she leaves it.' She did not return until thirty-one years later, playing a small part in support of her daughter, Mabel Terry-Lewis, with John Hare in *The Master*. Her only other appearance was in 1906 at her sister Ellen's Jubilee Commemoration at Drury Lane.

3 **Ellen Terry** followed her elder sister Kate into Charles Kean's company. After her debut in his production of *The Winter's Tale*, she was also a notable Puck, Prince Arthur (following Kate), and Fleance in *Macbeth*. She toured with Kate in *A Drawing-room Entertainment* and later joined her in Bristol, where the two sisters caused quite a stir in the town. At sixteen she met her first husband, the forty-seven-year-old artist G. F. Watts, when he was painting Kate. The marriage

was short-lived, and probably never consummated. The couple were separated and she was sent home in disgrace. Later she created a scandal by running away to live with Edward Godwin. After six years absence from the stage, the playwright Charles Reade persuaded her to return to play Philippa in *The Wandering Heir*. After her great success as Portia with the Bancrofts, Henry Irving asked her to become his leading lady in 1878, beginning with Ophelia to his Hamlet. During their partnership of twenty-four years, she gave memorable performances of Portia, Beatrice, Desdemona, Viola, Lady Macbeth, Cordelia, Imogen and Volumnia, as well as supporting Irving in many of the melodramas for which he was famous, some of them specially written for him. Portia was clearly a memorable landmark for her—the 1879 revival of *The Merchant of Venice* with Irving ran for 250 nights; in 1889 she appeared by Royal Command at Sandringham in the trial scene; she played Portia in 1902 at Irving's final performance at the Lyceum, and again in 1903, when she acted with Irving for the last time, in a special all-star performance for the Actors' Benevolent Fund.

Ellen's long partnership with Irving is thought now to have been more than just professional, though no breath of scandal touched either of them at the time. She had two other short-lived marriages to rather unsuccessful actors—Charles Kelly in 1878 and James Carew in 1906, when she was fifty-eight and he was thirty-two; but her deepest attachments seem to have been outside wedlock, first to Godwin and later to Irving.

She had a great success as Mistress Page in Beerbohm Tree's 1902 Coronation production of *The Merry Wives of Windsor,* and the following year made a near-catastrophic experiment in management at the Imperial Theatre, with her son Gordon Craig directing her in Ibsen's *The Vikings*, which only ran for twenty-four performances. A hasty revival of *Much Ado About Nothing* did little to diminish her financial loss. In 1905 she played Alice Grey in Barrie's *Alice Sit-by-the-Fire*, and in 1906 finally succumbed to Bernard Shaw's pleas to play the part he had written for her—Lady Cecily Waynflete in *Captain Brassbound's Conversion*. The Golden Jubilee of her first appearance on the stage was celebrated at Drury Lane, on 12 June 1906, by virtually all the leading figures in the artistic world—Coquelin, Réjane,

Caruso, Genée, Duse, the Bancrofts, Charles Wyndham, and twenty-two Terrys in the final masque. Ellen played scenes from *Much Ado*, with Fred Terry as Benedick and sisters Kate and Marion as Ursula and Hero, and Gordon Craig designed the decor and costumes. Her stage appearances from then on were infrequent, but her lecture-tours of America and Australia were very popular. John Gielgud saw her lecture at the Haymarket Theatre on 'Shakespeare's Heroines,' and in later years he approached his own 'Ages of Man' recital in much the same way, sketching in just an impression of some characters, and acting full-out only in the long set-piece speeches.

Ellen's last professional appearance in a London run was in 1919 as the Nurse in Doris Keane's *Romeo and Juliet*, and she was created Dame Grand Cross of the British Empire in the New Year Honours List for 1925. In 1928 the BBC marked her eightieth birthday by a programme in which John Gielgud was accompanied by members of the Terry family and other friends in Shakespearean scenes associated with Ellen Terry. Gielgud was heard as Bassanio, Horatio and Oberon.

4 **Edith and Gordon Craig**. Ellen Terry chose the name Craig for her two illegitimate children while on a Scottish holiday, after learning the name of a great rock off the coast of Ayrshire—Ailsa Craig. When Edith first acted with her mother at the Lyceum she was called Ailsa Craig. Edith travelled abroad as her mother's stage-manager and finally took up directing herself with some prestige but without much success. Gordon Craig also acted with his mother and Henry Irving, but after directing her disastrously in *The Vikings* he spent most of his life in different parts of Europe, drawing, designing, occasionally directing (*Rosmersholm* for Eleonora Duse in Florence in 1906, *Hamlet* at the Moscow Art Theatre in 1911, and Ibsen's *The Pretenders* at Copenhagen in 1926), and writing prolifically. He settled in Florence in 1908 where he founded and edited *The Mask*, a journal on the art of the theatre, and ran a school of acting in the Arena Goldoni. His books had a great effect on methods of production in Europe and America, and include *The Art of the Theatre* (1905), *Towards a New Theatre* (1913), *The Marionette* (1918), *The*

Theatre Advancing (1921), *Books and Theatres* (1925), *Henry Irving and Hamlet* (1930), *Ellen Terry and her Secret Self* (1931), and *Index to the Story of My Days* (1957). In 1922 he brought his International Exhibition of Theatre Art and Craft to London, Manchester, Glasgow and Bradford, where it was seen by over 350,000 people. But for most of his life he was neglected by his own countrymen, while his reputation grew throughout the rest of Europe, particularly Germany, and it was the French Government which bought his huge theatrical library for the Rondel Collection.

5 **Marion Terry** first appeared on stage in 1873, as Ophelia in Tom Taylor's perversion of *Hamlet*, which launched her on a long and successful career, even though she was overshadowed by Ellen's wider popular acclaim. She stepped into her role as Viola in *Twelfth Night* at the Lyceum when Ellen was suffering from a poisoned thumb in 1884, and substituted for her on several other occasions. She played for the Bancrofts, Beerbohm Tree, with Henry Irving in *Faust*, in several seasons with George Alexander, including creating a notable Mrs. Erlynne in *Lady Windermere's Fan*, and with Charles Wyndham. At the 1900 Stratford-upon-Avon Festival she played Rosalind and Portia, and in 1906 appeared at Eilen's Jubilee matinée with her brother and two sisters in the *Much Ado* excerpt; but her greatest successes were in light comedy, of which she was considered a great exponent, especially in Wilde she played Mrs. Arbuthnot in *A Woman of No Importance*—and she several times returned to her original part of Mrs. Erlynne in *Lady Windermere's Fan*. She appeared at Windsor Castle in 1907 in a Command Performance before King Edward VII, as Mrs. Sternhold in *Still Waters Run Deep*. She toured England and America, and was rarely out of work in a career that spanned fifty years. Her last part was as the Princess in *Our Betters* in 1923, but then she had to retire during the run because of ill-health.

She continued to support the family's appearances, and in 1930 wrote to her brother Fred: 'I have been to three of John Gielgud's performances of Shakespeare's plays at the "Old Vic" and I can't say how really thrilled I have been with the work he does, Macbeth—Oberon—Hamlet—the last without cuts!! I was in the *uncomfortable* stalls for Hamlet, for just *five* hours, and didn't *want* to move (tho' I'd have liked to do so but couldn't, the place was crammed), I wanted to go tomorrow, the last of his performances, but there is no seat to be had, and I hear today it's going to the West End in a fortnight, so I'll see it then—it's *very young*, very thoughtful (without dragging it with long pauses and mouthing), graceful without effort and every word distinct and of course he looks charming—I told him I was proud of my nephew, he replied he "was proud of knowing he had some of the Terry blood in him, and hoped to go on doing better".'

6 **Fred Terry** was the youngest child in the family which gave three famous leading ladies to the English stage, and would have given a fourth, had Florence not retired on her marriage. He first appeared at the Haymarket at the age of sixteen in the Bancrofts' revival of *Money*, and then played with his sister Ellen in *New Men and Old Acres*. After several tours he appeared with her again, playing Sebastian to her Viola in Irving's disastrous production of *Twelfth Night*. Irving's Malvolio was booed, Ellen collapsed from a horse-fly bite and was replaced by Marion, and only Fred's performance received unanimous praise. For the next sixteen years he played a variety of parts on tour and in London, from Cassio, Laertes and Charles Surface to the Duke Michael in *The Prisoner of Zenda* and many similar romantic costume-parts. In 1900 he went into management with *Sweet Nell of Old Drury*, playing King Charles to his wife Julia Neilson's Nell Gwynn. This was revived many times over the next twenty years in a repertoire that regularly included *The Scarlet Pimpernel*, *Henry of Navarre* and other historical melodramas; but, apart from Charles Surface again in the 'all-star' revival of *The School for Scandal* at Covent Garden in 1915, his only other classical part was Benedick in *Much Ado About Nothing*, which he played several times with great success.

7 **Henry Irving** at different times acted with five members of the Terry family—Kate, Ellen, Marion, Florence and Fred—but it is his long partnership with Ellen that is best remembered. Unlike the Terrys he did not have an instant success; his strange diction and rather

awkward gait were handicaps in his youth, and he was thirty-three before he found the part and the play that shot him to fame overnight—the haunted murderer Mathias in *The Bells*. He revived it again and again over the years, and Ellen Terry said it was the emotional strain of this part that finally killed him. For three decades he dominated the stage as a tragedian of great power and intensity, and a comedian of grim sardonic humour, and excelled in certain Shakespearean parts. His devotion to the theatre was single-minded— Ellen Terry described him as 'quiet, patient, tolerant, impersonal, gentle, close, crafty, incapable of caring for anything outside his work.' For this work, at the Lyceum and on tour in England and America, he was rewarded in 1895 with the first knighthood ever conferred on an actor.

8 **Frank Benson** made his first major appearance on the stage in a female role, Clytemnestra in Aeschylus' *Agamemnon* at Oxford in the original Greek, produced by him in 1880 and then taken to London where it was seen by Ellen Terry and Henry Irving, who said 'If any of you decide to adopt the stage as a profession, I shall be only too glad to give you any help I can'; Ellen Terry said, 'Come and enlist under our banner, and help us in the great work.' So his first professional appearance was as Paris to their *Romeo and Juliet* in 1882 at the Lyceum. In 1883 he went into management for the first time, and began the series of tours, mostly of Shakespeare plays, for which he became famous, eventually producing all of them except *Titus Andronicus* and *Troilus and Cressida*. Many of the productions came to London for short seasons and a regular fixture was the annual Stratford Festival, where Benson laid the foundations for a season in Shakespeare's birthplace that now runs for most of the year, but in Benson's early days was only a week long. At one time he had as many as four touring companies on the road under his name, and they became widely recognized as training grounds for all serious actors— the Old Bensonians became a formidable gallery of theatrical talent by the end. For the Shakespeare Tercentenary at Drury Lane in 1916, it was generally accepted that he was the proper choice to play the title-role in the full-length *Julius Caesar*, and that was the only oc-

casion when an actor has been knighted in a theatre (still wearing his blood-stained toga). Agate wrote: 'About Benson in his heyday I cannot, and will not, be dispassionate. He gave what, to a young playgoer, seemed tremendous things. The thwarted walk of Hamlet; the blood-encrusted, wholly barbaric Macbeth; the patrician in Coriolanus; the zoological, unsentimentalized Caliban. He had four things most modern actors lack—presence, a profile befitting a Roman coin, voice, and virility to make you believe that Orlando overthrew more than his enemies.' In 1933, Sir Frank was granted a Civil List pension in recognition of his work for the theatre.

9 **Herbert Beerbohm Tree** was the generally accepted successor to Henry Irving in the line of actor managers. He began his career as an amateur, turned professional in 1878, and first went into management for himself in 1887 at the Comedy Theatre, where he produced *The Red Lamp*, and in the same year he took over the Haymarket Theatre. Early productions included *Henry IV Part I* in which he played Falstaff, *The Merry Wives of Windsor, Hamlet, A Woman of No Importance* and his greatest success, *Trilby*, in which he played Svengali. This made so much money that Tree built Her Majesty's Theatre opposite, managing it from 1897 until he died in 1917. It was here that he staged his famous Shakespeare Festivals with huge casts, spectacular scenery and effects, and often real animals on the stage (rabbits in *A Midsummer Night's Dream*, and his King Richard II entering London on horseback). Virtually every leading Shakespearean player of the time appeared with Tree. He was a success in romantic and in character parts, but his productions relied heavily on spectacle and particularly his stage-manager. This casual approach led to a series of battles with Bernard Shaw over Tree's production of *Pygmalion* with Mrs. Patrick Campbell in 1914. In 1904 he founded the Academy of Dramatic Art (later RADA), and was knighted in 1909. On Irving's death he was elected President of the Theatrical Managers' Association.

Gerald du Maurier appeared as a young man with Mrs. Patrick Campbell in *The Notorious Mrs. Ebbsmith* in 1893 and again in 1900-

1901. He was very successful in Barrie's *The Admirable Crichton*, and *Peter Pan*, in which he created the parts of Captain Hook and Mr. Darling. He excelled in playing English gentlemen, especially as the master-cracksman Raffles, and the secret agent Bulldog Drummond. From 1910 to 1925 he was a highly successful actor-manager at Wyndham's Theatre, nearly always producing modern or recent plays; he was a notable Mr. Dearth in *Dear Brutus* in 1917. His naturalistic style of acting brought him a considerable following and he was a skilled director, particularly of actresses. He was knighted in 1922.

10 **Mabel Terry-Lewis** made her theatrical debut in 1895 aged twenty-three. After an absence of fifteen years she returned to the theatre and built a very successful career for herself; in spite of her new start aged forty-eight. She first appeared in New York in 1923, and in 1930 played Lady Bracknel in Wilde's *The Importance of Being Earnest*, with her nephew John Gielgud as John Worthing.

11 **Sir Squire Bancroft** (1841-1926), together with his wife Marie, successfully managed the Prince of Wales Theatre and later the Haymarket. They presented and played in many drawing-room comedies, and helped to put the acting profession on a securer footing by giving good salaries and paying for costumes.

Sir Johnston Forbes-Robertson was an even ꞁ ore successful actor-manager. Born in 1853, he appeared with the B ncrofts and went on to act with Irving. He took over the managemꞁ ꞁt of the Lyceum in 1895 and his Hamlet there was much admired particularly for the beauty of his voice and the grace of his movemeꞁ ꞁ. In the tradition of great acting families, he had three brothers and ꞁ nephew also on the stage. He was knighted in 1913, the year of his r tirement, and lived to be eighty-five.

12 **Eleonora Duse** was born in 1858 into an Itaꞁꞁan acting family—

the Duse troupe founded by her grandfather Luigi. Her first success came as Juliet at the age of fourteen in Verona, one of the rare occasions when an actress has succeeded in the part at the correct age. After seeing Sarah Bernhardt in Turin she began to act in several of Dumas's plays, and her fame began to rival that of her French contemporary, especially in *La Dame aux Camélias*. She was a naturalistic actress and seemed 'not so much to act as to live'. She refused to wear makeup, and was famous for being able to pale or blush at will. Her tours of Europe and the Americas brought her an international reputation. Chekhov was captivated by her Cleopatra, and the New York producer Daniel Frohman said, 'We are in the presence of an artist whose approach to acting will long exert a beneficial influence upon the work of the men and women of our stage.' Bernard Shaw described her performances as the best modern acting that he had ever seen.

Unconventional and unhappy in her private life, she was a charming comedienne, but excelled in the great tragic parts, and at the end of her career triumphed as Clytemnestra, Antigone, Electra, and as several of Ibsen's heroines, particularly Ellida in *The Lady from the Sea* and Mrs. Alving in *Ghosts*. Of her 1923 tour with these last two plays St John Ervine wrote: 'She has the power which no other actress, known to me, possesses, of transmitting physical qualities to her very clothes; when she drops her shawl from her shoulders at the end of the second act after a period of trouble, it seems to be as weary as she is, to have gathered weariness into its folds, so that it drops almost to the ground in sheer fatigue.' This tour continued in the United States to packed houses, but she caught pneumonia in Pittsburgh and died on 21 April 1924. She was given a funeral mass in New York, and a state funeral in Rome, when Mussolini declared a day of mourning for her.

13 **Sarah Bernhardt** began her career at the Comédie Française, but first attracted notice at the Odéon, France's second national repertory theatre, and after her success as the Spanish Queen in Victor Hugo's *Ruy Blas*, she was invited to return to the Comédie. Her performance as Racine's Phèdre made her the most talked-about actress

of her day, together with her eccentric private life and displays of temperament. She took up painting, sculpture and ballooning and, after the early death of her sister Regina, was said to keep her own satin-lined coffin in her bedroom and sometimes to sleep in it. When she arrived in England in 1879 with the Comédie Française she was met by Oscar Wilde who christened her 'The Divine Sarah,' and Irving and Ellen Terry sent greetings. Her performance as Phèdre received a tremendous ovation from the London public, and her individual success encouraged her to form her own company and tour America, where she triumphed as Camille in Dumas's play. In Paris she continued as her own manager, and had successes in plays by Dumas, Sardou and Rostand and in the title-roles of Hamlet and Lorenzaccio, which opened the Théâtre Sarah Bernhardt. She undertook frequent world tours, and drew huge crowds everywhere. Slim and striking to look at, her greatest attribute was her 'golden voice.' The French critic Francisque Sarcey described it as 'languishing and tender, her delivery so true in rhythm and so clear in utterance that never a syllable is lost, even when the words float from her lips like a caress.' After a stage accident, she had to have a leg amputated at the age of seventy, but continued to appear in recitals, sketches and an occasional play, even though she had to be carried to the stage. She died in 1923 at the age of seventy-eight.

14 **Madge Kendal** was the twenty-second child of an actor-manager, and sister of the dramatist T. W. Robinson, but is best-known for her long partnership with her husband William Kendal, and John Hare, at the St James's Theatre. A fine comedienne, she had a great success as Lady Gay Spanker in *London Assurance*, which she revived several times, as Dora in *Diplomacy* and as Dorothy Blossom in *The Elder Miss Blossom*. She is most remembered for her performances in contemporary plays, though she did play one or two Shakespearean heroines and other classical parts, including Mistress Ford in *The Merry Wives of Windsor* with Ellen Terry and Beerbohm Tree at His Majesty's in 1902, and again in 1911 at the Gala Performance at the same theatre. The latter was her only performance after her retirement in 1908. She was created DBE in 1926. The companies with

which she and her husband were connected were very well managed, proving an important training-ground for young actors and actresses, and their partnership, like that of Sir Squire and Lady Bancroft, was held up as a model for the profession. She died in 1935.

15 **Oscar Asche** was born in Australia in 1871 and sent by his Norwegian father to Norway to learn acting. He came to England and joined Benson's Company, and later Sir Herbert Tree. He partnered Ellen Terry in her disastrous venture into management, playing Sigurd in *The Vikings* and Benedick in *Much Ado*. Later under his own management he won great success. He took the Adelphi Theatre in 1904 with Otho Stuart, and in *The Taming of the Shrew* doubled Petruchio and Christopher Sly, with his wife Lily Brayton as Katharina. This production brought them overnight fame and was subsequently played for 1,500 performances at home and abroad. He followed it with Claudius, Bottom and Angelo, then took over His Majesty's while Tree was on tour, producing himself in *Attila*, as Jaques in *As You Like It*, as Othello, and in a revival of *The Shrew*. In 1911 he directed and acted in Edward Knoblock's *Kismet*, his first great oriental success. His Zulu show *Mameena* was a failure at the end of 1914, but in 1916 he launched his real money-spinner. He wrote the lyrics and the dialogue of *Chu-Chin-Chow* to music by Frederick Norton, and it was financed equally by Tree and Lily Brayton. Asche produced and starred in it with his wife, and it ran at His Majesty's for five years, bringing him well over £200,000 in royalties, which he quickly gambled away. He later staged many extravagant productions, both of musicals and Shakespeare, playing Falstaff in *The Merry Wives of Windsor* several times over the years, and touring his native Australia to packed homes and municipal receptions. But his five years in *Chu-Chin-Chow* seemed to have taken the fire out of his acting, as well as ruining his figure until he could play Falstaff without padding, and the public gradually lost its appetite for the lavish spectacles associated with him. He published his autobiography, *Oscar Asche, His Life*, in 1929.

16 **Harley-Granville-Barker** was one of the most influential the-

atrical figures of the early years of the twentieth century. Born in 1877, he went on stage at the age of fourteen, and toured with Lewis Waller, Ben Greet and Mrs. Patrick Campbell. He worked with Tree and with William Poel, and in 1900 Shaw chose him for the part of Marchbanks in *Candida*. Thereafter he played in and produced many of Shaw's plays, and several of his own. In *Man and Superman* he played John Tanner opposite Lillah McCarthy, a very talented actress who became his first wife. In 1904 he took over the management of the Royal Court Theatre with J. E. Vedrenne, and produced plays by Euripides, Shaw, Ibsen, Galsworthy and several of his own plays. He wrote *Waste*, *The Marrying of Ann Leete*, *The Voysey Inheritance*, *The Madras House*, *Rococo* and a number of adaptations. In 1910 John Masefield wrote to him saying, 'People have come to regard you as a kind of god.' Certainly it is difficult to overstate his influence on both actors and producers. His productions at the Savoy just before the First War of *The Winter's Tale*, *Twelfth Night* and *A Midsummer Night's Dream* broke away from Tree's expensive spectacular style of Shakespearean production and revolutionized the whole approach to the text.

In 1914 he went to America, fell in love with Helen Huntingdon and divorced his first wife to marry her in 1918. She persuaded him to give up active work in the theatre in order to write and lecture, a decision that his old friend and collaborator Bernard Shaw denounced at one of Granville-Barker's own lectures in 1925 as a public scandal. His most influential publications have been his five volumes of Prefaces to *Shakespeare* published between 1927 and 1947, but as early as 1907 he wrote with William Archer *A National Theatre: Scheme and Estimates* much of which was based on his experiences at the Royal Court, where it became clear to him that a classical repertoire, however popular, could only be paid for by state subsidy. His brief work with John Gielgud on *Hamlet* and *Lear* has been acknowledged by the latter as enormously helpful and profound. Several of his plays have been revived in recent years.

Chapter Two: 1922-1928

1 **Claude Rains** first appeared on stage as a child actor in *Sweet Nell of Old Drury* at the Haymarket in 1900, then worked his way up through call-boy and ASM to general manager for Granville-Barker in his 1914 tour of the USA, when he also played Spintho in *Androcles and the Lion*. After the First War he made a considerable name as a character actor as well as a leading man, playing Khlestakov in *The Government Inspector*, Cassius in *Julius Caesar*, and Dubedat in *The Doctor's Dilemma*. In 1923 he played with John Gielgud at the Regent, in *The Insect Play* and *Robert E. Lee*. He had a number of successes in Shaw's plays, and in 1926 went to America, where he toured as Lewis Dodd in *The Constant Nymph*, and after a number of seasons at the Guild Theatre in New York he made his film debut in 1933 as *The Invisible Man*, in which his face was bandaged throughout. For the next sixteen years he worked in films, notably *Crime without Passion*, *Anthony Adverse*, *The Adventures of Robin Hood*, *Mr. Smith Goes to Washington*, *The Sea Hawk*, *Casablanca*, *The Phantom of the Opera*, and *Caesar and Cleopatra*. In 1950 he returned to the stage in Philadelphia to play in a dramatization of Arthur Koestler's *Darkness at Noon*, and in 1954 played Sir Claude Mulhammer in Eliot's *The Confidential Clerk*. A subtle and versatile actor renowned for his voice, he had a considerable influence on the young John Gielgud both as actor and teacher. In later years he played small cameo parts in films, the most notable of which was Dryden in *Lawrence of Arabia*. He died in 1967.

2 **Sybil Thorndike** began her long and distinguished career with Ben Greet's company, playing many Shakespearean parts in the first years of this century. She was leading lady for several seasons at Miss Horniman's Repertory Theatre in Manchester, and went to the Old Vic first in 1914, returning there many times subsequently to play virtually all the great Shakespeare female roles and also some of the male ones—including Prince Hal in *Henry IV*, the Fool in *King Lear*, Launcelot Gobbo in *The Merchant of Venice*, Ferdinand in *The Tempest*, and Puck in *A Midsummer Night's Dream*. She had great successes in the Greek tragedies—Hecuba in *The Trojan Women* and as

Medea. In 1924 she created the role of *St Joan*, and played many of Shaw's heroines—he once described her as his ideal Candida. She gave notable performances in contemporary plays like *The Corn is Green*, *Time and the Conways*, *Waters of the Moon*, *A Day by the Sea* with John Gielgud, *The Sleeping Prince*, *Separate Tables*, *The Potting Shed* and *The Chalk Garden*. She often acted with, or was directed by, her husband Lewis Casson, and in later years they gave many dramatic or poetry recitals together all over the world. She was created DBE in 1931, and Companion of Honour in 1970, and will be remembered as one of the best-loved actresses of our time. She continued acting until her late eighties, though eventually her arthritis forced her to retire from the stage in 1969. She died in 1976 at the age of ninety-four.

3 **Nigel Playfair**, the son of a distinguished gynaecologist, first acted with the OUDS and other amateur societies, and abandoned his plans for a career in the Law when he joined the stage in 1902. He toured with Benson's company, appeared in several of Shaw's plays at the Court Theatre, in Shakespeare with Tree at His Majesty's, and played Bottom in Granville-Barker's famous production of *A Midsummer Night's Dream* at the Savoy in 1912. He ran the Lyric Theatre, Hammersmith from 1918 to 1932, and was knighted in 1928. He died in 1934.

4 **Noël Coward** was very successful as a child actor. He learnt his trade from Charles Hawtrey, the brilliant actor-manager and director. A prolific songwriter and playwright, his early plays were considered controversial and attracted large audiences. John Gielgud succeeded him in *The Vortex* in 1925, and again the following year as Lewis Dodd in Margaret Kennedy's play *The Constant Nymph*. They remained fast fiends until Noël Coward's death, but the only other time they worked together was in 1956 when Gielgud starred in Coward's play *Nude with Violin*. This, was a commercial if not a critical success, and ran for many months with first Michael Wilding and then Robert Helpmann taking over the leading role. Many of Coward's plays were great successes, but especially *Hay Fever, Bitter Sweet,*

Private Lives, Cavalcade, Design for Living, Tonight at 8:30, Blithe Spirit, and *Present Laughter,* several of which have been successfully revived in recent years, including his own production of *Hay Fever* at the National Theatre in 1964 with Edith Evans as Judith Bliss. He was knighted in 1969, and died in 1973.

5 **Gwen Ffrangcon-Davies** began her career as a singer, walking-on as a singing fairy in *A Midsummer Night's Dream* at His Majesty's in 1911, but her first big success in London was as Étain in Rutland Boughton's opera *The Immortal Hour.* She played the part several times, including Sir Barry Jackson's revival at the Birmingham Repertory Theatre, after which he asked her to stay on and play several juvenile leads. She was a well-established actress by the time she played Juliet to John Gielgud's first Romeo, but their professional paths have crossed several times since then. In 1929 they played together in *The Lady with the Lamp;* she played Queen Anne in *Richard of Bordeaux* from 1932 to 1934, was directed by him in *Queen of Scots* in 1934, and joined him again in 1938 to play Olga in *Three Sisters.* She played his wife in the wartime *Macbeth,* his daughter Regan in the 1950 *Lear,* and his mother in Graham Greene's play *The Potting Shed* in 1958. He directed her as Madame Ranevsky in *The Cherry Orchard* with Trevor Howard, and brought her into the American tour of his production of *The School for Scandal* to play Mrs. Candour, when he took over the part of Joseph Surface himself. In addition, she has played many classical and modern parts, including a notable Mary Tyrone in *Long Day's Journey into Night,* with Anthony Quayle, which won her the 1959 London Evening Standard Drama Award. She was created DBE when she was 100 years old, and continued acting until her death in 1992, aged 101.

6 **Mrs. Patrick Campbell** first appeared on stage at Liverpool in 1888. She toured with Ben Greet's company, and first caught the public's attention by an outstanding performance as Paula in *The Second Mrs. Tanqueray* with George Alexander in 1893. Later successes included Agnes in *The Notorious Mrs. Ebbsmith,* Juliet and Ophelia opposite Forbes-Robertson, Mélisande both in English and in

French, the latter with Sarah Bernhardt playing Pelléas. She played the title-role of Magda in London and New York, in which Matheson Lang thought her better than Duse. Bernard Shaw criticized her performance in that play, but wrote *Pygmalion* for her, and she created the part of Eliza Doolittle at the age of fifty, and revived it several times. She gave notable performances in several of Ibsen's plays, including Hedda Gabler and as John Gielgud's mother in *Ghosts*. She played Mrs. Chepstow in *Bella Donna*, Lady Macbeth, Madame Rosalie la Grange in *The Thirteenth Chair*, and her last famous creation— Anastasia in *The Matriarch* in 1929. In her youth she was outstandingly beautiful, and although she ran to fat later on, her talent and her devastating wit made her one of the great theatrical figures for several decades. She carried on a long correspondence, and possibly a love-affair, with Bernard Shaw; their letters, published after her death in 1940, formed the basis of the play *Dear Liar.*

7 **Lucien-Germain Guitry** (1860-1925) was a French actor-manager whose son, Sacha, became both actor and playwright, writing almost a hundred light comedies. Sacha directed himself in his own plays, often partnered by Yvonne Printemps, his second wife, who had been a revue actress and singer. Their first appearance in London was with *Nono* in 1920; in New York in 1926 she played the title role in Sacha Guitry's *Mozart*, with music by Reynaldo Hahn.

8 **Edith Evans** was discovered by William Poel, who offered her first a small part in his revival of a sixth century Hindu classic *Sakuntala* and then the lead opposite Esmé Percy in *Troilus and Cressida*, both in 1912. She was then twenty-five but she quickly made up for her late start. She toured with Ellen Terry, playing Mistress Ford in the basket scene from *The Merry Wives of Windsor* and Nerissa in the trial scene from *The Merchant of Venice*. She created the parts of the Serpent and the She-Ancient in Sir Barry Jackson's production of Shaw's *Back to Methuselah* in 1923, and joined the Old Vic in 1925. Her appearances with Gielgud include Juliet's Nurse, Lady Bracknell, Arkadina in *The Seagull*, Katerina in *Crime and Punishment* and Katharine of Aragon in *Henry VIII*. He has also directed her in *The*

Old Ladies and *The Chalk Garden*. Kenneth Tynan wrote of the latter: 'Dame Edith Evans...suggests a crested wave of Edwardian eccentricity vainly dashing itself on the rocks of contemporary life... In this production we see English actors doing perfectly what few actors on earth can do at all: reproduce in the theatre the spirited elegance of a Mozart quintet.' Her playing with Peggy Ashcroft was hailed as a 'partnership of glory'. She had many great successes in other modern plays such as *The Late Christopher Bean, Daphne Laureola, Waters of the Moon, The Dark is Light Enough*, and the National Theatre's revival of *Hay Fever* in 1964, but the playwrights with whom she will be most associated in theatregoers' memories are Shakespeare, Congreve, Wilde and Chekhov. She partnered Redgrave, Richardson and Olivier, but her most scintillating performances were with Gielgud. She was created DBE in 1946 and died in 1976.

Chapter Three: 1929-1930

1 **Harcourt Williams** made his first appearance on stage with Benson in *Henry V* in Belfast in 1898. He toured with Ellen Terry, H. B. Irving, and George Alexander and was seen in many notable new plays by Ibsen, Shaw and Granville-Barker. In 1916 he played Clarence to Martin Harvey's Richard III, and in 1925 the Player King to John Barrymore's Hamlet. In 1929 he was appointed producer at the Old Vic and between then and 1934 put on nearly fifty productions. He continued to act occasionally, appearing as Brutus and as Caesar, the Ghost in *Hamlet*, Gaunt in *Richard II*, the French King in *Henry V*, and Darnley in *Mary Stuart*. He based his Shakespearean productions on Granville-Barker's *Prefaces to Shakespeare*, and after initial criticisms his innovations were acclaimed. By persuading John Gielgud to join the company in 1929 he brought a wider theatre-going public across the river, and set an example that was followed by Olivier in 1936. Williams returned to the Old Vic Company as an actor at the end of the Second War when the company appeared at the New Theatre under the triumvirate of Lau-

rence Olivier, Ralph Richardson and John Burrell. He continued to act and produce until near the end of his life in 1957. In 1935 he published *Four Years at the Old Vic*.

2 **Lilian Baylis**, born in 1874, interrupted a musical career in South Africa in 1895, to return to England and help her aunt run a temperance hall, the old Victoria Theatre—to become the Old Vic. Her aunt died in 1912 and she devoted herself to turning the theatre into the fulfilment of her own ideals, a theatre where opera and drama could be brought to ordinary people. All Shakespeare's plays were produced there between 1917 and 1923. She opened Sadler's Wells in 1931 as a home for opera and ballet and it was equally successful, though money problems dogged her all her life.

3 **Hamlet** is the part most associated with the first half of John Gielgud's career. His first performance of it in 1929 was an instant success. Ivor Brown wrote: 'This performance puts him beyond the range of the arriving actors; he is in the first rank.' James Agate went further. 'This actor is young, thoughtful, clever, sensitive; his performance is subtle, brilliant, vigorous, imaginative, tender and full of the right kind of ironic humour. It has elegance of body and elevation of mind, it is conceived in the key of poetry and executed with beautiful diction. I have no hesitation in saying that it is the high water mark of English Shakespearean acting in our time.' Sybil Thorndike wrote to him after the performance: 'I never hoped to see Hamlet played as in one's dreams...tonight it was Hamlet complete. When you spoke your final word I said to myself what I said when I read the first chapter of *Moby Dick:* "This is too good to be true"...I've had an evening of being swept right off my feet into another life—far more real than the life I live in, and moved, moved beyond words.'

In 1934 Gielgud directed himself in the part for the first time at the New Theatre. He worked on the designs with the Motleys, and was much influenced by Craig and by Komisarjevsky's designs for his production of *Lear* at Oxford. The cast included Frank Vosper as Claudius, Laura Cowie as Gertrude, George Howe as Polonius, Jessica Tandy as Ophelia, Glen Byam Shaw as Laertes, Jack Hawkins as Horatio, and the young Alec Guinness as Osric. J. C. Trewin acclaimed it as 'the key Shakespearean revival of its period,' and it ran for 155 performances, a record beaten until then only by Henry Irving, and since by Richard Burton in New York in John Gielgud's own production.

In 1936 he played Hamlet in America for the first time in a production by Guthrie McClintic, Katharine Cornell's husband. Judith Anderson played the Queen and Lillian Gish Ophelia. He played and directed *Hamlet* again in 1939 at Kronborg Castle, Elsinore, and before leaving for Denmark played for a week at the Lyceum. Appropriately this was the last play ever performed at Henry Irving's old theatre. George Rylands directed him when he played the part for the last time in 1944 at the Haymarket, with Peggy Ashcroft as Ophelia and Leslie Banks as the King. Agate thought this was his best Hamlet: 'Mr. Gielgud is now completely and authoritatively master of this tremendous part. He is, we feel, this generation's rightful tenant of this "monstrous Gothic castle of a poem". He has acquired an almost Irvingesque quality of pathos, and in the passages after the play scene an incisiveness, a raillery, a mordancy worthy of the Old Man. He imposes on us this play's questing feverishness. The middle act gives us ninety minutes of high excitement and assured virtuosity; Forbes-Robertson was not more bedazzling in the "O, what a rogue and peasant slave" soliloquy. In short, I hold that this is, and is likely to remain, the best Hamlet of our time.'

4 **Leslie Howard** was the son of Hungarian immigrants, but came to epitomize the shy English gentleman, especially in his Hollywood career. After he was discharged from the Army in 1917 suffering from shell-shock, he quickly established himself as a leading man on the stage both in London and New York, where he scored a great success as Andre Sallicel opposite Tallulah Bankhead in *Her Cardboard Lover*. In the thirties he acted principally in America and mostly in films, with Bette Davis in *Of Human Bondage*, with Humphrey Bogart in *The Petrified Forest*, with Vivien Leigh and Clark Gable in *Gone With the Wind*, and with Ingrid Bergman in *Intermezzo*. His Shakespearean

roles were much less successful—his Broadway Hamlet suffered by comparison with John Gielgud's and the 1936 MGM film of *Romeo and Juliet*, in which he played Romeo to Norma Shearer's Juliet, was one of the most disastrous Shakespeare films to come out of Holly-wood. He was more successful as Professor Higgins in *Pygmalion* which he co-directed with Anthony Asquith in 1938, with Wendy Hiller as Eliza and Wilfrid Lawson as Doolittle. When the Second War broke out he returned to England and made a number of patri-otic films as actor-director—*Pimpernel Smith*, *49th Parallel*, and *The First of the Few* about the inventor of the Spitfire. He was killed in 1943 when his plane was shot down in a flight from Lisbon to Lon-don, in rather mysterious circumstances.

5 **Ralph Richardson** began his career with Charles Doran's company in 1921, and toured with them for four years before joining Barry Jackson at the Birmingham Rep. He joined the Old Vic in 1930, and his first part was Prince Hal in *Henry IV Part I* with John Gielgud as Hotspur. The two of them then played together as Caliban and Pros-pero, Bolingbroke and Richard II, Enobarbus and Antony, Bluntschli and Sergius, Don Pedro and Benedick, and Kent and Lear. Their dif-ferent styles of playing complemented each other so well that over the years whenever they have played together they have enjoyed a re-markable joint success with public and critics alike. In that first Old Vic season, Richardson attracted many good notices. The Morning Post remarked that 'Mr. Ralph Richardson's Enobarbus places him among the first Shakespearean actors on the English stage.' He him-self has said: 'An actor tackling classical roles is like a jockey on a fa-mous horse which many great jockeys have ridden, there's a 25 per cent chance you won't get it over the jumps. But as a professional you are used to being afraid. You accept fear.' When Gielgud left the Old Vic in 1931, James Agate declared that there were only two actors fit to take over his leading roles—one was Richard Riddle (son of Henry Ainley), the other was Ralph Richardson. In the next season he played Henry V, Petruchio, Brutus, Iago, and of *A Midsummer Night's Dream* Agate said: 'Most of the old players seem to have thought Bot-tom, with the ass's head on, was the same Bottom, only funnier.

Shakespeare says he was "translated", and Mr. Richardson translated him.' It is this ability of his to bring an other-worldly quality to certain parts that has marked some of his greatest performances. When he and Olivier led the revived Old Vic Company from 1944 to 1947 his most memorable parts were as Peer Gynt, Falstaff, Cyrano de Bergerac, and the strange Inspector Goole in *An Inspector Calls*. His notable associations with John Gielgud have been the latter's production of *The School for Scandal* with Richardson as Sir Peter Teazle, *Home* at the Royal Court, the Apollo and New York in 1970, and *No Man's Land* at the National Theatre, Wyndham's and New York in 1975. He died in 1983, two months short of his eighty-first birthday.

Chapter Four: 1931-1938

1 **Theodore Komisarjevsky** was born in Venice in 1882, brought up in Russia and gained his first experience in the pre-Revolutionary theatre there. His sister was the famous Russian actress, Vera Komisarjevskaya, and he did his first production at her theatre in St Petersburg in 1907, following Meyerhold as her artistic director. When she died in 1910 he ran his own theatre in Moscow, where he was made director of the Imperial and State Theatres. In 1919 he came to England to produce Borodin's *Prince Igor* at Covent Garden. He was also a very skilled designer, and his season of Russian plays at the tiny Barnes Theatre (in 1924-5) with John Gielgud attracted a lot of notice.

His later Shakespeare productions at Stratford-upon-Avon aroused rather more controversy: a *Macbeth* with aluminium scenery and modern uniforms, and *The Merry Wives of Windsor* with a Viennese background and fairies with lighted candles on their heads. But he had more success with *King Lear, The Comedy of Errors* and *The Taming of the Shrew*. After the poor reception of his production of *The Boy David* for Cochran and Elizabeth Bergner in 1936, he went to America. He wrote many books on the theatre, though in practice his considerable talents were sometimes hampered by his unpredictable temperament.

2 **Michel St-Denis** was the nephew of the great French director Jacques Copeau, and began his career with him at the Vieux-Colombier as stage manager and assistant producer. In 1931 St-Denis took over the direction of his uncle's company, reorganizing it as the Compagnie des Quinze. Although the company only lasted three years, it established a considerable international reputation. In 1935 he came to England and produced *Noah* in which John Gielgud acted, *The Witch of Edmonton* in 1936, *Macbeth* in 1937 and *The White Guard* in 1938. In 1938 he also directed the famous *Three Sisters* with Gielgud, Peggy Ashcroft, Michael Redgrave, Glen Byam-Shaw, Harry Andrews, Alec Guinness, George Devine, Leon Quartermaine, Angela Baddeley, Gwen Ffrangcon-Davies, and Carol Goodner for the season at the Queen's when John Gielgud was in management with his own company. The two of them worked together in Chekhov again in 1961, when St-Denis directed *The Cherry Orchard* for the Royal Shakespeare Company at the Aldwych, with Gielgud as Gaev and Peggy Ashcroft as Madame Ranevsky. A sensitive and imaginative director, he was deeply interested in the training of actors. He ran the London Theatre Studio from 1936 to 1939; after the Second War he was head of the Old Vic School, and when it closed he returned to France to direct the Centre Dramatique de l'Est in Strasbourg. In addition he was artistic adviser to the Lincoln Center Project in New York, and to the Royal Shakespeare Theatre. In 1960 he published *Theatre: The Rediscovery of Style*.

3 **Peggy Ashcroft** has been directed by John Gielgud, or played opposite him, on a number of notable occasions throughout her long and distinguished career. In 1932 she and Edith Evans played Juliet and the Nurse in his production of *Romeo and Juliet* for the OUDS, and again under his direction in his 1935 New Theatre season, when he alternated with Olivier as Romeo and Mercutio. In his 1937-8 season at the Queen's Theatre she played the Queen in *Richard II*, Lady Teazle, Irina in *Three Sisters* and Portia in *The Merchant of Venice*. She

has played Ophelia to his Hamlet, Cordelia to his Lear and, most memorably, Beatrice to his Benedick. J. W. Lambert described *Much Ado* as follows: 'Resolving itself into a dance duet between Sir John and Miss Ashcroft, the revival was enchanting throughout in Mariano Andreu's hard but sparkling sets. Nothing in the theatre could be more exhilarating than their joint capitulation in the garden, when she is sent to bring him into dinner. Benedick, pride and fire, in Sir John shows swagger melting into ardour; Beatrice, no shrew, ever, but flame and starlight, in Miss Ashcroft shows *diablerie* transmuted into peace.' Peggy Ashcroft once said, 'Three people have influenced me enormously in Shakespeare: Edith Evans with her supreme understanding of what a voice can do with the flow and rhythm of words, Komisarjevsky by his analytical approach, and John Gielgud with his imaginative conception of the sweep of the play as a whole.' Her performances in Ibsen, Chekhov, Henry James' *The Heiress*, Beckett's *Happy Days*, Enid Bagnold's *Chalk Garden* and Rattigan's *The Deep Blue Sea* attracted both critical and public acclaim. She appeared at the Old Vic in 1932 as Cleopatra, and acted there for two seasons. In 1976 she played Lilian Baylis in the National Theatre's farewell to the Old Vic *Tribute to a Lady*. She has also played many seasons at Stratford-upon-Avon, where George Rylands said 'she did not act Cleopatra, she *was* Shakespeare's Cleopatra,' to Michael Redgrave's Antony; she was Emilia to John Gielgud's 1961 Othello, and in 1963 her Margaret of Anjou in *The Wars of the Roses* trilogy aged her from a seventeen-year-old girl to an old crone, sometimes in the course of one whole day when all three parts were played: in the morning, afternoon and evening. Created a Dame in 1956, she was also honoured by having the Ashcroft Theatre at Croydon named after her in 1962, when she spoke the prologue at the opening production. The stage was always her first love, but in her seventies she won a massive new following by her screen performances in *Caught on a Train, Jewel in the Crown* and *A Passage to India*. She died in 1991, at the age of eighty-three.

4 **Marie Tempest** trained as a singer and starred in comic opera between 1885 and 1899, and then abandoned her singing career to be-

come the leading comedienne of the next four decades. She had great success as Nell Gwynn, Peg Woffington, Becky Sharp, and the title role in *The Marriage of Kitty*, which she played many times in London and on a world tour that lasted five years and took in America, Australasia, South Africa, India, China and Japan. After her return in 1922 she reappeared triumphantly in London and became famous for her playing of comedy roles such as Judith Bliss in the first production of *Hay Fever*, Olivia in *Mr. Pim Passes By*, Fanny Cavendish in *Theatre Royal* and Janet Fraser in *The First Mrs. Fraser*. Gielgud played with her in *Dear Octopus* for ten months, and after he left the cast in June 1939 it continued for several months with Hugh Sinclair in his part. Marie Tempest was created DBE in 1937, and continued acting until she died in 1942 at the age of seventy-eight.

5 **Violet Vanbrugh** was the elder of the Vanbrugh sisters. She toured America with the Kendals, joined Irving at the Lyceum in 1891, had a great success as Anne Boleyn in *King Henry VIII*, and understudied Ellen Terry as Cordelia in *Lear* and Rosamund in *Becket*. She married the actor-manager Arthur Bourchier in 1894 and appeared for him in many farces and comedies; in 1910 she was engaged by Tree to play Queen Katharine, Mistress Ford and Lady Macbeth. But later she only played in Shakespeare occasionally and she was most successful playing a series of society ladies.

Irene Vanbrugh was five years younger than Violet, and was even more successful than her sister. She played with most of the great actor-managers over the years. In 1894 she toured with Alexander in *The Second Mrs. Tanqueray*, played Gwendolen in *The Importance of Being Earnest* at the St James's, then joined her brother-in-law Arthur Bourchier to play in England and America, and made her first great success in 1899 with John Hare at the Globe, playing Sophie Fullgarney in *The Gay Lord Quex*. She became recognized as an outstanding interpreter of the plays of Barrie and Pinero, and had successes in plays by Wilde and Maugham. Her rare excursions into Shakespeare included Gertrude in *Hamlet* at the Haymarket in 1930 and 1931, and Mistress Page partnering her sister in *The Merry Wives* in 1934 and 1937. She was created DBE in 1941.

6 **Madge Titheradge** was born in Melbourne in 1887 and first appeared on the London stage as the Second Water Baby in *The Water Babies* in 1902. She made a number of notable appearances with the actor manager Lewis Waller, playing Princess Katherine in *Henry V*, and later the Chorus as well; the title-role in *Peter Pan*, Fisher in *The Admirable Crichton*, and included in her classical parts Desdemona, Beatrice, and Nora in *A Doll's House*. She specialized in playing grand titled ladies, and carried much of her grand manner over into her private life. She died in 1961.

7 **Lillah McCarthy**, the first wife of Harley Granville-Barker, appeared with him at the Royal Court, and also created the leading roles in many Shaw plays, including Ann Whitefield in *Man and Superman*, Jennifer Dubedat in *The Doctor's Dilemma*, and Lavinia in *Androcles and the Lion*. She went into management at the Little Theatre in 1911, playing Hilda Wangel in Ibsen's *The Master Builder*, and with her husband at the Savoy, where she played Shakespearean roles. She wrote two books about her experiences, *My Life*, published in 1930, and *Myself and My Friends (1933)*.

8 **Ruth Draper**, an American actress born in 1884, specialized in dramatic monologues written by herself. She performed them privately for some time but went professional in 1920. She spent the rest of her life touring to great acclaim, continuously evolving her act but faithful to the same formula. In some sketches she acted several different people (as in *An English House Party*) and in others the wit lay in her response to invisible characters (as in *Opening a Bazaar*).

Chapter Five: 1939-1945

1 **Baroness Blixen** was born Karen Dinesen, in 1885. She grew up in her native Denmark but left to study English at Oxford University and painting in Paris and Rome. In 1914 she married her cousin, Baron Blixen, and went with him to run a coffee plantation in British East Africa: When they were divorced, in 1921, she took over the management of the farm herself and 'began to write to amuse myself in the rainy season'.

She had to leave East Africa and return to Europe in 1931 and in 1934 she published *Seven Gothic Tales* under the name of Isaak Dinesen. This was followed by *Out of Africa* in 1938 and by *Winter Tales* in 1942.

After she returned to Denmark, Baroness Blixen continued to write profusely, in Danish and in English, was visited by many younger writers and praised by many older ones. She died in September 1962.

2 **Hugh 'Binkie' Beaumont** was probably the most successful impresario of the twentieth-century British Theatre. As managing director of H. M. Tennent Ltd., he was the most powerful theatrical manager of his time, and Tyrone Guthrie once said that more than any other single individual, he could make or break the career of almost any worker in the British professional theatre. Born in 1908, he began his career as an assistant manager with the Howard and Wyndham theatre chain and later became a director of Moss Empires. In 1936 he went into management with H. M. Tennent and on the latter's death in 1941 succeeded him as managing director. Notable for his shrewdness in matching plays with the best possible actors, directors and designers, he was probably most famous for his association with John Gielgud, including his classical seasons at the Phoenix and the Haymarket during the Second War, and at the Phoenix and the Lyric, Hammersmith, in the nineteen-fifties. Among the shows he put on were *Dear Octopus, The Heiress, The Lady's Not For Burning, A Day by the Sea, Nude with Violin,* and *The Potting Shed*, which starred

or were directed by Gielgud, and the playwrights he championed included Thornton Wilder, Terence Rattigan, Tennessee Williams and Robert Bolt. His successful musicals were *Oklahoma!*, *Irma La Douce*, *West Side Story*, *Hello Dolly!* and *My Fair Lady*. Before the days of the big subsidized companies he dominated the London theatre, with his unique talent for producing brilliant shows that were both critically and commercially successful. By the time of his death in 1973 it needed four columns of *Who's Who in the Theatre* to list all his productions.

Chapter Six: 1946-1954

1 **Esmé Percy** acted with Granville-Barker in 1908 at the Court, and then with Annie Horniman, the great promoter of repertory theatre, at the Gaiety in Manchester. He also produced over 140 plays for the troops in the First War. He was an authority on Shaw and in 1949 became President of the Shaw Society.

2 **Peter Brook**, born in 1925, has often aroused controversy with his productions, especially of Shakespeare, and his experimental methods. Between 1946 and 1955, his productions included *Love's Labour's Lost*, *Romeo and Juliet*, *Salome* at Covent Garden designed by Salvador Dali, *Measure for Measure*, *Titus Andronicus*, Anouilh's *Ring Round the Moon* and *The Lark*, Otway's *Venice Preserv'd* and Fry's *The Dark is Light Enough*. He directed Paul Scofield as Hamlet in 1955, and as Lear in a famous production for the Royal Shakespeare Company in 1962, which toured abroad to great acclaim and was later filmed. Later productions included Weiss' *Marat/Sade* and, in 1966, *US*, a documentary on the American presence in Vietnam. His most influential recent Shakespeare production was *A Midsummer Night's Dream* for the RSC, which used trapezes, jugglers and other circus techniques.

In recent years he has experimented with new forms of drama

taking international companies to the people in Iran and Africa, using legend, myth and contemporary documentary techniques woven together with music and mime. His experimental studio is based in Paris.

3 During the run of *Venice Preserv'd* John Gielgud's knighthood was announced in the Coronation Honours List. His first line in the play was 'My Lord, I am not that abject wretch you think me,' which stopped the play the night of the announcement with an ovation of cheering and applause that carried on for several minutes.

Chapter Seven: 1955-1978

1 **Alain Resnais** decided to make *Providence*, his first English-dialogue film, as soon as he saw David Mercer's script, although Eric Shorter speculated in *The Daily Telegraph* that 'perhaps English is not the right language for the expression in the cinema of high-flown sentiments and low-tone comedy which shows an actor of Gielgud's quality in situations of Wildean irony and uninhibited agony'. *Sight and Sound* described his performance as 'the Sutherland portrait of Maugham come to life' and, after saying that in the film 'there is a degree of soul-baring unheard of outside one of the more minor plays of the English school or of Albee' ended its review with this tribute: 'The dream cast perform together superbly, each voice contributing its particular sonority to the ensemble: Resnais has spoken of a quintet in which Bogarde would be piano, Ellen Burstyn violin, Gielgud cello, Warner viola and Elaine Stritch bass. Miklos Rosza's score is perfect.' In 1977 the film won most of the French cinema awards, for best French film of the year, best direction, script, sound,

editing, music, and design, and shortly afterwards the New York film critics voted Sir John Gielgud the Best Actor of the Year for his peformance as Clive Langham.

2 **Orson Welles** shot *Chimes at Midnight* very quickly, but he had conceived it over many years. In his early days with the Mercury Theatre in New York he once combined eight of Shakespeare's history plays into a cut-up version of his own called *Five Kings*. In 1960 he put *Chimes at Midnight* on the stage in Belfast, and by 1964 he had raised the money for the film, which he completed in 1966. It draws together a selection of the Falstaff scenes from both Parts of *Henry IV* and *The Merry Wives of Windsor*, plus dialogue from *Richard II*, *Henry V* and Holinshed's Chronicles. Welles described it as a lament for the death of Merrie England. He only had Gielgud for two weeks to shoot his scenes as the King, a part that was nearly as long as Falstaff's in the film, so he shot no retakes, and used doubles for all of Falstaff's own scenes. In spite of all these constraints, it is generally considered one of Welles' finest films, with particularly moving performances by Gielgud, Welles, and Keith Baxter as Prince Hal. Several critics hailed it as a masterpiece, ranking it with *Citizen Kane* and *The Magnificent Ambersons* among Welles' greatest cinematic works.

Chapter Eight: Impressions of America

1 **Judith Anderson** was born in Australia in 1898 and went to America at the end of the First War, where she had her first great success as Elise in *The Cobra* in 1924. She succeeded Lynn Fontanne as Nina Leeds in the Theatre Guild presentation of *Strange Interlude* in 1928, and was chosen by the Guild to star in another O'Neill work in 1932—the trilogy *Mourning Becomes Electra*. Her first Shakespearean role was Gertrude with John Gielgud in 1936. She said then, 'There is no more devastating scene in drama than the "closet scene" between Hamlet and his mother.' The great critical acclaim that

greeted her performance as the Queen led her to speculate, 'Now that I have begun my classic education, do I dare breathe that I have dreamed of Lady Macbeth and now—as a matter of fact—I want to act Lady Macbeth.' Her wish was to be granted several times. She first played the part a year later in London with Laurence Olivier at the Old Vic, with Maurice Evans in 1941 in New York, and twice on television for NBC's *Hallmark of Fame* in 1954 and 1960. The *New York Times* critic Jack Gould found this last performance 'alternately vibrant, calculating, cruel, regal and pitiful; the intricacy of the characterization was knitted so faultlessly that it had a thrilling power'. It was this power to project evil that made her such a notable Medea in 1947, in the production which she invited Gielgud to direct and to co-star as Jason. She has acted in a number of films over the years, but still her best-remembered cinema performance is as Mrs. Danvers in Hitchcock's *Rebecca*. She was created DBE in 1960.

2 **Helen Hayes** was born in 1900 and began her career as a child actress, making her first appearance at the age of five as Prince Charles in *The Royal Family*. She first attracted notice in 1918 in *Dear Brutus* and her first great success was in another Barrie play—*What Every Woman Knows* in 1926. The following year she starred in Jed Harris' production of *Coquette* in New York and then on tour. A year later she married the playwright Charles MacArthur but it was another author, Maxwell Anderson, who wrote a play especially for her—*Mary of Scotland*. It opened in 1933 and ran for 248 performances on Broadway before going on tour. After the doomed Scottish Queen she turned to the role of the English Queen with which she is most famously associated, in *Victoria Regina*. This opened in December 1935 and broke many box-office records in New York and on its tour of forty-three American cities. It finally played until January 1939, by which time Helen Hayes had played a part in which she aged eighty years at each performance 969 times. Maxwell Anderson wrote: 'She gave us such moving young grace and such heartbreak in the final scenes that many count *Victoria Regina* their happiest experience in all modern theatre.' Her first performance in London was as Amanda Wingfield in John Gielgud's production of *The Glass Menagerie*. In

the cinema she appeared in *The Sin of Madelon Claudet, A Farewell to Arms, What Every Woman Knows, Anastasia* and *One of our Dinosaurs is Missing*. One of the actresses to be graced with the title 'First Lady of the American Theatre' she also received the compliment in 1955 of having a Broadway theatre named after her but sadly it has since been torn down. However, another Broadway theatre has since been named after her. She died in 1993.

3 **The Lunts** formed their famous partnership when they married in 1922. Lynn Fontanne was born and brought up in England, where she had some acting lessons with Ellen Terry, but she had her first success in America in 1916 when Laurette Taylor asked her to join her company for a series of plays she was planning. The new arrival was soon attracting as much notice as the established star. Alfred Lunt came from the mid-west and made his name on tour in the United States, playing with Margaret Anglin and, on one occasion, opposite Lillie Langtry. The Lunts' first appearance together after their marriage was in the 1923 revival of *Sweet Nell of Old Drury*, playing King Charles II and Lady Castlemaine, but their first joint success came when the Theatre Guild offered them the starring parts in Molnar's play *The Guardsman*. This ran for nearly twice as long as any play the Lunts had ever appeared in separately, and from then on they determined to play together all the time if possible. The public flocked to see them together in *Caprice, Elizabeth the Queen*, and *Reunion in Vienna*. In 1933 they joined Noël Coward in his play *Design for Living*, which he produced, although Coward is on record as saying 'Nobody directs the Lunts.' Their performances in *The Taming of the Shrew, Idiot's Delight, Amphitryon 38*, and *The Seagull* established them as unquestionably the most famous acting team on the American stage, and they became just as popular in London, both for their acting and for their insistence on appearing at the height of the Blitz in the Second War in Sherwood's *There Shall be No Night* and Rattigan's *Love in Idleness* (later retitled *O Mistress Mine*). Most famous for their comic playing, their unique trick of overlapping their lines and their torrid lovemaking on stage, they surprised their public in 1959 with Dürrenmatt's *The Visit*, a sombre revenge-drama directed by

Peter Brook, who said: 'Alfred reminds me of John Gielgud. Alfred, like Sir John, is a brilliant improviser, who arrives at a role by intuition and trial and error.'

4 Irene Worth was born and educated in America, but after her 1943 Broadway debut in *The Two Mrs. Carrolls* she was persuaded by Elizabeth Bergner to go to England for her theatrical training. She studied with Elsie Fogerty and made her London debut in *The Time of Your Life*. In 1919 she created the part of Celia in T. S. Eliot's The *Cocktail Party* at the Edinburgh Festival, and then in New York, where Brooks Atkinson in the *New York Times* wrote: 'Irene Worth finds the lonely depths in the character of the other woman in a remarkably skillful, passionate and perceptive performance.' She joined the Old Vic to play Desdemona, Lady Macbeth and Helena in *A Midsummer Night's Dream*. In 1953 she was acclaimed for another Helena—in *All's Well That Ends Well*—at the inaugural season of the Stratford Ontario Festival, which, Herbert Whittaker wrote some years later, 'has become a legend, and is still celebrated for its deep-throated poignance, its grace and its wit'. The same year she worked for the first time with John Gielgud, in his production of *A Day by the Sea*. They have played together several times since, mostly in modern plays—*The Potting Shed* and *The Ides of March* in London, *Tiny Alice* in the USA, for which she won a Tony Award, a recital *Men and Women of Shakespeare* with which they toured North and South America, and Seneca's *Oedipus* at the National Theatre in London, in which she played Jocasta. She is most memorably associated with tragic parts—Argia in *The Queen and the Rebels, Mary Stuart*, and Goneril in the Brook/Scofield *Lear* for the RSC; but she has also been acclaimed for her Rosalind at Stratford Ontario, and Hesione Hushabye in *Heartbreak House* at the Chichester Festival, which prompted Walter Kerr to write: 'I really must stop seeing Miss Worth. She leads to disappointment with practically everyone else.' Her power and sensitivity have given her successes in the other media—radio, television and the cinema—but she chose to work mostly in the English theatre, with appearances abroad at intervals, until recently, when she decided to return to the country of her birth where she has continued to gather the plaudits of critics and the public.

Chapter Nine: 1979-1989

1 **James Mason** was born in Yorkshire in 1909. Educated at Marlborough and Cambridge, he quickly found that his First Class Degree in Architecture was little help in finding work in the depths of the Depression in 1931, so he turned to acting as a better prospect. After playing in repertory and at the Old Vic he began to make his name in a series of rather routine British films, frequently as the aristocratic scoundrel with a sadistic streak. He became a British star when he horsewhipped Margaret Lockwood in *The Man in Grey*, and an international star when he smashed a cane on Ann Todd's fingers as she played the piano in *The Seventh Veil*. This brought him the invitation to Hollywood. The *New York Times* said he was 'one of the very few actors it is worth taking the trouble to see, even when the film encasing him is so much cement'. In a list of over a hundred films some fitted that description, but he will be remembered for a brooding presence on the screen in films as diverse as *Odd Man Out* (his own favourite), *The Prisoner of Zenda*, *20,000 Leagues Under the Sea*, *North by Northwest*, *Rommel Desert Fox*, *Five Fingers*, *Pandora and the Flying Dutchman*, *Lolita*, *The Deadly Affair*, *Spring and Port Wine*, and *The Autobiography of a Princess*. He always tried to resist the attempts to typecast him as the suave villain, and his performances as Brutus in the 1953 *Julius Caesar*, in *A Star is Born* with Judy Garland, with Paul Newman in The *Verdict*, and in his last film *The Shooting Party*, reveal his considerable range as an actor. He was nominated three times for an Oscar, which he never won, but the great American pioneer director of the silent film, D. W. Griffith, paid him a singular tribute: 'That Mason is the finest actor.' He published his autobiography *Before I Forget* in 1982, and died in 1984.

2 **Alexander Korda** began his film career in Budapest at the age of twenty-two, after he was invalided out of the army in the First War. By 1919 he was the star producer in Hungary. Arrested by the Horthy regime, he was released with the help of a British official. Gratitude for this blossomed later into an intense patriotic love of his adopted country. He pursued his film career in Vienna, Berlin, Paris and Hollywood before coming to England in 1931, where he had his first real success with *Service for Ladies*. He secured enough financial backing to found London Films in 1932, and had a huge international success with *The Private Lives of Henry VIII*, which made a star of Charles Laughton. His talent-spotting eye also fell on Robert Donat, Merle Oberon (whom he later married), Ralph Richardson and many others who first attracted notice in films made by his various companies. He built Denham Studios, bought his way into United Artists, worked with MGM British Studios and was Chief Production Executive of British Lion. The last film he directed himself was *Rembrandt* in 1936, again starring Laughton, which was a commercial flop but is now seen as something of a classic. Thereafter he worked as producer or executive producer on a variety of mostly romantic or patriotic films—*The Scarlet Pimpernel, Sanders of the River, Things to Come, The Drum, The Four Feathers* and *The Thief of Bagdad*. *Lady Hamilton* was made in 1941 with the Oliviers in America and was one of Churchill's favourites. His support of directors like Carol Reed, Michael Powell and David Lean produced films as notable as *The Fallen Idol, The Third Man, The Sound Barrier* and *Hobson's Choice*. His interest in bringing Shakespeare to the screen made possible Olivier's *Richard III*. He made, and lost, several fortunes in pursuit of his often extravagant film ambitions. He was the first man to be knighted for services to the film industry, in 1942, mainly because of his patriotic films for the war effort. He died in 1956.

3 **Gore Vidal** was born at West Point in 1925. He wrote his first novel, *Williwaw*, during the Second War when he was nineteen, serving in the American army in the Pacific. It was instantly acclaimed as one of the best American war novels. In 1948 *The City and the Pillar* was the first American novel to deal openly with homosexuality. In

the fifties he wrote for the theatre, films and television. *Visit to a Small Planet* began on television and moved on to Broadway, *The Best Man* was first a play and then filmed with Henry Fonda in the title-role. His novels continued to reach the bestseller lists on both sides of the Atlantic—*Julian, Washington D.C., Myra Breckinridge*, and his American historical series with *Burr, 1876, Lincoln*. His attempts at a political career were impressive but not crowned with success; in the 1982 California Democratic Primary for the US Senate he came second in a field of nine with half a million votes. A man of strong views, often caustically expressed, he was so chagrined when he saw the final film version of *Caligula* that he sued to have his name removed from the credit titles.

4 **Richard Burton** was born Richard Jenkins in 1925 in Pontrhyd-fen, South Wales, and later adopted the surname of his schoolmaster benefactor. He was discovered by Emlyn Williams, who gave him his first professional part in *Druid's Rest* at the Royal Court in Liverpool, which later came to London. He went up to Oxford University in 1944, where he played Angelo in the OUDS production of *Measure for Measure*. After service in the RAF, he returned to the stage at the Lyric Hammersmith in *Castle Anna*, and then played with John Giel-gud for the first time in *The Lady's Not for Burning*. It ran for over a year and marked Burton's Broadway debut when it transferred in No-vember 1950. He made a considerable impression in the 1951 Strat-ford-upon-Avon season of the History plays. Kenneth Tynan wrote: 'A shrewd Welsh boy shines out with greatness the first this year...His playing of Prince Hal turned interested speculation to awe almost as soon as he started to speak...Burton is a still, brimming pool, running disturbingly deep; at twenty-five he commands repose and can make silence garrulous.' He first played Hamlet in 1953 with the Old Vic Company, also playing Philip the Bastard in *King John*, Sir Toby Belch, Coriolanus and Caliban. He returned to the Old Vic in 1956 to alternate the parts of Othello and Iago with John Neville. The fol-lowing year he played opposite Helen Hayes on Broadway in *Time Remembered*, and in 1960 appeared there in his first stage musical—*Camelot* with Julie Andrews. His film career had begun early—in

1948, again with Emlyn Williams, in *The Last Days of Dolwyn*, making his Hollywood debut with Olivia de Havilland in *My Cousin Rachel* in 1952. He followed this with *The Desert Rats, The Robe*, and *The Prince of Players* as the great American actor Edwin Booth. The best known of his later films are *Look Back in Anger, Cleopatra, Becket, The Spy Who Came in from the Cold, Who's Afraid of Virginia Woolf?, The Taming of the Shrew, The Comedians* and *Where Eagles Dare*.

An admirer of Gielgud from his earliest days (in 1944 he went to see his Hamlet at the Haymarket five times in one week), his own first Hamlet at the Old Vic was described in the *Evening Standard* as 'the most effective—and authoritative—Hamlet that any actor under thirty has achieved on the London stage since Gielgud's first performance twenty-four years ago.' His 1964 Hamlet divided the critics. The *Toronto Star* attacked Burton as 'artistically impotent' but the *Toronto Telegraph* acclaimed it: 'Burton's performance is a masterpiece. He is the closest we shall come in this generation to the complete Hamlet.' Commercially it was a smash-hit. It took over $400,000 in four weeks in Toronto, in Boston it was a sell-out, on Broadway it was the most profitable Shakespeare stage production ever. Walter Kerr in the *Herald Tribune* had one reservation after acclaiming this Hamlet's display of 'all of the myriad qualities which the man Hamlet requires. All except one. Mr. Burton is without feeling.' But Howard Taubman in the *New York Times* applauded it as 'a performance of electrical power and sweeping vitality'. The production was put on record and on film, and its eventual gross takings reached the figure of $6,000,000. He died in 1984.

Epilogue

1 **Laurence Olivier** was born in 1907 and at the age of ten was noticed by Ellen Terry in a school production of *Julius Caesar*—'the small boy who played Brutus is already a great actor'. At fourteen his Kate in *The Taming of the Shrew* attracted the notice of the press, and after training under Elsie Fogerty at the Central School he was re-

cruited by Barry Jackson for the Birmingham Rep. He played Bothwell in *Queen of Scots* in 1934, directed by John Gielgud, and the following year they appeared for the first, and last, time together on stage in *Romeo and Juliet*, alternating Romeo and Mercutio. In 1937 he went to the Old Vic to play Hamlet there and later at Elsinore, and this and other Shakespearean parts made his reputation. In 1944 he and Ralph Richardson were released from the Royal Navy to lead the revived Old Vic Company at the New Theatre. His *Richard III* was such a success that John Gielgud presented Olivier with the sword used by Kean and Irving in the same role. When his Old Vic contract was not renewed in 1949 he took the St James's Theatre as an actor-manager, where the productions included Christopher Fry's *Venus Observed*, the Orson Welles *Othello*, and a Shaw/Shakespeare pairing of *Caesar and Cleopatra* and *Antony and Cleopatra* in which he starred opposite his wife Vivien Leigh. The Stratford season of 1955 was as important for him as that of 1950 had been for Gielgud; he had two of his greatest successes with Macbeth and Titus Andronicus. After startling audiences with his Archie Rice in Osborne's *The Entertainer* he returned to Stratford in 1959 with a powerful Coriolanus that ended with one of his characteristically dangerous death-leaps. In 1961 he became the first Director of the new Chichester Festival Theatre, and two years later he became the first Artistic Director of the National Theatre at the Old Vic. The personal acting highlights of his ten years there include Astrov in *Uncle Vanya*, Brazen in *The Recruiting Officer*, *Othello*, Tattle in *Love for Love*, Edgar in *The Dance of Death*, Shylock, and James Tyrone in *Long Day's Journey into Night*. His film career has embraced commercial successes, and flops, and his own productions of, mostly, Shakespearean films. From early successes like Heathcliff in *Wuthering Heights*, and Max de Winter in Hitchcock's *Rebecca*, he moved to directing the wartime *Henry V*, *Hamlet* in 1948, *Richard III* in 1955, and *The Prince and the Showgirl* opposite Marilyn Monroe in 1957. Later films include *The Devil's Disciple*, *Spartacus*, *The Entertainer*, *Term of Trial*, *Khartoum*, *The Battle of Britain*, *Marathon Man*, and *Sleuth*. Increasing ill-health restricted his performance on stage and screen. His last major role was King Lear for Granada television. He was knighted in 1947, and made a Life Peer in 1970. He died in 1989.

Index

Ralph Richardson
An Actor's Life
Updated, Revised and Expanded

GARRY O'CONNOR

"STUNNING . . . THE BEST BIOGRAPHY OF AN ACTOR I'VE EVER READ."
— *NEW YORK TIMES BOOK REVIEW*

"INDISPENSABLE IN ANY THEATRE COLLECTION."
— *LIBRARY JOURNAL*

"*EXEMPLARY: carefully researched, sensitively attuned to the subject, agreeably written and well documented . . . it reads effortlessly.*"
— *WASHINGTON POST*

"*This is a book to be grateful for, an account of art and life joined into unusual integrity.*"
— *SUNDAY LONDON TIMES*

"*This is* **THE MOST EXCITING THEATRICAL BIOGRAPHY I HAVE EVER READ.** *It is an astounding book, original in form and fascinating in content.*"
— *SIR HAROLD HOBSON*

"*Garry O'Connor's biography is as* **DELIGHTFUL AS ITS SUBJECT**"
— *RICHARD SCHICKEL, TIME*

CLOTH • ISBN 1-55783-300-1

The Real Life of Laurence Olivier

"A PASSIONATE AND MONUMENTAL CELEBRATION OF A GENIUS."
— ARTHUR MILLER,
Front Page, *London Sunday Times*

ROGER LEWIS

"This book confirms Lewis as the most ferociously attentive describer of stage and screen acting since Ken Tynan. It's MAGNIFICENT." — *NEW STATESMAN*

"Forget the standard show business 'life.' Lewis has reinvigorated [the] genre. This is the biography of the year! UNMISSABLE." — *CITY LIFE*

"Dammit, this book is very, very, seductive!" — *KALEIDOSCOPE*

" . . . A MARVELLOUS WORK . . . YOU WILL BE CAPTURED AND CAPTIVATED . . . A MASTERPIECE. DO READ IT." — *THE WESTMINSTER REVIEW*

"Lewis delivers ONE OF THE BEST BOOKS YET ON THE FINE OLD CRAFT OF ACTING." — PATRICK HUMPHRIES, *EMPIRE*

CLOTH • ISBN: 1-55783-298-6

APPLAUSE

SLINGS AND ARROWS

THEATER IN MY LIFE

by Robert Lewis

"A decidedly good read. Breezy, intelligent, and chatty. A stylish, entertaining, and above all theatrical book."
> —*The New York Times Book Review*

"He's a marvelous storyteller: gossipy, candid without being cruel, and very funny. This vivid, entertaining book is also one of the most penetrating works to be written about the theater."
> —*Publishers Weekly*

"The most interesting book about the theater since Moss Hart's *Act One*."
> —**Clifton Fadiman**

"A superior performance."
> —*The Los Angeles Times*

paper•ISBN 1-55783-244-7